AN EYE
TO
THE HILLS

AN EYE
TO
THE HILLS

Cameron McNeish

Foreword
by ***Chris Townsend***

SANDSTONE PRESS

First published in Great Britain in 2022 by
Sandstone Press Ltd
PO Box 41
Muir of Ord
IV6 7YX
Scotland

www.sandstonepress.com

ISBN: 978-1-913207-86-1
ISBNe: 978-1-913207-87-8

Sandstone Press is committed to a sustainable future.
This book is made from Forest Stewardship Council ® certified paper.

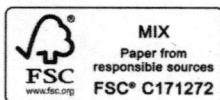

MIX
Paper from
responsible sources
FSC® C171272
FSC
www.fsc.org

Jacket design by Raspberry Creative Type, Edinburgh
Typeset by Iolaire, Newtonmore
Printed and bound by CPI Group (UK) Ltd, Croydon, CR0 4YY

Contents

Acknowledgements

I mostly walked alone when compiling my various weekly newspaper offerings, but the articles would never have reached publication without the encouragement of others. Even confirmed loners have to rely on team efforts from time to time, so a huge thanks to the staff and the editors of the papers I worked for over the years, especially the late Ken Jones, Ken Smith and Gavin Musgrove of the *Strathspey and Badenoch Herald* and Andrew Jaspan, Richard Walker, Calum Baird and Darren Bruce at the Sunday Herald and Newsquest Ltd. Special thanks to Gavin and Darren for giving me permission to reproduce those essays that first appeared in their publications.

A sincere thanks to my good friend, editor and publisher, Robert Davidson. Without his constant encouragement and his own specialist hill-going knowledge, not to mention his excellent editing skills, this book would have been all the poorer. The whole team at Sandstone have been a joy and a delight to work with.

Thanks also to Anne MacLeod for permission to reproduce her poem, 'Coming Back to Meall Fuar Mhonaidh'.

An inspiring presence in my working career as an outdoors writer over the past forty years or so is my good friend and erstwhile colleague Chris Townsend, and I'm thrilled he has written the foreword to this book. Chris and I began working together on my own magazine, *Footloose*, in the early eighties and, when I became editor of *The Great Outdoors* magazine in 1990, Chris was the writer I desperately wanted on board with me. Britain's most prolific long-distance backpacker, three-times Munroist and the first man to climb all the Munros and Tops in one continuous expedition, Chris is not only the UK's most experienced hiker but probably our wisest. I'm delighted his name will grace this book alongside my own.

As always, thanks to my wife Gina for putting up with all the foibles of an outdoor writer for half a century. She's always been there for me when hill days haven't gone the way I expected, and she's always been there to lift me up when I was down. Fifty years of married life – wow, who'd have believed it?

Finally, this book is dedicated to the other two 'G's in my life, my two sons, Gordon and Gregor.

List of Illustrations

Foreword

by Chris Townsend

Many decades ago, a keen young backpacker and hillwalker was nervously planning his first trip to the Scottish Highlands. Everything he'd heard about this then almost mythical land said it was much vaster and more serious than the English and Welsh hills he knew. This was back when the Internet only existed in science-fiction, so he wrote a letter to someone whose writing about Scotland he'd seen in the journal of the Backpacker's Club. I was the young walker and the person to whom I wrote the letter was Cameron McNeish. I'm pleased to say he wrote a helpful and encouraging reply and I went to the Scottish Highlands, had a great time, and fell in love with the mountains and the wildness.

Not so many years later I met Cameron at an outdoor event, probably a trade show which we both used to attend regularly to look at new gear and meet others in the outdoor business. By then he was writing regularly for walking and climbing magazines, something I was just starting out doing. We got on well and have been friends ever since. As well as helping inspire my writing Cameron also taught me cross-country skiing in those long-gone days when snow from the glens to the summits was taken for granted. I remember he was a patient teacher – I was not a natural skier and some of the others in the group weren't much better. We learnt enough for him to take us up Creag an Leth-choin in the Cairngorms and I was enthralled. A mountain on skis! What could be better? I'm still not sure I'll ever forgive him for leaving us at the top of the Cairngorm ski resort and saying 'make your own way down' though. That descent is still one of the most terrifying I've ever done!

Later I wrote for Cameron for many years when he was editing outdoor magazines. He took this work seriously and raised the standard of outdoor journalism as well as using his platform as editor to campaign on conservation and access issues. Sadly, as this book shows, many of the matters he raised, and continued to raise over the years, are still urgent concerns.

Over the years we've been on several trips together, from day walks to overnight camps – I remember a December plod through the Gaick Pass in sombre, sleety conditions where only Cameron's companionship gave enjoyment – to two weeks on the challenging GR20 long-distance path down the rocky spine of Corsica, where Cameron's confidence and joy on steep rock gave me the nerve to deal with places a little beyond my comfort zone. Well outside Cameron's comfort zone, though for vastly different reasons, was a mountain marathon we did together in the Peak District. After two days running round peat bogs and groughs on Kinder Scout and Bleaklow, Cameron swore he'd rather have spent the weekend walking round the streets of Manchester, and he was never coming back. And he didn't for twenty years, until a rather more pleasurable visit described in this book.

On these walks and adventures we discussed a wealth of thoughts and ideas about the outdoors and nature. We shared our love of writers who'd influenced us both such as John Muir and Colin Fletcher, both of whom I'm pleased to see appear in these essays. We talked of conservation and politics – the last can't be ignored if you're concerned about the first – and wondered about the world we were bequeathing to the future. But the main thing I remember is the companionship of someone who shared my passion and joy in the hills and wild places.

As well as editing magazines Cameron also contributed regular columns to the *Sunday Herald* and the *Strathspey and Badenoch Herald* for many years and it's those that he's collected together for this book. I read most of them at the time, especially those in the *Strathy,* as this became my local newspaper when I moved up to Strathspey a decade before the twentieth century ended. Reading them again I'm impressed with the breadth of knowledge and diversity of interest reflected in them. As well as hillwalking and mountaineering there are essays covering natural history, the weather, mythology, history, outdoor people, islands, conservation and more. There is so much packed in here. Anyone wanting to learn about Scotland, and the vast majority of the essays are about Scotland though there are a few dips south of the border, will learn a great deal here, all imparted in Cameron's easy going fluent style that conjures up everything he describes so well.

Cameron is usually regarded as an 'outdoor' writer, that is someone who writes about hillwalking, mountaineering, and adventures in wild places. A current trend is for 'nature' writing, which is about wildlife, and interactions with nature, apparently separate from the 'outdoors.' I've never liked this division, this pigeonholing. So many writers cover both. Cameron certainly does. There are deep thoughts here about conservation and wildlife as well as exciting adventures in the hills. This book is both nature writing and outdoor writing. And all expressed with passion, energy, and enjoyment.

Having all these essays together in one place gives them a power and significance greater than they had as individual stand-alone pieces. Themes can be followed, Cameron's developing thought processes revealed. Divided into sections, each with a new introduction from Cameron, it's fascinating to read decades of words on wildlife or mountain people or islands all together. This is an important collection of work.

Introduction

Professional outdoor writing is an unusual occupation, an existence dominated by obsession and yearning, ambition and reality, occasional feasts and many famines. On one hand you earn a living from doing those things you love best, but on the other your livelihood depends on being outside at all times of the year and in all weathers. If illness or injury strike, your means of earning a living are considerably reduced. In addition, whilst days on the hill or mountain are creatively inspiring, the downside is having to spend almost as much time in front of a computer screen at home, putting words to the experience so others may enjoy it vicariously. The sheer delight of simply going out for a hillwalk for its own sake fades to almost nothing.

My lifelong passion has been climbing hills and mountains, both at home and abroad. At various times I've obsessed on rock climbing, winter climbing, ski touring, backpacking and that most manic and inexplicable game, Munro-bagging. I moved my family to the Scottish Highlands to be close to the hills and, after working for the Scottish Youth Hostels Association in Aviemore, became an outdoor instructor, writing articles and books first thing in the morning and last thing at night. I quickly understood that doing both jobs wasn't sustainable in the long term, so I chose to write.

I chose wisely. It was a risky thing to do but I was fairly comfortable with risk. Fundamentally part of the climbing game, mountaineers learn how to manage it through experience and the gaining of skills, processes that apply as fully to the rest of life. Risk management in the writing game essentially boils down to two things: finding a regular source of freelance work to fit beside, if possible, full-time employment. When I began writing professionally, very few newspapers were interested in outdoor topics and full-time jobs as an outdoor writer were as rare as hen's teeth. Purely by chance I met a man by the name of Stephen Young who owned the Northern Scot group of newspapers. One of his titles was the *Strathspey and Badenoch Herald* and I managed to convince him that, as more and more outdoor enthusiasts were moving to the Aviemore area, which was fast becoming one of the 'adventure capitals' of Scotland, the local paper should serve them with a weekly outdoors column. He agreed and I wrote my first column for the '*Strathie*' in early 1979, a weekly essay I contributed for thirty-two years.

A few years later I become the Deputy Editor of *Climber & Rambler* Magazine for a company called Holmes McDougall Publishing Ltd who paid me a regular salary. I became editor the following year and, in 1990, became editor of *The Great Outdoors* magazine, a role I enjoyed for the next twenty years. In addition to my weekly *Strathie* column I became the outdoor columnist for a newspaper called *Scotland on Sunday* between 1996 and 1999.

The company that owned *The Great Outdoors* magazine also owned a couple of newspapers and were intent on launching a new Scottish Sunday title called the *Sunday Herald* to compete with *Scotland on Sunday*. A well-known and respected editor called Andrew Jaspan was brought in to launch and run the new paper. We happened to be standing side by side in the men's loo, doing what comes naturally, when he asked me why I was writing for a competing newspaper. 'Because they asked me,' I answered simply. 'If I asked you to write a weekly column for us would you do it?' he retorted. I said I would and jumped ship to contribute a weekly 'walks' column to the *Sunday Herald* for the next fifteen years.

Writing a weekly local newspaper column is a huge privilege, but not always easy. It takes considerable commitment and it's difficult not to repeat yourself, so the content of my *Strathie* column changed over time. From walk descriptions I became more campaigning in my output, commenting on a range of environmental subjects. To reflect this, Ken Smith, one of my editors, changed the title of the column from 'Out of Doors' to 'McNeish at Large', and I became the voice of dissent amongst local landowners, developers and politicians. I was extremely critical of ski developments on Cairn Gorm and my thoughts didn't win me many friends among the ski community in Aviemore. On one occasion, while taking a group of schoolchildren into the Northern Corries I was confronted by Bob Clyde, the General Manager of the ski-lift company who told me to 'get off ma mountain'. I had one even more vociferous critic during my time with the *Strathie*, the late Donnie Ross, a local shepherd whom I admired greatly. Sadly, my admiration was not reciprocated. In me he saw everything that threatened his traditional way of life. Critical of sheep-farming, I called them 'hooved locusts', just as John Muir had done in Yosemite. I advocated for more woodland instead of monoculture grouse moors, and thought there were too many red deer and they should be culled. Worst of all in Donnie's eyes, I wasn't a local highlander but came from Glasgow.

Life as a columnist on the *Sunday Herald* brought less criticism. Who could take offence at someone describing a walk in the wild places? My 'Peak Practice' column necessitated a lot of travelling as it was important to cover routes in all parts of Scotland and even a few in the north of England. Occasionally I would jump in my old campervan and spend a long weekend in some part of the country, walking two or three routes over the weekend and storing them for future use when the weather was particularly bad.

Compiling some of these old newspaper columns into a book has been a fascinating and revealing experience and has confirmed something to me that I long suspected. Progress in terms of environmental management and conservation in Scotland is an extremely slow process. I was writing about land reform, raptor persecution, ski development and deer fencing over thirty years ago, and there has been little positive development on any of these issues in the intervening years. In a *Strathie* column in 2002 I wrote critically of Highlands and Islands Enterprise's ownership of the Cairn Gorm estate, suggesting that as a Government development agency they should withdraw and transfer ownership to either the local community or the incoming National Park board. As Highlands and Islands Enterprise (HIE) they are still on Cairn Gorm, controversially pumping millions in public funds into a succession of tenant ski companies that have all gone bust. Now they are bailing out a funicular train that has failed spectacularly, an uplift scheme that I described as a white elephant as far back as 2002.

In 1997 I wrote about the extravagant cost of deer fencing to the public purse and how much more effective deer culling and the removal of sheep would be in allowing young trees to grow. Today there are literally hundreds of miles of new fencing going up throughout Scotland as landowners cash in on the Scottish Government's Forestry Grant Scheme to implement new woodland creation. On the one hand it's encouraging to see the Scottish Government prioritising new woodland growth, but it subsequently demoralising to realise that much of this new growth will be for timber production with its associated issues of clear-fell and increased road freight. As I discovered to my cost only recently, many landowners are erecting miles of fencing but failing to put in regular access points, one of the fundamental requirements for landowners and managers in the Land Reform (Scotland) Act 2003. The responsibilities contained in the Scottish Outdoor Access Code are supposed to work two ways: we walkers have responsibilities, but so do landowners and land managers. Many of them are failing in these responsibilities by excluding people from vast tracts of land. Claiming millions of pounds of taxpayers' money to fence out not only the deer and sheep, but also those same taxpayers.

It's not all bad news though. There is much more awareness of raptor persecution in Scotland today, although I'm not sure how many more sea eagles, golden eagles, buzzards, hen harriers, red kites and peregrines have to be poisoned or shot before our Governments decide to do something positive about it. Likewise, recent years have seen the reintroduction of beavers to some of our rivers, albeit a tightly controlled reintroduction with an insane licensing system that allows some farmers to shoot them if they feel they are adversely affecting their land. It's taken decades of campaigning for beavers to be reintroduced in Scotland. I hate to think how long it might take before politicians approve of reintroducing the lynx. As for wolves – forget it!

Perhaps the biggest change I've seen in almost fifty years of writing about our hills is our nation's general attitude to the outdoors and nature.

The dark cloud that was the Covid-19 pandemic and its associated lockdowns had an unexpected silver lining. It increased awareness of the basic need we have for nature and the natural world. During the crisis of 2020 and 2021 we heard much about 'mental health'. The term covers a huge range of conditions but, on this occasion, I'm referring to those issues caused by the restrictions of lockdown: worry, stress, loneliness and isolation. To some folk these are merely an irritant, but for others they can become chronic mental health issues that require treatment.

I've been convinced for many years, and have written about it for just as long, that regular encounters with the natural world can reduce the stresses caused by living in a highly pressurised society in which many elements are beyond our immediate control, or as in the Covid crisis, a sense of entrapment, loss of freedom or even deep concerns about the long-term future.

Many who have lost their jobs and income, and particularly those who have lost loved ones to this deadly virus, may react negatively or even angrily to my suggestion of going for a walk in the woods. I am overwhelmingly aware that I may sound trite and condescending, but even in such awful circumstances an exposure to the natural world can alleviate stress, depression and even grief.

There have been many studies that have shown the positive

relationship between exposure to the natural world and well-being. Whilst nice views and pleasant countryside appeal to our sense of beauty there are also chemical reactions taking place in our body that create a natural drug-like effect in our brain. A natural high, as potent and addictive in its own way as cannabis or crack cocaine! But, and it's an enormous but, as more and more people discover this phenomenon, as more people tune into nature as never before, the natural world itself has been on the receiving end of what has been described as 'lockdown surge', and we have to be reminded of our responsibilities. Most important of all, we must recognise that we are not divorced from the natural world but part of it and, because we are part of it, have to treat it with love and respect. If we do that, we will be rewarded with those mental health benefits I mentioned, benefits and blessings that are lost if we have to wade along footpaths covered in litter and cold campfire remains, or become part of an uncaring public that gathers in popular tourist hot spots to the detriment of everything that made the place special in the first place.

It's good to remember the wonderful quotation from the American forester, writer and ecologist Aldo Leopold: 'We abuse the land because we regard it as a commodity belonging to us. When we see the land as a community to which we belong, we may begin to use it with love and respect.' I hope the essays that follow will reflect some of that love and respect, and in reading them some of that appreciation of our wild places may rub off on you. We have entered a crucial period in our custodianship of a planet that we haven't loved and respected very successfully to date. I published my first article about global warming in 1978 and our battle against it hasn't advanced much in the intervening years. Global climate change is the biggest test any of us has ever faced and it can't be left to politicians to sort out. The fightback begins with us, you and me, and we can begin by gaining an understanding of the workings of a natural world that includes us, affects us, and depends on us, not for the survival of the planet itself, but for the survival of mankind on the planet. Earth could cope very well without us.

The following essays (with dates of original publication) also reflect some of the delights, joys and challenges the outdoor life can offer, written over a period of forty years or so. While nothing in life is as constant as change, the hills themselves thankfully remain largely inviolate and immutable, their spirit of ancient mightiness still offering life-affirming experiences. The title of this book, An Eye *to the Hills* reflects that longevity but it also reflects something else. Psalm 121 includes the popular lines: 'I to the hills will lift mine eyes, from whence doth come my aid?' Unfortunately, many people ignore the question mark. The psalmist is asking a question, not making a statement. His aid doesn't come from the hills but he gives the answer to his question in the next line of the psalm: 'My help cometh from the Lord, who heaven and earth has made.' What I like about this psalm is the recognition that the hills may not provide the immediate aid, but can provide something else. The psalmist lifts his eyes to the hills for inspiration, for revelation, for illumination, something that I and many others have been doing for a long, long time. I hope they will bless you in the same way.

Here endeth the lesson.

CHAPTER ONE

The Big Days

There are big days on the hill and even bigger days. Some may be long in terms of distance, although shorter days in terms of mileage can still be big because of the amount of climbing involved. Then there are the days that are big because of an element known as the 'long walk-in'.

Because of our extensive road network, even in the more remote parts of the Scottish Highlands and Islands, long walk-ins are now relatively rare. Indeed, one of the attractions of hillwalking in Scotland is that you can usually climb your hill, or group of hills, and be in the pub by opening time, but that's not always the case. The Fisherfield Munros include a spot near A' Mhaighdean that is thought to be the most remote in the land, so that and its neighbours require a long walk-in from Kinlochewe, Poolewe or Corrie Hallie near Dundonnell. These particular long routes are generally on good tracks where a mountain bike may be useful.

The Cairngorms, their northern remoteness diminished nowadays by easy access to the Cairn Gorm Mountain car park in Coire Cas, once necessitated a very long walk-in from Coylumbridge. Even today the big hills of the southern Cairngorms still require a hefty trek from the Linn of Dee or Allanaquoich to reach them. The Knoydart Munros, on their wild peninsula between Loch Nevis and Loch Hourn, the lochs of heaven and hell, require a long walk-in from either Kinloch Hourn in the east or Inverie in the south. Hardier types, or masochists, may prefer the wilder route from Glen Dessarry via the rain-soaked and boggy Mam na Cloich Airde to Sourlies at the head of Loch Nevis.

There are strong arguments in favour of the long walk-in, both from the points of view of physical readiness and deeper appreciation.

The Cairngorms require long and steady ascents through forests, climbing steadily below a canopy of Scots pines, through alpine zones into alpine-arctic zones with associated wildlife and vegetation, to the higher realms through skirts of ancient pines that become more storm-tossed and stunted the higher you climb, eventually beyond the tree line. Here you can comprehend the different types of landscapes in a holistic sense, experiencing their connectedness as you ease yourself upwards. Exiting the trees also begins another stage, climbing the lower slopes into glacier-scooped corries by way of narrow ridges onto the vast arctic spaciousness of plateaux that are as remote and isolated as they were a century ago. No such experience is possible when you step out of a heated vehicle onto a tarmac car park with dozens of other cars, coaches and buses, and shivering tourists.

The seven-mile walk from Kinloch Hourn to Barrisdale is a coastal adventure I'm particularly fond of, following the shoreline of Loch Hourn past the abandoned homes and former townships at Skiary and Runival, beyond the old and now roofless church at Barrisdale to the wonderful view of Ladhar Bheinn across the waters of Barrisdale Bay. Loch Hourn, often described as the grandest of the fissures that tear into Scotland's west coast, reaches far and deep inland from the Sound of Sleat, winding into the heart of the country like a Norwegian fjord. The great highland writer Seton Gordon compared it to a 'lake of the infernal regions', and the comparison is not at all fanciful. Loch Hourn has acquired an aura of mystique through Gaelic mythology as the ancestral home of Domhnull Dubh, the Devil. One school of thought suggests that Hourn is a corruption of Iutharn, which means Hell. Another interpretation is that the name is possibly Norse, meaning Horn, which could perhaps be corroborated by the curving sweep of the loch. Whatever the meaning the walk along its rocky shores is always wonderfully evocative. It is to be entertained by oystercatchers, herons and gulls and there is always the chance of spotting an otter or a stravaiging sea eagle.

The long walk-in to climb a hill, or group of hills, occasionally requires the use of a tent or a night in a bothy, which can add to the experience, and I must confess to a hint of envy for those super-fit trail runners I see so much of on the hills these days, hill-athletes who are capable of jogging over huge swathes of hill country with comparative ease. The exploits of these folk leave me breathless with admiration.

Many years ago, inspired by an article I had read in the *Scots Magazine*, I attempted to walk from Ben Nevis over the Munros of the Aonachs, the Grey Corries and the Mamores and back to the summit of the Ben within twenty-four hours, and almost made it but ran out of time and energy just below Stob Ban. The route is known as the Tranter Round, and was first completed in 1964 by the late Philip Tranter who sadly died in a car crash while returning overland from a mountaineering trip to the Hindu Kush. His time for this forty-mile route, with over 20,000 feet of climbing, was later superseded by the fell-runner Charlie Ramsay who extended it by adding the five Munros that surround Loch Treig: Beinn na Lap, Chno Dearg, Stob Coire Sgriodan, Stob a' Choire Mheadhoin and Stob Coire Easain. With profound serendipity this created a challenge of twenty-four Munros in twenty-four hours, an astonishing distance of fifty-six miles with 28,000 feet of ascent, almost the height of Everest.

The Glen Shiel area of Wester Ross is another rich in multi-Munro big days. A Tranter-like round starts at the Cluanie Inn and traverses the South Glen Shiel ridge followed by a tough re-ascent to take in the Five Sisters of Kintail and the ridge of Ciste Dubh. Many hillwalkers are happy to confine their big days to the completion of the South Glen Shiel Ridge, with seven Munros for the tick list, or a traverse of the Five Sisters of Kintail with three Munros. A boggy walk-in to the SYHA hostel at Alltbeithe from Melvich or Cluanie gives access to the big hills of Affric and the potential for even more.

Not all big days require a long walk-in though. Some, although relatively short in distance, require a lot of climbing, those roller-coaster routes that take in several summits in a day. I've described a couple in this chapter, the Ros-Bheinn group and the Tyndrum Corbetts are good examples, the latter being a hill round I often used to gauge my hill fitness when preparing for big backpacking trips abroad.

Another big day that will test your mountaineering skills to the limit is a traverse of the Cuillin Ridge on Skye. Only six or seven miles in length, its eleven Munros will task you with over 13,000 feet of climbing, not to mention the other sixteen non-Munro tops en route. Much is on exposed, rocky ridges and you'll have to negotiate some sustained rock scrambles along the way including the highlight of the route. The Inaccessible Pinnacle is the most technical Munro on the list, requiring rock-climbing and abseiling skills for which you will have to carry a rope, slings and the paraphernalia of the climber.

In the following essays I've described a range of longer days I've enjoyed over the years, routes that will not deter any hill-walker of reasonable fitness, but outings that blessed me richly at the time, even though I was on my knees at the end of several of them.

ROIS-BHEINN
JUNE 1981

Superb examples of all that is good about the Corbetts, the Scottish hills between 2500 and 2999ft, are to be found amongst the rocky bluffs and rugged landscape of the Moidart peninsula. These lower hills begin more or less at sea level, and provide good, hard days that would be worthy of the higher Munros. This route is only ten miles in length but the amount of up and down makes it a pretty tough challenge.

There are no footpaths to speak of in Moidart, and no

three-thousand footers, which means no erosion paths, no lines of cairns, no roadside car parks and few people. There are however, ten fine Corbetts. Five peaks rise from a horseshoe-shaped ridge that dominates the north-west corner of the peninsula, and three of those are Corbetts. Sgurr na Ba Glaise (874m/2884ft), Rois-Bheinn (878m/2897ft) and An Stac (814m/2686ft) are the highest points on the ridge that curves around Coire a' Bhuiridh, the yellow corrie, just south of Lochailort.

These hills were my birthday treat a number of years ago. I camped on the shores of Loch Ailort where I was entertained by one of the most stunning sunsets I've ever seen. The dying sun set over the Cuillin of Rum in a burst of yellows and reds and, within moments, the waters of the sea loch were running blood red. I lay on the shore in a shimmer of primroses and violets with a glass (okay, a mug . . .) of equally blood-red wine, the toast of heroes, and drank to Fionn MacChumhaill, Ossian, Diarmid and all those warriors of legend who passed the enchanted loch on their final journey to Tir nan Og. It was a good omen.

I've never returned to these hills, partly because the day that followed was well nigh perfect and I've never wanted to break its spell, one of the finest days the Corbetts have to offer.

A farm track runs in an east-north-east direction from Inverailort to cross a burn that foams and splutters from the low bealach between the hillock of Tom Odhar and the north-east ridge of Seann Chruach. Follow the footpath through the col and onto open moorland beyond where the Allt a' Bhuiridh chuckles down from the corrie above. Cross to the east bank of the river and climb the western slopes of Beinn Coire nan Gall, heading towards the bealach between it and Druim Fiaclach. From the bealach climb to the summit of Fiaclach by its steep north ridge. Druim Fiaclach is made up of two long and narrow ridges. The best route lies along the south western one where you can enjoy the airy spaciousness, with far-flung views in every direction and where you can gaze down into the depths of its great, wide-open southern corrie. From here the route rollercoasters up and down, along broad, then narrow, sections of ridge. Ahead lie the big climbs up onto Sgurr na Ba Glaise, the peak of the grey cow, and the highest hill of the day, Rois-Bheinn itself. From Sgurr na Ba Glaise, descend the steep slopes that lead down to a wide col, the Bealach an Fhiona. From here an ancient dry-stone wall follows the steep and very rocky slopes of Rois-Bheinn to its eastern summit and trig point.

The views are fantastic, out west along the length of Loch Ailort to the open sea where the isles of Eigg and Rum dance on glistening waters.

By the time you return to the Bealach an Fhiona you will be even more aware of the great lump called An Stac (814m/2671ft), which effectively blocks your homewards route. Its ascent involves more steep and rocky slopes, the steepest yet and the longest too, a good pull of a thousand feet at the end of what has already been a strenuous day.

From the summit descend north, then north-north-east down rocky slopes to Seann Cruach, then down its north-east ridge to the woods above the Tom Odhar col. Descend through the woods to the col and make your way back to Inverailort.

SGURR EILDE MOR, BINNEIN BEAG & BINNEIN MOR, MAMORES, AUGUST 1989

After the horrors of monsoon rain with its associated landslips and blocked roads it was great to see the weekend arrive with wall-to-wall sunshine. As I made my way up the stalkers' path above Loch Eilde Mor, I couldn't help recall some of the land-slips I had seen over the years. Most vivid was an experience in the Hindu Kush of Pakistan where, following forty-eight hours of heavy rain, a great brown river of mud, soil and rocks swept past our campsite with only yards to spare. Closer to home, in the Cairngorms, another swept down a steep corrie wall bring-ing with it boulders the size of a car. I fervently hoped not to see another today in the Mamores.

I was certainly aware of how waterlogged the ground was. It was more like spring after a big snowmelt than high summer, and the loch below Sgurr Eilde Mor was full to overflowing when normally, at this time of the year, it shrinks in size. Possibly I was being slightly paranoid because, as I wandered past the still waters and saw the dumpy peak of Binnein Beag ahead, my fears evaporated and I began to enjoy the wonderful situation of the hills at the eastern end of the Mamores ridge.

Sgurr Eilde Mor (1010m/3314ft), Binnein Beag (943m/3094ft), and Binnein Mor (1130m/3707ft) form a trio of peaks that surrounds the great corrie that drains north to Tom an Eite at the head of Glen Nevis. Views from all three summits are far-reaching with the open expanse of Rannoch Moor to the east and a whole cluster of high peaks to the south, west and north with the massive bulk of Ben Nevis dominant, crouching as it does over the curving outline of the Carn Mor Dearg Arete.

The stalkers' path descends slightly from Loch Eilde Mor before climbing onto the broad bealach that separates the two Binneins. I hadn't bothered with Sgurr Eilde Mor today, wanting to get high on Binnein Mor to grab some photographs of the ridge and, in turn, to climb Binnein Beag to get photos of Binnein Mor, the shapeliest of all the Mamores peaks.

I wasn't disappointed. From the summit Ben Nevis looked close enough to touch although, despite its dominant bulk and presence, it didn't compare to the beautifully sweeping ridges of Binnein Mor whose tiny square-cut summit is formed by curved ridges and corries into a classic, archetypal mountain shape with sparkling lochans filling its corries. I climbed past them, travers-ing the hill's north-west slopes to reach the north ridge, a long, narrow highway to an impressively narrow summit with barely enough room for the cairn.

From here another long ridge swept away to a subsidiary summit, then flowed on in a graceful curve to the double-topped Na Gruachaichean, the maiden. The other tops of the Mamores piled up against one another and layer after layer of mountain skyline rolled on into the sun-kissed west.

A broader ridge carried me down to Sgurr Eilde Beag where a wonderfully engineered stalkers' path dropped to the outward path from Kinlochleven. Away in the south dark clouds were building up and the paranoia returned. Could this be the next storm moving in from the Atlantic? Only time would tell.

LADHAR BHEINN, KNOYDART
MAY 1995

Exactly 150 years ago, factor James Grant and his henchmen, under orders from Josephine Macdonnell of Glengarry, began tearing down the thatched cottages and killing the livestock of the cotters who lived on the shores of Loch Hourn and Loch Nevis in Knoydart. The Macdonells of Glengarry had run up huge debts and the Knoydart folk were forced to take up an offer of paid transport to the New World so the family could sell the land.

The flockmasters soon took over with their black-faced sheep and, when that became uneconomical, the entire peninsula was given over to deer stalking. Knoydart became a man-made wilderness.

As we tramped along the shore of Loch Hourn last week the ghosts of the past were still present in the low-walled remains of Skiary, by the little sanctuary of Runival and in the roof-less church at Barrisdale Bay. On the tidal burial-isle of Eilean Choinnich tiny shards of granite were all that remained of the gravestones. Only the high tops offer redemption from the past and Ladhar Bheinn, Knoydart's highest, is symbolic of a new era in Knoydart's history.

In 1987 the mountain was bought by the John Muir Trust, a conservation organisation that took a leading role in the eventual community buyout of Knoydart, reversing history by putting the future of the area firmly back into the hands of the folk who live and work there. Ladhar Bheinn (1020m/3346ft) is also symbolic of those ingredients that make west highland hills so special.

The most westerly Munro on the mainland, it offers excep-tional sea views to the islands of the west and the blend of sea and mountain air is intoxicating. A big hill with a complexity of corrie and ridge, Ladhar Bheinn can be climbed from several directions: from Folach in Gleann na Guiserein, by Coire a' Phuill from the Mam Barrisdale or by the magnificent Coire Dhorcaill. Having climbed it by all directions I'd recommend the latter route, after the seven-mile lochside preamble from Kinloch Hourn.

There's a good bothy at Barrisdale, where the estate charges a couple of quid a night for a dry shelter with light and a flushing toilet. Alternatively, you can camp outside.

Just beyond the bothy a wooden bridge crosses the river and a well-used track runs off across salt flats to a stalkers' path that climbs to the shoulder of Creag Bheithe, before turning south-west into the lower reaches of Coire Dhorcaill, a magnificent bowl that's partly enclosed by the subsidiary peaks of Stob a' Chearcaill and Stob a' Choire Odhar. Between these tops lies a horseshoe of ridges and peaks that makes a fabulous, high mountain walk, but unless you're experienced on steep, danger-ous terrain avoid Stob a' Chearcaill. The rocky slopes of this top can be lethal when wet.

The Druim a' Choire Odhair forms the north-west boundary of Coire Dhorrcail and can be reached by a steep and relentless climb from the corrie floor. The ridge then rises comparatively gently in a series of rocky peaks, each eyrie outlook confirming upward progress above the fjord-like Loch Hourn far below.

As the ridge gains height it narrows appreciably, ultimately to its own top, Stob a' Choire Odhair. From here a scythe-shaped ridge links to the summit ridge, with a fairly steep but easy scramble up the final few feet. The summit is on the west-north-west ridge just a short distance from this junction.

Experienced scramblers will follow the corrie rims right round to Stob a' Chearcaill where the top's north-facing slopes offer a tricky descent, but others are advised to follow the corrie rims down to the Bealach Coire Dhorrcail, round the head of another steep corrie before the junction with the long Aonach Sgoilte ridge, and down to another bealach before Stob a' Chearcaill. From here grassy slopes drop to the summit of the Mam Barrisdale from where a good track takes you back to Barrisdale. Bear in mind when planning that Barrisdale is seven miles from the car parking area at Kinloch Hourn and the walk from Barrisdale up and over Ladhar Bheein is another nine miles. A big day indeed if you don't stop over at Barrisdale.

LUINNE BHEINN AND MEALL BUIDHE, KNOYDART
JULY 1995

A few weeks ago I wrote glowingly of the seven-mile trek alongside Loch Hourn to Barrisdale in Knoydart from where most folk climb Ladhar Bheinn, the most western Munro on the mainland. The bothy at Barrisdale is used increasingly to access two other Knoydart Munros, Luinne Bheinn and Meall Buidhe.

I know from speaking to many Munro-baggers that they are often faced with something of a dilemma when considering the best approaches to these two hills. If you want to make a good weekend of it, with a long and glorious walk-in, the Barrisdale approach is best, both scenically and aesthetically. The alternative is to catch the 10.00am ferry from Mallaig, which gets you to Inverie in Knoydart at 11.00am, climb the hills, and return to Inverie for an overnight stay, returning to Mallaig next morning.

Luinne Bheinn and Meall Buidhe, along with Ladhar Bheinn, are the big hills of Knoydart. The first two rise from extremely rough and rocky corries and are separated from Ladhar Bheinn by the high pass of the Mam Barrisdale. A good track, which runs all the way from Inverie to Barrisdale, crosses the pass, the summit of which gives excellent access to the north-west ridge of Luinne Bheinn (939m/3081ft).

Although I personally prefer the Barrisdale route the southern one from Inverie is probably slightly easier, if a little longer. Meall Buidhe is best accessed from the Mam Meadail, the pass that runs from the Inverie River to Glen Carnoch. It's a relatively short climb to Meall Buidhe's south-east ridge, which leads easily to the summit. From the hill's eastern top, a knobbly,

undulating ridge leads roughly north-east to Luinne Bheinn and
from there it's only a short descent to the summit of the Mam
Barrisdale and the track that runs all the way back to Inverie.
It's a distance of seventeen to eighteen miles.

The route from Barrisdale is considerably shorter, but
Barrisdale is, of course, seven miles from the roadhead at Kinloch
Hourn. A track runs to the summit of the Mam Barrisdale, and
easy slopes climb east onto the Bachd Mhic an Tosaich, from
where the ridge to Luinne Bheinn both narrows and steepens in
a rough and rocky climb to the summit ridge. A lower, muddier
path has evolved in recent years, which follows a line of old fence
posts onto Luinne Bheinn's south-west ridge, a path that's better
used in descent, but I'll come to that in a moment.

It's interesting that the name Luinne Bheinn has been translated as meaning the hill of anger, or the hill of melody, or even
the hill of mirth – an emotional mountain apparently. I think it
was Hamish Brown who suggested it should just be the hill of
moods. The summit sits proudly at 939m/3080ft, with a long
ranging view down the length of Gleann an Dubh-Lochain and
out beyond Loch Nevis where, shimmering on a flat sea, lie the
contrasting outlines of mountainous Rum and flat-topped Eigg.

At the east end of the summit ridge a steep southern flank
drops down to a broad, undulating ridge that forms a back wall
to the rugged, rocky corries that lie between the two Munros.
This ridge eventually borders the remote and desolate north
corrie of Meall Buidhe, and leads to the obviously defined north-
east summit ridge. The highest of the two tops is the western
one, at 946m/3104ft.

With both summits now bagged, the main problem is how to
get back to Barrisdale. If you descend by a southern route, or by
any route to the west, you're faced with another long climb over
the Mam Barrisdale. The best return route, I've found, involves
more climbing but takes you through the remarkably rugged
landscape that lies between the two Munros.

Descend Meall Buidhe's north ridge and make your way
gradually north-east, down long rocky ribs into the heart of this

wonderfully rough and rugged mountain bowl. A short climb up grassy slopes leads to a pair of high-level lochans and from the second one a long easy angled gully leads back to Luinne Bheinn's south-west ridge. It's only a short traverse now to the muddy path I mentioned earlier, and those old fence posts that lead down to the summit of the pass. From there it's downhill all the way back to Barrisdale.

A'MHAIGHDEAN, WESTER ROSS
AUGUST 1997

The poet Milton once referred to 'wilderness' as a place of abundance. Gary Snyder, the poet laureate of the American ecology movement, agrees, but with the corollary that wilderness has also 'implied chaos, eros, the unknown, realms of taboo, the habitat of both the ecstatic and the demonic. In both senses, it's a place of archetypal power, teaching and challenge'.

The Letterewe Deer Forest between Loch Maree and Little Loch Broom is probably as close to that description as anything we have in Scotland. The north shores of Loch Maree are rich in oak wood and associated undergrowth and the glens are full of wild flowers: orchids, bog asphodel, lousewort and milkwort. Higher up, the quartzite and Torridonian sandstone ridges, crags and tops offer all the challenge Snyder could ask for and at the very heart of this so-called Letterewe Wilderness lies the remotest Munro of all, A'Mhaighdean, the Maiden (918m/3012ft).

The ascent of A'Mhaighdean demands something more than a day trip. You can ride a mountain bike from Poolewe as far as the bothy at Carnmore from where a good path climbs the mountain but there is an argument to suggest it's better to ease yourself in gently, either from Poolewe by way of Kernsary and the Fionn Loch, or by Dundonell, Shenavall and Gleann na Muice Beag in the north, or from Kinlochewe and Loch Maree.

In a couple of previous visits I've climbed A'Mhaighdean as part of a long rosary of Munros from Shenavall: Beinn a'

Chlaideimh, Sgurr Ban, Mullach Coire Mhic Fhearchair, Beinn Tarsuinn and then A'Mhaighdean and its close neighbour, Ruadh Stac Mor. That's certainly a big, big mountain round.

This time though, I wanted to combine A'Mhaighdean with other aspects of this Letterewe deer forest: the marvellous oak woods of Loch Maree where there was once a thriving iron smelting industry, the cathedral-like grandeur of the Fionn Loch below the steep crags of Beinn Airigh Charr, Meall Mheinnidh and Beinn Lair and the empty quarter around lonely Lochan Fada before returning to Kinlochewe above the narrow gorge of Gleann Bianasdail.

It turned out to be a memorable outing, even if the three mile walk along the trackless shore of Lochan Fada was tougher than expected, but the undoubted highlight was the ascent of A'Mhaighdean from Carnmore. Although a superb stalkers' path traverses across the steep slopes of Sgurr na Lacainn and makes its tortuous way up the mountain's north-east corrie we chose to scramble up the steep, stepped north-west ridge. The stalkers' path took us as far as Fuar Loch Mor from where we skirted the loch's western bank and took to the rock. There was plenty of good, steep scrambling but all the real difficulties can be avoided.

In essence, this was a stairway to heaven, a heaven with some of the best views imaginable, arguably the finest in the country, out along the length of the crag-fringed Fionn Loch to Loch Ewe and the open sea. To witness such a view, with the western sun sinking beyond the Hebrides in a riot of colour, is heaven indeed.

MAOILE LUNNDAIDH, WESTER ROSS
OCTOBER 1998

It's as though one of the lumpen Cairngorms has been transported to the Achnashellach Forest and dumped alongside the west's more 'pointy' peaks. Maoile Lunndaidh (1007m/3304ft) is one of Scotland's most remote Munros and would be well at home above the Braes o' Mar or Badenoch. Typical Cairngormian, her flat summit plateau is surrounded by several impressive corries, particularly the steep-sided Fuar-tholl Mor, and as you march across her dome-like plateau you might, for all the world, be striding across the Braeriach plateau.

This impression is probably made more vivid if you include Lunndaidh's close neighbours, Sgurr Choinnich (999m/3277ft) and Sgurr a 'Chaorachain (1053m/3455ft) in your day's outing. Sgurr a' Chaorachain, in particular, is as well defined as Lunndaidh is rounded, although you could be forgiven for putting this one in the Cairngorm category too. Whatever characteristics they may share, the three can be combined to offer a big challenge of some twenty miles.

A forestry road runs from the hostel at Craig on the A890 (two and a half miles east of Achnashellach) all the way up beside the Allt a' Chonais and means you can start and finish your day by bike. Ride as far as the bridge over the Allt a'Chonais, and pick it up on your way back down. A long freewheel through the forest makes a fine end to the day when the feet are beginning to nip a bit.

If you have the ability to cycle and gaze at the scenery at the same time (I always end in the ditch) then enjoy the massive, rocky face of Sgurr nan Ceannaichean as it frowns down on you. The mountains in front are Sgurr Choinnich and Sgurr a' Chaorachain, divided by a steep col. While you could cross the river at Pollan Buidhe and climb up through the rough corrie to the col, a more satisfying route follows a footpath south-west to the Bealach Bhearnais to where Sgurr Choinnich's west ridge can be picked up. Climb this ridge, which becomes increasingly rocky as you ascend, to the narrow, level summit ridge.

Now head south-east along and drop down for a short distance in the same direction before turning west-north-west where the corrie edge is followed down to the col below Sgurr a' Chaorachain. Follow the ridge directly to the summit where you have a choice of route – you can either continue east to Bidean an Eoin Deirg, which can be descended steeply north-north-east to a col at about 600m, or descend off Sgurr a'Chaorachain's north ridge for half a kilometre before turning north-east onto the Sron na Frianich above the waters of the dark Lochan Gaineamhach. Drop down the eastern slopes of the Sron to the bealach and its many peat hags.

To continue to Maoile Lunndaidh, climb the long western ridge of Carn nam Fiaclan and follow the narrowing neck of ridge between the head of the impressive Fuar-tholl Mor in the north and Toll a' Choin in the south, to the huge, gravelly plateau of Maoile Lunndaidh.

Once you've found the summit cairn, a dodgy operation in misty conditions, drop down the broad heather-covered slopes of the north ridge into Gleann Fhiodhaig just east of the ruined Glenuaig Lodge. Follow the track back to the Allt a'Chonais and that long promised downhill bike ride back to the start.

THE TALLA BHEITH CORBETTS, PERTHSHIRE
NOVEMBER 2002

The track that runs the length of Coire Dhomhain through the hills of the Dalnaspidal Deer Forest normally provides a pleasant approach to the Munros of Sgairneach Mhor and Beinn Udlamain. Today it was leading me into low cloud and snow showers.

I was heading for the Corbetts of Stob an Aonaich Mhoir (855m/2821ft) and Beinn Mholach (841m/2775ft), two of the least visited hills in Scotland. While both summits can be tackled independently via tracks from Loch Rannoch-side in the south I thought I'd take two days to climb both, camping out overnight in one of the emptiest quarters in Scotland.

The Scottish Mountaineering Club Guide to the Central Highlands is not very flattering to either hill. In the eleven lines that describe the route to Beinn Mholach the guide manages to say virtually nothing about the hill itself, although it does say it lies in the heart of a wasteland'. It doesn't say much more about Stob an Aonaich Mhoir, but does tentatively suggest that this area of the Talla Bheithe deer forest between Loch Garry and Loch Ericht 'will attract only the confirmed seeker of solitude'.

This area of rounded hills and shallow glens is certainly pretty desolate, particularly on a dour mid-November weekend when low clouds and frequent snow squalls cut visibility to less than a hundred metres.

It's often when expectation is at its lowest that the mountain magician creates beauty out of nothing. Descending a narrow, steep-sided glen into Coire Bhachdaidh I looked up to see the cloud suddenly lift and expose a marvellous scene. A sinuous stream, sparkling in the sudden light, twisted its way down the length of the corrie all the way to a white house, Coire Bhachdaidh Lodge, on the shores of Loch Ericht. Beyond the dark waters the hills of Ben Alder Forest were bathed in mellow sunshine.

The real bonus was that I could now see my first top and was soon climbing snow-covered slopes to its summit, perched precariously above the steep crags that drop into Loch Ericht. Old Rannoch tales claim that a village was once drowned in the waters of the sixteen-mile-long loch. Apparently, a great earthquake caused a cataclysmic rush of water to submerge the parish of Feadaill at the south end and all its inhabitants perished. Local folk say that on a still day you can see the steeple of the church below the surface of the water.

Beinn Mholach lies south-east of Stob an Aonaich Mhoir, five miles of bog-trotting over a shallow, waterlogged pass to the upper reaches of the Allt Shallainn. From the headwaters of the burn it was a fairly straightforward climb over heather slopes to Mholach's rocky summit, but it was dark by the time I reached the big summit cairn. Too high to camp I had to descend to the river and find a campsite with the aid of my head torch.

It snowed during the night and, come morning, I had a fairly easy, if damp, descent to Loch Garry where the land rover track took me back to Dalnaspidal Lodge and the A9. This round would make a hefty day out during the long hours of summer but, for those who would rather not camp, both hills can be climbed independently from Loch Rannoch. Distance from the Bridge of Earn road to Stob an Aonaich Mhor is sixteen miles and from Annat to Beinn Mholach it's eleven. Beinn Mholach from Dalnaspidal is twelve miles. For lovers of solitude you won't get much better than this.

TYNDRUM CORBETTS, STIRLINGSHIRE
JUNE 2006

For some years the round of the five Corbetts just north of Tyndrum has been my little test piece. The round of Beinn Odhar (901m/2955ft), Beinn Chaorach (818m/2685ft), Cam Chreag (885m/2903ft), Beinn nam Fuaran (806m/2645ft) and Beinn a' Chaisteal (886m/2907ft) is only about twelve miles in terms of distance but the traverse of all five hills involves a whopping 1980m/6500ft of climbing. That's about one and a half times the height of Ben Nevis.

Climb that lot in the normal nine or ten hours and your legs will know they've been working overtime. Try it when you're unfit and you'll think you're going to die . . .

I'm in training at the moment for a two-week jaunt along the GR20 in Corsica.[1] The route is probably the toughest in France's Grande Randonée trail system with a lot of climbing and scrambling involved. Someone recently described it to me as a two-week-long Cuillin ridge. I suspect that is a slight exaggeration but I'm not taking it lightly. I've been adding a bit of running to my weekly exercise routine and trying to get in some longer walks with a heavy pack. I thought a round of the Tyndrum Corbetts would be a good check on my fitness as well as a tough training day.

The hills are situated north of Tyndrum and to the southeast of the Auch Glen. The first hill of the round, Beinn Odhar, impresses as the rather fine conical peak you see as you drive towards Bridge of Orchy from Tyndrum on the A82. Indeed, many people mistake it for Beinn Dorain, the Munro to the north.

1. Chris Townsend and I hiked the GR20 the following month and loved it, despite the heat. Chris described it as the toughest waymarked trail in the world.

This is as fine a clutch of Corbetts as you'll find, and probably the only group that will give you five ticks in your Corbetts book, but give yourself plenty of time. I left the car at 8.00am and even at that time the West Highland Way had a steady procession of hikers on it. Once I left the popular trail I only saw one other walker the whole day.

Beinn Odhar got the legs working and the descent down to the bealach below Beinn Chaorach was longer than I remembered it. The 400m of climbing to Chaorach's summit ridge was a good, steady pull and I still felt good as I reached the trig point. A chance now to enjoy the views of the Bridge of Orchy hills as I strode down the wide ridge to the bealach below Cam Chreag. I never feel this hill really belongs in this group. Its natural home is with the Mamlorn hills of Creag Mhor and Ben Challum, but at least its long north ridge gives access to what is always the toughest hill of the round, Beinn nam Fuaran.

It's a long climb, about 400m, from the bealach to the summit of Beinn Fuaran but it always feels longer because you know you have another hill to climb after it. It's also a difficult hill to descend because, by this time, your legs are likely to be turning to rubber and several little rock bands require extra care.

The final climb to Beinn a' Chaisteal, thankfully, isn't too steep but it feels long. All you can do is enjoy the view across the Auch Gleann to dark and craggy Beinn Dorain and plod upwards. Don't even think of the steep descent that comes after the summit, that'll come soon enough. By the time I reached the top I felt surprisingly good and convinced myself that maybe, just maybe, I was fit enough for the GR20.

THE STRATHFARRAR FOUR, EASTER ROSS
AUGUST 2007

I had started comparatively late in the day but didn't mind too much. I wanted to camp high in the hills to feed my habit of wilderness connection, but the on-duty warden at the entrance to the Strathfarrar National Nature Reserve at Inchmore said

I couldn't leave my car in the reserve overnight. Could I leave it beside his house and walk in? He relented and it was a deal.

I didn't have to camp until it became dark so I had all afternoon and evening at my disposal. Besides, while walking along a normal tarmac road can be purgatory, I didn't mind this one. With the lively dipper-infested River Farrar for company, and the luminescent pale-green birch growth contrasting with the darker greens of the Caledonian pines, I had plenty to occupy my attention.

Access to Strathfarrar is by Struy, at the north end of Strathglass, and the road that runs into the glen is closed to cars.[2] I suspect this restriction actually benefits Strathfarrar. It's a peaceful place, although it wasn't always so. Two hundred years ago the residents of the glen were savagely cleared, the native Caledonian pine forest was burnt down to make grazings for sheep and, more recently, hydro-electric workings have left their visual scars. Despite that, Strathfarrar is still worthy of a visit, particularly to climb the four Munros that make up its northern boundary wall, an airy traverse of Sgurr na Ruaidhe, Carn nan Gobhar, Sgurr a' Choire Ghlais and Sgurr Fhuar-Thuill.

After five miles on the road, which wound its way steadily into the glen, I took to the heather. In front of me lay the big climb of the day, up a hydro track into the empty acres of Corry Deanie and the un-named ridge that flows east from Sgurr na Ruaidhe.

Most Munro-baggers climb the Strathfarrar Four from a point just east of Loch a' Mhuillidh, but I left the road a tad earlier, at Deanie Lodge. I wanted to approach the first of the Munros, Sgurr na Ruaidhe, from its long eastern ridge, which simply seemed a more logical way of climbing the complete Strathfarrar ridge.

The eastern hills of this ridge are well rounded and offer easy walking. Sgurr na Ruaidhe (993m/3258ft) and Carn nan Ghobhar (992m/3255ft), the peak of redness and the cairn of the goats are paired together in the east and separated by the

---

2. The latest access information for Strathfarrar can be found at
   www.mountaineering.scot/access/special-arrangements/strathfarrar

Bealach nan Bogan. From there a broad curving ridge lifts you onto the scree-covered wastes of Carn nan Ghobhar from where a short descent and a steep climb brings you to Sgurr a' Choire Ghlais (1083m/3553ft), whose summit boasts two large cairns and a trig point, the highest position being a little to the south-south-east of the main ridge on a broad platform that gazes down a broad sweep into the depths of Strathfarrar. The ridge continues with western views opening up those wild, empty lands that surround lonely Loch Monar.

From Sgurr a' Choire Ghlais the ridge drops again and narrows considerably before rising over the top of Creag Gorm a' Bhealach, the crag of the blue pass, and continues to Sgurr Fuar-Thuill (1049m/3442ft). Although this is the final Munro of the day it's well worthwhile wandering onto the top of Sgurr na Fearstaig, the peak of the sea-pinks, for the view to the west, Loch Monar and a clutter of hills, before going south along the ridge towards Sgurr na Muice for a few hundred yards until an easy descent down a scree gully carries you to the stalkers' path below.

This track disappears for a short section just before you reach the Loch Toll a' Mhuic (where I camped) below the steep crags of Sgurr na Muice. The next day gave me a long walk-out back to my car at Inchmore.

A MONADH LIATH TRAVERSE, INVERNESS-SHIRE
MAY 2008

If you were an eagle and you chose to fly north from the Badenoch village of Newtonmore some twenty-five to thirty miles of wild, uninhabited hill country would pass below your wings before you reached Strathnairn, just south-west of Inverness.

This is the Monadh Liath, the grey hills, a vast area of some 700 square miles, a mountain wild land area that attracts few admirers. Most Munro-baggers stick to the craggier edges of the south, where A'Chailleach (930m/3051ft), Carn Sgulain (920m/3018ft), Carn Dearg (945m/3100ft), and Geal Charn (926m/3038ft) are all relatively accessible from Newtonmore or Laggan.

Linking these Munros together in one outing, a long twenty mile trot, offers a pretty good introduction to the special characteristics of the Monadh Liath, characteristics that have not always been recognised by mountain writers. The Munro guidebooks tend to give these hills a bad press suggesting they are 'tedious', or 'uninspiring puddings' although Munros guru Hamish Brown did once suggest that you can't exhaust the potential of even the dullest hills in Scotland.

A couple of winters ago I climbed Geal Charn by its steeply flanked north-east corrie. Under snow and ice it was an unusual and committing route to what is regarded as an easy Munro. I've also ski toured between all the Munros, the best ski tour I've enjoyed in Scotland. The potential for good days is certainly there.

In his excellent book, *Wilderness Dreams*, author Mike Cawthorne admitted to being a Monadh Liath aficionado. 'It may have betrayed an early obsession with maps but the Monadh Liath, least known of regions, hundreds of miles from where I lived, found a place in my imagination as early as adolescence. Hanging on my bedroom wall between red and white shirted footballers and glossy celluloid stars was an unfolded Ordnance Survey (OS) map of the entire range, a mass of contours and squiggly blue lines that gave the appearance of a vast earth-bound lung. It seemed alive with possibilities.'

Alive with possibilities it certainly is. The traverse of the four Munros is a good introduction to the area, but make sure you carry your map and compass. It's for no small reason that Cawthorne refers to the Monadh Liath as 'Terra Incognita'.

A'Chailleach is easily climbed from the road-end in Glen Banchor above Newtonmore, a Munro-baggers path has evolved over the past few years climbing the hill from the Allt a' Chaorainn. From the summit an easy descent leads to the defile that contains the bubbling Allt Cuil na Caillich and once you've crossed that it's a straightforward climb up grassy slopes to Carn Sgulain.

It's from here that you begin your long westward trek, over

an undulating and broad ridge that crosses over a series of rounded tops, with vast, ever widening views all around you. Gaze north into the interior of Cawthorne's Terra Incognita and allow its anonymous spread, its jumbled sprawl, to tease your mind. Trace imaginary routes through the hidden glens, over the bulbous tops and wonder if you could cope with the isolation, the remoteness and the anonymity of it all? Enjoy it while you can. Appreciate it's wild qualities, for all that you see has been designated as a 'preferred area for onshore windfarm development'.[3] It could soon lose its remoteness and isolation as a network of bulldozed tracks are created to service the windmills.

Leave the main ridge to visit the shapely Carn Dearg, high above lonely Loch Dubh, then return for the last, long peat-hag ridden stretch over a jumble of hills that surround the head of Glen Markie. Geal Charn is the last summit, perched above its craggy north-west corrie, before a long descent drops you down to the Feith Talagain and the footpath to Garva Bridge. You might have experienced something of the wild quality of the Monadh Liath, but you will also have experienced the tough nature of its terrain. You might not have fallen in love with it, but you will have learned to respect it.

---

3. The threat of windfarms in and immediately around the Monadh Liath Munros was removed in 2013 when the Scottish Government changed planning legislation to prevent windfarms being built in National Parks or recognised Wild Land areas in Scotland.

CHAPTER TWO

Hands Required

Back in the 1980s scrambling became fashionable: climbing steep, rocky slopes without the use of a rope or other gear. What had been considered a risky, although exhilarating, thing to do suddenly became acceptable. Wild-eyed rebels of the climbing scene had been scrambling up steep rock for generations but, when someone wrote a guidebook, it became a kind of subculture of the mountaineering genre, just as skinny-dipping evolved into 'wild swimming', or using a tent somehow makes you a 'wild camper'. The outdoors media has much to answer for.

Scrambling fills the grey area between walking and climbing, requiring the use of hands as well as feet, ascending steep or steepish rock before it becomes too vertical and so requires the use of a rope. It didn't take long for a grading system to be introduced, and guidebooks were published on places like Lochaber, the Cairngorms and the Lake District. Hillwalkers were encouraged to leave the well-trodden footpaths and tackle ground they previously considered beyond their abilities and, for many, this opened up a new and exhilarating mountain world, far from the madding, overcrowded footpaths and onto the vertical realms of the climber.

Routes like Curved Ridge on Buachaille Etive Mor, Ledge Route on Ben Nevis and Afterthought Arete in the Cairngorms became popular and were recognised as good standard scrambling routes. While many walkers felt uncomfortable and unprotected on such steep, rocky terrain, others acquired new confidence on steep ground and made the progression to proper rock climbing and winter mountaineering.

Scrambling isn't for everyone though. It requires a good head for heights, a reasonable sense of balance and, most important, the ability to navigate your way up steep rock. There are no signposts on scrambling routes and choosing decent hand and footholds is critical. The scrambling grading system has three, sometimes four grades, from Grade 1 to Grade 3 with a few more difficult routes, essentially moderate rock-climbing routes, gaining a Grade3(S). All but the most experienced and competent would use a rope on these most severe scrambles.

A Grade 1 scramble requires the occasional use of your hands and you will generally be able to walk off the route should you choose to. Grade 2 routes are steeper, more akin to climbing where it is necessary to use your hands for more sustained stretches. Exposure is likely to be more obvious at this grade and retreat from the route may be difficult. Grade 3 routes should be considered as advanced scrambles, requiring moves on steep rock in exposed situations where some may prefer the protection of a rope. Occasional moves of 'moderate' rock climbing standard may be required. The ability to abseil is pretty much essential to exit these routes, so it's wise to carry a rope on these grades . . . and, of course, know how to use it. Most of the time you'll find these more difficult routes on north-facing cliffs and corries where the air is likely to be chilled and the rock is more often than not damp or greasy. Such routes call for a greater commitment as escape routes are few and far between.

While I was a hugely enthusiastic rock-climber in my youth I was never an accomplished climber. Only managing to achieve a reasonable standard on routes up to VS (Very Severe) and occasionally HVS (Hard Very Severe), I did excel at scrambling. Loving the exhilarating freedom of moving confidently over steep ground, and the awareness that I was in control in what were exposed situations, these experiences on Scottish mountain routes prepared me for bigger mountain routes in the Alps. I wouldn't have climbed the steep and crumbly Hornli Ridge of the Matterhorn without feeling at home on steep, exposed, rocky ground. As it was, my ascent of the Matterhorn, that most beautiful of iconic mountains, became one of the most cherished and memorable highlights of my whole mountain career.

That said, scrambling isn't everyone's cup of tea. I'm always slightly surprised at how many keen hillwalkers suffer from various grades of vertigo, and amazed at how many succeed in climbing all the Munros. Probably many don't suffer from vertigo at all, but simply have an aversion to heights, a condition known as acrophobia. Most of us have such aversions, to a greater or lesser extent and in various forms. I can happily swarm up a Grade 3 scramble but become extremely nervous climbing a ladder. On holiday in Paris many years ago, I felt extremely uncomfortable looking down from the Eiffel Tower but, as with any phobia, the effects of acrophobia can be alleviated by facing the condition head on. Go scrambling with an experienced partner, perhaps using a rope for protection until you feel more comfortable.

It's also useful to bear in mind that vertigo is a symptom, rather than a condition in itself, a sensation that everything is spinning around you. You may feel nauseous too. Vertigo is commonly caused by a problem with the way balance works in the inner ear, although it can also be caused by problems in certain parts of the brain. The dizziness may be barely noticeable, or so severe that you find it difficult to keep your balance. If you find dizziness is severe when you are in steep or high places it might be worth consulting your GP.

Most of Scotland's hills do not require the use of hands to climb them. Hills like An Teallach, Liathach and the Horns of Alligin offer alternative paths to avoid the scrambling difficulties, but there are some, even amongst the Munros and Corbetts, where mild scrambling is unavoidable. If you really are uncomfortable with exposure don't try these hills on your own but go with an experienced companion or, even better, hire a qualified guide. Indeed, a sizeable number of Munro-baggers hire professionals to guide them over the Munro summits of the Skye Cuillin where some of the routes require rock-climbing skills rather than mere scrambling skills. Hiring a qualified guide has a number of additional benefits. These folk have a wide range of skills they are usually willing to pass on, and have built up a vast knowledge of the mountain environment including geology, birdlife, flora and fauna. Likely they will also have a few good stories to share, and your guided experience will amount to considerably more than just a few ticks in your Munro book.

The routes in the following essays include some well-known and popular mountains, all of which require at least some minimalist scrambling. Try not to fear it, but see it as an opportunity to experience the mountain in a slightly different way. I remember teaching a man and his wife scrambling skills and noticing her bright red, manicured fingernails. My heart sank but, before long, she was scrambling up the rock with the rest of the group, wearing gloves to protect them. A few months later she sent me a letter listing all the rock climbs she had done that summer, and some were impressive. There was a PS: 'I don't wear gloves anymore, to hell with the manicures.'

THE RING OF STEALL, GLEN NEVIS
APRIL 1987

The nine-mile long Mamores Ridge has long been considered one of the great Scottish hillwalking outings, with Glen Nevis separating it from the Grey Corries in the north and long slopes running down to Kinlochleven in the south, all well served by a marvellous network of good stalker's paths.

The ridge itself is narrow and sustained, almost alpine-like in winter and spring conditions. The full traverse, from Sgurr Eilde Mor in the east to Mullach nan Corein in the west, is a big day out, but a shorter round takes in the dramatically named Devil's Ridge along with four of the Mamores Munros: An Gearanach (983m/3222ft), Stob Choire a' Chairn (981m/3218ft), Am Bodach (1032m/3386ft), and Sgurr a' Mhaim (1099m/3606ft). The Devil's Ridge lies between two subsidiary tops, Sgor an

Iubhair and Stob Choire a' Mhail and, despite its name, is far
from evil, although in winter conditions it can give several
heart-stopping moments.

This truncated Mamores route is known as the Ring of Steall
as the route follows the high ridges around Coire a' Mhail,
whose waters feed the Grey Mare's Tail which falls into the
Steall meadows below. The route traverses four other 3,000ft
tops including Sgorr an Iubhair, which was demoted as a Munro
by the Scottish Mountaineering Club in their latest bout of
'adjusting' a few years back. Despite the loss of the Munro, nine
miles and over 4,000ft of climbing offers an unforgettable day
with close-up views of Ben Nevis, the Aonachs, the Grey Corries
and across Loch Linnhe to the hills of Argour and Morvern.

Even the preamble to this route is memorable. From the
Polldubh car park a trail weaves through the trees above the
roaring Himalayan-like Nevis Gorge, a place W. H. Murray once
described as the 'best half mile in Scotland'. Suddenly the path
is squeezed out into a flat, green meadow in which the Water of
Steall flows gently, as though unaware of what the Nevis Gorge
has in store below. At the head of the meadows a white slash of
water falls for three hundred feet into the river and close by a
triple hawser-wire bridge crosses the river to a footpath running
east past the Steall Hut, below the Grey Mare's Tail and a tree-
clad buttress into Coire Chadha Chaoruinn.

Once past the Allt Coire Chadha Chaoruinn another path
climbs uphill in long zigzags, eventually carrying you to the
north-west spur of An Gearanach, which roughly translates as
the complainer (maybe because it used to be unmarked on the OS
map!). A short and narrow ridge runs south to An Garbhanach
from where another ridge continues in a south-west direction
before rising to the summit of Stob Choire a' Chairn. Big drops
fall southwards into Coire na Ba, eventually to the Heights of
Kinlochmore and Kinlochleven. The long Mamores ridge now
undulates towards Am Bodach, before swinging west and north-
west to reach the peak of the yew tree, Sgorr an Iubhair.

The drama increases as you approach the Devil's Ridge. From

its high point at Stob Choire a' Mhail it narrows considerably in its link with the southern stony slopes of Sgurr a' Mhaim. At its narrowest section, a footpath drops down the east side, avoiding the rocky difficulties of the ridge crest, before taking a scrambling route back onto the ridge again. Finally, an awkward scramble drops you onto a high bealach below the quartz-covered summit slopes of Sgurr a' Mhaim. The descent follows a gently curving ridge, usually beautifully corniced well into the spring, above Coire Sgorach before a final knee-trembling descent eases down the nose, the Sron Sgurr a' Mhaim, and takes you back into Glen Nevis about one and a half miles west of the car park at Polldubh.

THE CUILLIN OF RUM
JUNE 1990

They called it Ruiminn in the seventh-century annals of Ulster, and there have been suggestions that the Vikings called it Romoy. Victorian whim changed the name to Rhum and in the past few years the Ordnance Survey, and the owners of the island, Scottish Natural Heritage, have reverted to plain and simple Rum.

One of the group of islands known as the Small Isles, Rum is mountainous, whereas its close neighbours, Eigg and Canna, are considerably flatter. Rum also boasts a rather incongruous castle, constructed from imported stone and built on the instructions of an eccentric Victorian industrialist who insisted the builders wear kilts, a mausoleum, and best of all, its own, curling, Cuillin ridge. A traverse of the whole ridge, from the Bealach Bairc-mheall near Kinloch Castle to Sgurr nan Gillean in the south, returning to Kinloch either by the Dibidil path or the track from the Harris Mausoleum, takes between eight and twelve hours.

I first visited the Rum Cuillin with an old mate, the mountain photographer John Cleare. We stayed at Kinloch Castle, not in the castle itself (which was once run as an hotel by the National

Trust for Scotland) but in a less salubrious part of the building, the old bunkhouse at the back.[1]

Our day started wet and windy, and we battled against the elements all the way up Coire Dubh to the Bealach Bairc-mheall where the rain didn't seem quite so heavy. From there we pushed on over the first of our hills, Hallival and, with the weather improving, battled up the narrow north ridge of Askival (812m/2680ft), the highest of the Rum Cuillin, where we came across the first major obstacle of the ridge.

An ominous black tower blocked the way ahead, looking menacing in the wind-torn mist. Closer at hand it didn't seem quite as grim and an easy scramble led to the base of a twenty-foot wall, split by a wide crack. Holds were plentiful and, despite the exposure, we were up it in minutes.

The remainder of the ridge was sheer joy. By this time the mists had cleared and the sun was shining, illuminating magnificent seascapes in every direction. A long craggy ridge descended to the wonderfully named Bealach an Oir, the golden pass, from where we climbed again to the double-peaked Trallval. A big drop followed, down over rough rock and scree to the Bealach an Fhuarain from where a great, grey buttress reared alarmingly. We threaded a route up through various walls and cracks, real exploratory scrambling, and trounced up the narrowing ridge to the summit of Ainshval.

The last top, Sgurr nan Gillean, was only a stone's throw away now, after which followed the ridge of Leac a' Chaisteil to Ruinsival and the long walk back to Kinloch via the little mausoleum at Harris. The Victorian industrialist, Sir George Bullough built it, a Greek-looking structure which should look out of place on a Hebridean island, but doesn't. With the sun lowering on the western horizon, the grass a verdant green and the sea a rich blue, we could have been strolling by the Aegean

---

1. I believe the bothy in the castle is now closed but there are a number of new facilities on the island that offer accommodation, including camping pods, a bunkhouse and B&B.
   Check out www.isleofrum.com/placestostay.php

Sea rather than the Minch. This was the Bullough's Parnassus which, for the moment, was ours too.

THE ROUND OF COIRE LAGAN, ISLE OF SKYE
FEBRUARY 1992

The round of the peaks that frown on Coire Lagan on the Isle of Skye is to many Munro-baggers the stuff of nightmares. A long scree climb, awkward scrambling, an exposed ledge, the potential for difficult route-finding, and a rock climb followed by a long abseil are the ingredients of what is probably the most technical hillwalk in the United Kingdom.

It's nothing less than a full day's mountaineering, and the experience of negotiating narrow ridges and Britain's best-known pinnacle remains a considerable achievement.

Few would argue that the finest way to climb the eleven Munros of the Skye Cuillin is in one continuous expedition, starting at the south end of the ridge on Sgurr nan Eag and working your way north through some of the most spectacu-lar mountain scenery to be found anywhere, finishing on the airy upthrust of Sgurr nan Gillean. That said, most hillwalkers are content to break the ridge into four separate expeditions. Arguably the most challenging of these hikes-and-climbs is the round of Coire Lagan, taking in Sgurr Alasdair (992m/3256ft), Sgurr Mhic Choinnich (948m/3110ft) and the Inaccessible Pinnacle of Sgurr Dearg (986m/3235ft).

The In Pinn is technically the most difficult ascent of the Munros. A narrowing blade of rock, it leans against the summit crest of Sgurr Dearg, an impressive feature that will either delight or scare the pants off you. Essentially, there are two routes.

The short, steep western face involves a rock climb of about Difficult standard, where the longer east ridge, a Moderate rock climb in technical terms, is seriously exposed. If you're an experi-enced climber you'll romp up this eastern ridge, exhilarated by its position and exposure, but if you've never climbed you'll need a rope, climbing gear and an experienced companion. However you climb, you have to abseil from the top, an 18m/60ft drop to Sgurr Dearg. The ascent of the Inaccessible Pinnacle is, without question, one of the highlights of any round of the Munros.

The most obvious approach to the Round of Coire Lagan is by the Great Stone Chute, which drops down in a cataract of stone from the gap between Sgurr Alasdair and Sgurr Thearlaich. Alasdair is reached from the gap by an easy arête scramble on the right, while the best way onto Sgurr Thearlaich is to descend for a short distance to the east of the gap and climb an obvious crack on your left. This takes you onto Thearlaich's southern rib, which can be followed to its slabby summit.

From here descend some tricky grooves and slabs to the Bealach Mhic Choinnich where the ascent of Sgurr Mhic Choinnich looks terrifyingly formidable. Don't despair though, you only have to climb a few feet and traverse the west face of the buttress by the exposed Collie's Ledge (Moderate difficulty) to reach the mountain's north-west ridge. This is followed to the summit. Walkers who don't wish to tackle Collie's Ledge are best descending to Coire Lagan by the Great Stone Chute between Sgurr Alasdair and Sgurr Thearlaich, regaining the ridge by the An Stac screes.

From the summit of Sgurr Mhic Choinnich descend to another bealach above the An Stac screes. Drop down a little to reach a cairned path through said scree that leads below the west edge of An Stac's tower. Staying close to the base of its wall climb to easier ground. Continue on the main ridge and climb the Inaccessible Pinnacle by its east ridge. On the tiny summit a convenient boulder provides an anchor for an 18m/60ft abseil off the west side, before a long euphoric descent to Glen Brittle by Sgurr Dearg's west ridge.

AN TEALLACH, WESTER ROSS
JULY 1995

It was an extraordinary scene.

To our left the sky was blue and clear and the great mountains

of Fisherfield stood out starkly against it, but below our feet great
billows of smoke-like cloud fumed up from the corrie's depths,
momentarily hiding the rotten teeth of the mountain skyline.
As we descended from the rounded summit of Sail Liath, one of
An Teallach's numerous tops, my companion, John Mackenzie,
waxed lyrical about the redness of the mountain's Torridonian
sandstone. When the sun sinks over the western horizon, he
claimed, these slopes glow fiery crimson like coals in a roaring
furnace. The Gaels named An Teallach because of these mists
that swell from Toll an Lochain, its deep and cavernous corrie,
and the analogy of the roaring furnace is a good one. We both
agreed 'The Forge' was a good translation.

The mountain dominates the Strathnasheallag Forest south
of Little Loch Broom, its serrated crest reaching a high point
on Bidein a' Ghlas Thuill (1062m/3484ft). Another of its peaks,
Sgurr Fiona (1060m/3474ft) is also a Munro, but the mountain's real attraction is the long ridgeline around its deep toll or
'hollow', particularly the section known as the Corrag Bhuidhe
Buttresses, a sinuous edge which offers the finest ridge scramble
on mainland Scotland.

John and I had been making a Wilderness Walk television
programme and our ascent of An Teallach was the climax. Lord
John, Earl of Cromartie and Chief of Clan Mackenzie, eulogised
on the character of the hill, which I admitted was my favourite
mountain, yet we were both aware of it as a rotten, peeling
carcass. The sandstone crumbles below your feet, and the spires
and pinnacles of the wonderful Corrag Bhuidhe Buttresses, to
which we escaped from the badly eroded footpath, have loose
holds which turn a simple scrambling excursion into one of
considerable drama.

John, a passionate rock climber, was desperate to get to grips
with the steep and awkward corners of Corrag Bhuidhe, even
in the dank swirling mists. The first steep slab was a delight,
climbing the rounded sandstone 'woolpacks' that are piled high
on each other for a good thirty feet. This was followed by a level
stretch of grassy scree that leads to the crux, a steep and shallow

chimney, scraped and marked by crampon scratches. An abseil sling at the top suggested the regular use of a rope, particularly sensible in winter conditions. A tiptoe traverse along the narrow crest had us whooping with delight before the climb onto the overhanging spire called Lord Berkeley's Seat. Apparently, the good Lord was a gentleman who, for a bet, sat on the spire's summit block with his feet overhanging the edge. John was better informed; he claimed his fellow peer was a nineteenth-century empirical physicist.

For the obvious reasons of height and exposure, most walkers avoid the Corrag Bhuidhe Buttresses and Lord Berkeley's Seat, instead using the eroded footpaths that neatly skirt these obstacles before climbing Sgurr Fiona by means of a long staircase of sandstone blocks. From there you descend north-north-east down a rocky ridge to the wide, slabby col. There are no real obstacles left now, other than a long pull onto the highest summit, Bidean a'Ghlas Thuill.

The normal descent route continues north from the summit to the obvious col and then drops steeply eastwards into Coire a' Ghlas Thuill. Follow the north side of the stream to the Garbh Allt waterfalls from where a good path takes you back to the A832 and the reward of a pint or two in the Dundonnell Hotel.

LIATHACH, TORRIDON
OCTOBER 1997

Many years ago, when I was young and newly in love with mountains, I arrived in Torridon one late afternoon and wandered up the hillside on the south side of the glen. Climbing higher, my attention was captured by the massive mountain wall that lay across the glen. It looked impregnable. Liathach, the grey one, that day seriously unsettled me. Tiers of sandstone stacked high into the sky, it was and remains one of the great cathedrals of the earth. No matter how I tried I couldn't trace a route up its sheer flanks. It looked impossible, but I knew that one day I'd have to try and climb it.

That day arrived several years later, after I learned from experience that hillsides often appear vertical when you look at them head on. Liathach is not impregnable, but it is a very serious hill. With two Munro summits tempting the baggers, it always surprises me that more hillwalkers don't come to grief on this giant. Its ridge is convoluted, crossing six lesser tops as well as the two Munros, Spidean a'Choire Leith (1055m/3461ft), and Mullach an Rathain (1023m/3356ft).

The usual ascent route starts just east of Glen Cottage and climbs to the steep upper slopes of Toll a' Meitheach, a shallow corrie high on the hill's sandstone flanks, the path running alongside the Allt an Doire Ghairbh as it rushes down over its rocky steps. Rocky slopes mingle with steep grassy slopes before the path climbs over a break in a rock band, and then it's a steep scramble into the upper reaches of the corrie where a scree-filled gully gives access to the ridge itself, just west of Bidein Toll a' Mhuic. This is a good place to stop, the sweaty part of the day over. In front of you the long ridge of the adjacent Munro, Beinn Eighe, stretches eastwards.

In the other direction, Liathach's twisting ridge wriggles towards the triangular-shaped face of Spidean a' Choire Leith, the first of its Munro summits. Despite the rock and loose scree the ridge poses little difficulty, first of all flowing in a north-westerly direction, then west over a couple of subsidiary tops, before the final boulder-covered slope to Spidean's summit.

The views are extensive, all the way from Ben Hope in the north to Ben Nevis in the south but, chances are, you won't notice because your eyes will be on the spectacular outline ahead, where the ridge narrows for a good mile with much of its length broken and shattered into the series of spectacular spires known as the Fasarinen Pinnacles, the ancient sentinels of Liathach.

These quartzite gendarmes fall dramatically into Coire na Caime on the north side, one of a number of north-facing corries that make up the other face of Liathach, a more broken and less austere aspect that is hidden from the tourists in Glen Torridon. A traverse across these pinnacles is a wonderfully airy and exposed scramble and those with some experience of rock climbing will seek out the holds willingly. Everyone else will be happy to follow the exposed but well used footpath that contours the southern side of the pinnacles. This path leads to the second Munro of the hill, Mullach an Rathain, the aptly named 'hill of the row of pinnacles'.

A wide, grassy ridge leads to the summit and the Ordnance Survey pillar. To the north a short, stony arête runs out to the highest of the pinnacles and the lower peak of Meall Dearg overlooks Coire na Caime. A long ridge runs westwards down to the subsidiary top of Sgorr a' Chadail, with fabulous views across Loch Torridon, but the best descent route goes west and south of the summit cairn, dropping towards a broadening slope of broken, scree-filled gullies and worn terraces, then down to the road alongside the Allt an Tuill Bhain. After that it's only a short walk back to the car. Somehow the steep sandstone flanks appear less forbidding now.

SGURR NAN GILLEAN, ISLE OF SKYE
AUGUST 1997

It was Sorley MacLean, the bard of the Gael, who referred to the 'antlered Cuillin'. He could well have been describing the three peaks that form the northern portals of the Cuillin itself, Bruach na Frithe, Am Basteir and Sgurr nan Gillean.

This triple stack of mountains forms the classic view of the Skye Cuillin from Sligachan. The bare, rocky walls of Coire a' Bhasteir form an impressive north-facing rampart, bounded on either side by prominent pointed peaks, the magnificent Sgurr nan Gillean on the left and the lower Sgurr a' Bhasteir on the right, and are dominated by its central peak, Am Basteir, the Executioner, and its distinctive 'tooth.'

I first gripped the rough gabbro rock of the Cuillin as a teenager. During a week-long camping and climbing adventure, still innocent of any knowledge of Munro-bagging, we climbed the peaks simply because they were there. More recently, with a bunch of mates, we traversed these three northern Cuillin on a wet and cloudy day, returning to the Sligachan bar just before closing time. A rather overambitious and adventurous descent of Am Basteir had delayed us.

We had to use the rope to abseil through swirling mist into the narrow gap between the summit and the Basteir Tooth, from there to down-scramble on wet and slippery ledges into the Lota Corrie. It was perhaps just as well the mist obliterated the sight of the big drops.

More recently I climbed the trio with a friend from Cumbria. David Powell-Thompson, a strong fell-runner and experienced climber, had never before been to Skye and I caught some of his excitement as we scampered up the length of the Fionn Coire (between Sgurr a' Bhasteir and Bruach na Frithe), the dark walls of the mountains on either side pressing in as we climbed higher over oceans of rock and boulder scree.

It didn't take long to reach the crest, and we wandered to the summit of Bruach na Frithe rejoicing in the alpine-like surroundings. David had never, in his own words, seen anything to compare with this view.

Am Basteir was next. We retraced our steps to the Bealach nan Lice and followed the rough path round the foot of Am Basteir to where the normal route climbs the rocky ridge to the summit, dropping at one point into a narrow recess which calls for a fairly agile bit of scrambling, or an abseil if you have a rope. This gap in the ridge has been made worse by a rockfall and many Munro-baggers now avoid it by following a series of ledges on the south side of the ridge.

Nicholson's Chimney, a steep eighty-foot gully, offers access to Sgurr nan Gillian's west ridge and our third summit. The ascent is probably more of a rock climb than a scramble but we went for it anyway, relishing big solid holds in the steep chimney and delighting in the narrow, steep and sinuous ridge crest that took us to the tiny summit of the mountain. This has to be the finest mountain summit in the country, an airy crest thrown up by steep rocky slopes on all sides. It was no wonder the great

Skye-based scribe, Sheriff Alexander Nicholson, once described it as 'the *upheaval* of Sgurr nan Gillean'.

CIR MHOR, ISLE OF ARRAN
JUNE 1998

The outline of the Arran hills from the Ayrshire coast is one of my earliest recollections of Scottish mountains. On our regular family holidays to Saltcoats I would often gaze across the Firth of Clyde at the unmistakable outline of the 'sleeping warrior'. Like another world, it was a romantic landscape of rocky mountainsides, rushing burns and vast seascapes that transfixed my young imagination and created an inexplicable excitement within me that I couldn't quite understand. Ten years were to pass before I set foot on the island.

My first view up Glen Sannox had a salutary effect. Here was wildness in the raw. Steep and rocky slopes leading upwards to a serrated skyline that terrified me, yet at the same time thrilled me. I wanted to climb every peak I could see, but my older and wiser companions suggested we reserve our energies for the western side of the glen. I was too excited to argue.

Soon we were crossing the bare moors towards a broad, crag-littered ridge. This was the north-east shoulder of Suidhe Fhearghas, and it offered a good, if fairly strenuous, route to the main Caisteal Abhail ridge. Nowadays a rather eroded footpath approaches the rounded summit of Suidhe Fhearghas, but make the most of it for beyond this summit the character of this walk changes dramatically. Ahead lies Caisteal Abhail, the 'Castles', and its notorious Ceum na Caillich, the Witch's Step.

With my experienced companions I had taken a direct descent into the gap of the Witch's Step. In my youthful ignorance I simply assumed this kind of vertical rock was what hillwalking was all about. I know better now, and this is not the route to follow if you're not an experienced scrambler. Far better to descend on the north side where a footpath takes you to the bottom of the cleft. The scramble itself begins in a groove immediately right of the main summit boulder and, lower down, an exposed slab is the crux.

From the bottom of the cleft, some straightforward scrambling took us over a succession of rocky tors to the summit of Caisteal Abhail at 859m/2835ft. It's a fairly extensive summit, with four ridges radiating from it in different directions. A crescent of rocky tors marks the highest tops and the central tor is the highest.

The easiest route to the top is on the east side. Some paths on the south side of the ridge avoid the main scrambling difficulties but we ignored them. From the summit an awkward line of crags bars the way, so we retraced our steps to turn the crags on their right where much more benevolent slopes sweep around the head of the glen to the foot of Cir Mhor, arguably the most impressive mountain on the island. The ascent to the spectacularly airy summit was simple enough, but the descent from the summit to the Saddle was steep and awkward, requiring use of the hands on some of the higher sections and a lot of care on loose screes.

Unless you plan on continuing to Goat Fell, Arran's highest peak, you're best to descend in a north-easterly direction from the saddle into upper Glen Sannox, where a steep and stony footpath makes full use of an eroded basalt dyke to make its way through a band of cliffs to the boggy upper reaches of the glen, where a footpath follows the river all the way to the old barytes mines, and the bridge that meets the outward track. Follow it back to the A841 and, as we did all those years ago, begin planning your climbs on the other fabulous peaks of Arran.

THE AONACH EAGACH, GLEN COE
SEPTEMBER 2001

The serrated edge of the ridge looked as though it was tearing the clouds apart as the wind blew them over the crest. Swirling masses of mist curled into the sky and, each time a gap was torn in the cloud, a long fin of rock, grass and scree appeared dramatically before us. Even on the best of days the Aonach Eagach can be a daunting sight. On a day like this it looked darkly threatening.

The traverse of the Aonach Eagach, the notched ridge, is one of the classic scrambles of Scotland but the tightrope route along its narrow crest has formed the nadir in the fortunes of many a Munro-bagger. As John Manning and I climbed up the hillside above Glen Coe I suggested that, other than the initial descent onto the ridge from the first summit, Am Bodach, the rest of the route was a doddle. It's curious how selective the memory can be. Over two miles in length and boasting four summits, two of which are Munros, the Aonach Eagach forms the north wall of Glen Coe. There used to be a sign, warning hillwalkers not to descend from the ridge itself but it's long since gone.

As if to prove the frailties of my memory we nipped down the ledges and grooves of the descent from Am Bodach onto the ridge like mountain goats. Generally considered the crux of the route, it is in effect a sixty-foot drop-off that looks much worse than it actually is.

We were on the crest of the ridge in no time, striding purposefully along the fairly easy gradient to a top beyond which lie the slopes of Meall Dearg, at 953m/3127ft, the final Munro summit of the Rev. A. E. Robertson, the first person to climb all the 3000'ers exactly one hundred years ago.

Between Meall Dearg and Stob Coire Leith, a number of rocky towers, the 'Crazy Pinnacles', prevent straightforward progress. While the path and the crampon marks of generations of climbers make route-finding relatively easy, we quickly understood that we weren't going to get things all our own way. The rocks were greasy and slippery in the autumnal dampness and the narrow chimneys and gullies, so delightful in dry, summer conditions, were muddy and wet. Everything seemed steeper and harder than I remembered, but nevertheless the exposure and scrambling were exhilarating. We were both mildly disappointed when, with the last of the pinnacles behind us, all that was left was a rather steep trudge to Stob Coire Leith. From there it was an easy walk on a broad ridge to the second of the ridge's Munros, Sgorr nam Fiannaidh, 967m/3173ft.

From the summit of Sgor nam Fiannaidh there are several descent options but, with the sun just managing to pierce the grey clouds, we elected to stay high and continue to the logical end of the ridge traverse, Sgorr na Ciche, the Pap of Glencoe. We weren't being purist. A reasonable path runs down to the old Glen Coe road from the Pap of Glencoe, and it is preferable to the steep, scree-scabbed, knee-wrenching descent that runs down to the road beside the Clachaig Gully. The only advantage to that route, the normal descent route from Sgor nam Fiannaidh, is that it takes you straight to the front door of the Clachaig Inn. That said, I'd rather enjoy my post-walk pint with my knees intact.

THE COBBLER, ARROCHAR
MARCH 2003

I'm wary of inventing personalities for our mountains but there is little doubt that some hills do have particular characteristics, tempting us into twee anthropomorphism. A good case in point is the Cobbler near Arrochar, a hill that's often described as an outrageous, audacious and impertinent wee thing. Despite its relatively lowly height of 884m/2917ft it's an awesome mountain and even has the cheek to make us rock-climb to reach its summit.

Curiously surreal, the Cobbler dominates its neighbours despite its inferior size, but it's the mountain's outlandish profile that gives it its commonly used name. Some think it resembles a cobbler working at his last. Its Sunday title is Ben Arthur, its Ordnance Survey name, but I don't know anyone who calls it that. It has three distinct tops: the left one, formed into a leaning pyramid; the Central Peak, the true summit, is a tiny exposed platform; while the North Peak is formed by an immense overhanging prow, a remarkable feature that boasts many of the mountain's best rock-climbs.

Snow and ice on the path that runs up the hill's eastern corrie reminded me of another reason this hill is special. This was the mountain that inspired the late W. H. Murray to become a mountaineer. Murray, the finest of all Scottish mountain writers, overheard a conversation between two people and was mesmerised by their discussion of a mountain climb in Wester Ross. It had never occurred to him that here was a whole world of which he knew nothing, that was apparently quite accessible and close at hand. He decided to investigate, but the only mountain he knew was the Cobber, so he went there in ordinary shoes and everyday clothes. He found the mountain covered in snow but he carried on, soon finding himself in wintry conditions in the corrie that leads to the summit ridge. He was frightened by the ice and the exposure but continued to the top where his trepidation melted away as he gazed over a panorama of hills and mountains spread before him like a white-topped sea. In his own words, he was 'hooked for life'.

That initial experience eventually profited all of us for Bill went on to become a renowned mountaineer and writer and his books, particularly *Mountaineering in Scotland*, became classics, inspiring a generation of hill-goers.

I had climbed up from Loch Long alongside the Buttermilk Burn, past the Narnain Boulders, into the corrie, where long, blue icicles hung from the crags and spindrift blew off the summit ridge like spumes of smoke. Below the ice-encrusted prow of the North Peak I relived something of Murray's trepidation.

This is an awesome place of rock and ice where an eroded path climbs steeply through the snow wreaths to the summit ridge. With the hard work over I followed it through the rocks and boulders to the table-flat top of the North Peak, a natural eyrie with vertiginous drops on three sides. To the south Ben Lomond and its loch dominates the view and to the north and east Ben Ime and Beinn Narnain stand out in sharp relief against the jumble of mountains beyond. Across the corrie the crags of the central peak rise high above the dark arm of Loch Long, winding its way down to the sea.

For most walkers this is effectively the summit of the Cobbler. The Central Peak is a little higher but the route to the top isn't evident and involves some rock climbing. From the summit ridge a window in the rock above you represents the portal to the top. You have to squeeze through this 'fat man's gap' to find a narrow ledge that traverses off to the left. By following this around the back of the rock, a couple of easy moves take you onto the small summit platform. In winter conditions it can be particularly awkward, and I was happy enough to ignore it, fighting off the temptation to think the mountain had defeated me. The insolent pup . . .

CREISE AND MEALL A' BHUIRIDH, ARGYLL
MAY 2006

A few weeks ago a minor brouhaha broke out when a member of the Munro Society, the club that exists for those who have climbed Scotland's Munros, suggested the majority of members are fakes. Professor Findlay Swinton, a retired chemistry professor from Dundee, claimed that only a minority of hillwalkers have actually climbed all the Munros under their own steam.

'These are people who have led or soloed all the Cuillin tops. Being dragged eighty feet up the Inaccessible Pinnacle on Skye, then lowered off by a professional guide or a friendly rock climber, surely doesn't count as a genuine ascent,' he said.

I was chewing these thoughts over as I descended onto the great connecting rib between Creise and Meall a' Bhuridh, the two Munros that form part of the great western wall that fringes the Rannoch Moor, thinking how silly such an attitude was when, in essence, we climb hills for fun. My own first ascent of the In Pinn, as a spotty youth, was on the end of someone else's rope, and nobody would have convinced me then that I was a fake. I've since taken numerous people up and wouldn't for a moment consider their ascent was anything other than genuine.

By a curious coincidence I happened to meet a couple of Munro-baggers on the Meall a' Bhuridh ridge, two guys who said they had just taken the chairlift to the summit of Meall a' Bhuridh (3635ft/1108m). From there they were heading for Creise, to 'bag' the Munro. It was on the tip of my tongue to question their use of the chairlift, but I stopped myself. The guys were enjoying their day out, they were appreciative of the wonderful surroundings and, as far as they were concerned, the use of the chairlift to Meall a' Bhuridh was completely legitimate.

Our conversation made me realise that there isn't really such a thing as a 'genuine ascent'. I make frequent use of the Cairn Gorm car park at 2500 feet, or the Ben Lawers high-level car park. Is that cheating? Climbers on Everest fly in to Lukla, at a height of 12,000 feet. The only 'genuine' ascent of Everest I could think of was Phil and Pauline Sanderson's recent climb when they and some friends cycled to Nepal from the lowest point on Earth, beside the Red Sea in Jordan, then climbed the highest mountain in the world. But did the fact that they used bikes to get from Jordan to Nepal negate any claim of a 'genuine ascent'?

Of course not, it's all silly speculation and the important thing about hills and mountains is in the being there, not how many peaks you can bag. Here was I, seriously considering all this nonsense, in one of the most spectacular settings in the western highlands.

If you gaze across at Creise and Meall a' Bhuiridh from the Black Corries on the edge of the Rannoch Moor, you'll see one of the finest mountain panoramas in Scotland, together with the deep defile of Glen Etive and the familiar triangular shape of the Buachaille Etive Mor. Creise itself, at 1100m/3609ft, is a steep-sided hill that offers some superlative scrambling up the steep north nose of Sron na Creise. The rocky ribs that spill down eastwards into the Cam Gleann provide an easier way to the top, although there is still good scrambling to be found here too.

That had been my route to the summit ridge. I'd started at Blackrock Cottage, the Ladies Scottish Climbing Club hut on the road that leads to the White Corries ski grounds. I'd crossed the boggy heather moorland around the north slopes of Creag Dhubh to the mouth of the Cam Ghleann to reach the rocky slopes of Sron na Creise. Contouring west to avoid the rocky difficulties, I'd enjoyed some easy scrambling up the steep, rocky ribs that spill down from Stob a' Ghlais Choire, the start of a long and scenic ridge that eventually terminates at Stob Ghabhar in the south.

Less than a kilometre from Ston a' Ghlais Choire lay the summit of Creise, beyond which the flat top of Mam Coire Easain gave way to a stony rib which descends to a high bealach which, in turn, leads to Meall a' Bhuiridh, the Glen Coe ski mountain. It's an easy climb to the summit of Meall a' Bhuiridh with a straightforward descent straight back down to Blackrock Cottage by way of the ski grounds. Of course, at the weekends you have the option of an easier descent, by the chair lift, but that would be cheating, or would it . . .

CHAPTER THREE

Birds and Beasts

I recently read a blog by a young and excellent outdoor writer named Alex Roddie which raised a curious question: 'Has outdoor culture become too detached from nature?' A reader had apparently made contact, requesting him to stop writing about the natural world in his articles, contending that 'people wanted to read about the "outdoors", not about birds and plants'.

This chimed a chord with me. During my twenty years' editorship of *The Great Outdoors* magazine, essentially a magazine aimed at the UK's hillwalkers and backpackers, I received a number of similar requests, sincere responses from people who saw the outdoors as some kind of sporting arena, a place to enjoy a good day out with your mates, or a list of hills to climb, tick off and take a selfie by the cairn to show off on social media.

Nothing wrong with any of that, and I accept that for some people an awareness and appreciation of the natural world is secondary to some kind of 'personal achievement'. Lots of hill-goers view the outdoors as a sporting arena where the number of peaks you climb is the *raison d'être,* or the completion of a long-distance trail is only successful if you walk or run it faster than anyone else. I get that, and I fully understand the racing mentality of some fell-runners, but most fell-runners I know have a deep love and appreciation of the natural world. I guess that's why they run up and down hills rather than round an urban running track.

I also understand the list-ticking mentality of the baggers. Been there and done that and I've written books about the

Munros and the Corbetts. I even have a Munros T-shirt! I recall being too totally wrapped up in the excitement of exploration and discovery to notice the very ground I was walking on, never mind birds and plants, and the sheer thrill and challenge of mountaineering closed my mind to those things I shared the mountain with: the birds, the plants, the rocks and the geomorphology.

I suspect most of us have an awareness of the natural world. For me it eventually became a vital part of my overall outdoor experience, an added motivation to climb hills and explore wild places. Perhaps I was lucky. I came to the hills through a slow evolving of skills and outdoor awareness, a city kid who immediately felt at home amongst the bracken and heather, most probably due to a childhood in which I was thrown out the front door after breakfast and told not to come back until dinner was ready. In that precious time my pals and I explored the green fringes of our suburbs, cycled into the countryside and played at Huckleberry Finn in the woods and on the river. As a young teenager I roamed the lowly hills of the Campsie Fells where I learned mostly from my mistakes. Later I joined the Lomond Mountaineering Club and learned from older, more experienced climbers. We spent much of our time in Glen Coe and, when the weather was bad, we 'padded' around the tops rather than rock-climb on wet, greasy rock. It was during those outings that I first learned to distinguish between a golden eagle and a buzzard, or between a ring ouzel and a blackbird, a meadow pipit and a skylark.

During our climbs I learned the difference between schist and quartzite, andesite and granite, and during one impromptu geology lesson from an old gangrel (he was probably about thirty but seemed old to me) I sat flabbergasted as he explained how the rock I was climbing on was part of an ancient volcano that erupted through and onto a land surface of Dalradian metamorphic rocks about four hundred and twenty million years before. My very first geology lesson, and the subject has fascinated me ever since. Those early years taught me the natural world is infinitely more than just a playground or a gym. It's an incredibly ancient, evolving home for countless other creatures and plants. I accept it's difficult to learn these things if you are taught to climb on an indoor climbing wall.

I'm not a noted ornithologist as Tom Weir certainly was, and I'm no great wildlife writer and observer as my good friend Jim Crumley is, but I am aware that birds and beasts are part of the rich fabric of the great outdoors, and I've always delighted in their company. In watching a squirrel scampering up a tree, or wondering at the majestic flight of an eagle, I've become aware of the simple magic of the moment. Many of you will know the sheer delight of watching a family of otters slipping and sliding into a river from a muddy bank. Or been stunned by the aerial speed of a peregrine falcon tearing the sky in two. To lie on the sun-warmed red granite of the Cairngorm plateau and watch a snow bunting feed her chicks in a nest almost hidden by rocks and boulders is a special and humbling experience, and to discover a patch of purple and pink moss campion blooming amidst the harsh and austere barrenness of the summit screes of Nevis or Macdui is a reminder that beauty and charm can exist in the most inhospitable of surroundings. A metaphor for life perhaps, a message of hope from the hills?

Some of the best cliff and scree flowers are found high in the magnificent cliff buttresses, ridges and deeply indented gullies of the highest hills. A number of rare species grow here too, including alpine saxifrage, highland saxifrage, highland cudweed, hare's-foot sedge and curved woodrush. Where snow lies late into the spring amazing 'snow-bed' communities of plants develop, adapted to survive the harshest of conditions. Alpine lady-fern and wavy meadow-grass join a rich diversity of rare mosses and liverworts, including snow fork-moss, scorched rustwort and monster pawwort, and it doesn't take the nature-loving hillwalker long to realise the biggest and most obvious threat to these high mountain communities of birds and plants is climate change. As temperatures rise, the available area in which these plants can grow and birds can thrive becomes increasingly restricted. Worryingly, many can't move upwards or further north: they are often on the very edge of their range. In addition, high deer numbers means that many grazing-sensitive species are now found only on inaccessible ledges, while muirburn (heather management by burning) can be disastrous for these slow-growing plants. It doesn't take long to appreciate that hills and mountains, including their associated wildlife, are an indicator of change and mutation in our climate and the risk such change imposes on all of us.

An awareness of, if not a love for, the plants, birds and beasts of the natural world, reminds us of what we have and prompts us to understand that with a slight change of focus things could be immeasurably better. Through it all one vital factor stands clear. Nature Reserves, National Parks and Sites of Special Scientific Interest are all fine, but nature doesn't operate in silos. An often used example is that red squirrels should be able to move from the Borders to the Highlands along a continuous band of woodland without restriction. What's more, what is good for the natural world is good for us too. We're not different and we're not separate. Our very existence depends on a healthy ecosystem because we are part of that ecosystem and if one part of it is not functioning properly it will have a negative effect elsewhere. As the poet Francis Thompson once wrote: 'thou canst not stir a flower, without troubling of a star'. I like that because it graphically illustrates the nature of this web of creation, the interdependence of mankind and the other creatures that live on the planet in forests, mountains and rivers. Or, if you like, the land itself.

A BADENOCH SPRING
APRIL 1986

A reader kindly phoned me a couple of nights ago to tell me she had seen her first swallow of the year. Could this be a record? I checked and some ornithologist friends told me they had already spotted several near the Insh Meadows.

It seems ironic to be writing about sightings of swallows because, as I write this, snow is being thrashed against my office window by gale-force winds and it feels more like Christmas Eve than Good Friday. If I remember correctly, I spent last Christmas Eve walking in the rain on a mountain called Streap in Lochaber, thinking that it didn't feel at all like Christmas. Perception against reality, things aren't always as they seem.

One thing is certain. Summer is always later arriving in Badenoch than in many other parts of Scotland. In years past I've seen swallows on the west coast in mid-April and, one late Easter, I recall fishing with my two sons on the waters of a West Highland loch when we were startled by the dive bombing of screaming swifts, taking insects on the wing in that magical acrobatic display of theirs.

The following morning though, as I took a pre-breakfast wander along the shores of the loch, I heard my first cuckoo of the year. It was a rather miserable effort I must admit, but it was unmistakably cuckoo. I was lucky enough to see it too, as it flew from some beeches chased by agitated chaffinches, its long, white-tipped tail and falcon-like shape giving it away.

Swallows arrive from southern Africa, having travelled all the way across the Sahara, Morocco, eastern Spain, the Pyrenees, western France, and England before arriving in Scotland usually sometime in May. House martins and swifts also arrive from Africa at around the same time although swifts only stay long enough to breed before migrating back to Africa as early as late July.

With all these thoughts of summer bird song it was a bit of a shock to take the brunt of a full-scale winter assault the other day as I walked up to Creag an Leth-choin, or Lurcher's Crag, the rather imposing little peak that dominates the eastern portals of the Lairig Ghru. No sooner had I reached the open expanse known as Lurcher's Meadow than a great black curtain of cloud literally poured itself over Braeriach and Sron na Lairige, filled up the great chasm that is the Lairig Ghru, and proceeded to deluge Lurcher's Meadow with a blinding snowstorm. The suddenness

of the storm and the vehemence of the wind took me completely
by surprise, reiterating all too clearly how the apparent closeness
of summer in the glens bears little consequence on the hill. The
storm didn't last long, and I sat it out, huddled against a boulder,
wishing I had brought some more winter clothes.

The cloud and snow, which for a while had seemed like an
impenetrable white curtain, lifted as quickly and suddenly as
it had dropped, leaving the long glen of the Lairig looking as
though it had just been given the first coat of a whitewash job.
To add to the atmosphere of changing seasons I spotted my first
wheatear of the year as I descended to Glenmore.

BIRDS OF SUPERSTITION
NOVEMBER 1989

Legend claims that our little orange-breasted robin was once
as drab as a city speug. It was when he tried to wrest the crown
of thorns from the head of the crucified Christ that his breast
became saturated in the blood of Jesus, giving the red breast the
identifying feature we know and love today.

Just as the valiant robin tried so hard to relieve Jesus of his
discomfort so he was helped by another little bird who tried his
best to pull the nails from Christ's hands and feet. So hard did
he try that all he managed to do was get his mandibles crossed,
ending up with a rather deformed-looking beak. Today, of
course we recognise the crossbill, the Scottish parrot that can
be seen in the pine woods of Strathspey, effectively using his
'deformity' to remove seeds from tough pine cones.

Other birds have religious connections too. Take Gille Bride,
the servant of St Bride. This is the oystercatcher who apparently sheltered Jesus with his wings as he was trying to avoid
the dark forces of Satan. For his brave deed the oystercatcher
was taken under the protection of St Bride, the patron saint of
all birds. In some areas the skylark is supposed to have an even
more exalted patronage. In Eriskay, for example, he is known as
uiseag Mhuire, or Mary's lark.

According to the poet Longfellow, when Noah decided that the waters had begun to subside and land must be close, he sent a dove to search. A kingfisher, who at that time was apparently clad in dull grey feathers, was sent out shortly after the dove, but the kingfisher had decided that life on the ark was not particularly to his liking and had little intention of returning. Unfortunately, the mountainous land that he discovered didn't look very appealing either. Instead, he flew higher and higher until the very sky turned his back blue and the sun burned his breast bright red. He flew so high that he lost the ark and, in a wild panic, descended to the land in search of his ertswhile home ... which suddenly didn't appear so bad after all. Even today, the kingfisher spends all his time flying up and down rivers in search of the lost ark.

Not all birds have positive religious connections. The scurrilous magpie is associated with evil, the preponderance of which is associated with the number seen at any one time. Magpies are certainly increasing in numbers, especially in urban areas, so this legend doesn't auger well for the future of our cities. It was the Brahan Seer who once claimed: 'Chunnaic mi Pioghaid is dh'eirich leam, Chunnaic mi dha's gum b'iarguinn iad, Chunnaic mi tri a's b'aihearach mi, Ach ceithir ri m'linn ch'n iarainn iad.'

Translated, the Seer's words claim: 'I saw a magpie, to me then luck did die, I once saw two and they troubled me, Great joy was on me when once I saw three, But four forever let me not see.'

A contemporary rhyme is similar: 'One for sorrow, two for joy, three for a girl, and four for a boy.' Doesn't say a lot for the male sex though ...

SILKY SMOOTH AND SLEEK
JULY 1994

In years of outdoor wandering I have rarely seen an otter. A couple of times on the west coast and once in Loch Hourn in Knoydart, so when I heard the low whistle I was immediately attentive. The sound was barely perceptible over the whisper of

the riverside trees but it was enough to make me stop and freeze
and reach for my binoculars, hoping the low light was yet pale
enough to allow me the privilege of seeing.

This was a stretch of riverbank I knew well, for I've often
waited and watched here while gazing at voles, dippers, sand-
pipers, oystercatchers, and, aye, even the occasional leaping
salmon. There haven't been any salmon for a while but for all
that I'm not going to say where it is for there are still those who
see otters as vermin, and will blame them for the lack of big fish.

It was as well I knew this part of the river, because I noticed
a rock, midway out in the slow-moving current, that appeared
to have sprouted a round, rumped protuberance. It moved, and
there was a flash of scaly white belly: the otter was feeding. I
slowly sunk down in the bracken and settled myself.

She (I'll call her a she because although I honestly couldn't tell
the difference her silky-smooth shape was all wrong for mascu-
line) was ebony-coloured and sleek with that round flat-nosed
face that is such a delight. And she was a restless eater. Holding
the fish with her front paws she tore at the meat almost savagely,
and then slithered round for a better grip. After three or four
minutes of this tearing and ripping, feasting and slithering, she
stopped and sat bolt upright, her long weasel neck outstretched.
It was then I heard the low whistle again, this time a bit louder
than the last, but still muffled and a little wheezy. I followed her
gaze with the glasses and saw what she saw.

From the opposite bank, where great tree roots grip the water's
edge like talons, a long wedge-shaped ripple appeared and at its
apex, a flat head and whiskered nose. She, on the rock, begins to
show some signs of excitement and dances about in that slinky
way of hers while he (again I could be wrong but a 'he' fits into
the plot much more neatly) slides onto the boulder alongside her.
Curiously, he doesn't feed on the remains of the fish but looks as
though he's fairly content, sitting with a non-committal air while
she slides into the water, turns on her back and does backwards
somersaults without as much as a splash to suggest that she's
dived. Only the tell-tale ripples tell of her passing.

Soon she is back, half rolling as she swims, sinuous, silent and sleek, as though suggesting that he joins her. But he is happy enough where he is, a dark silhouette on a dark rock on a dark river. I could just make out the ripples of her passing on the water's surface, but by now the gloom had made it difficult to see her flat head. It was while I searched the surface for a hint of her shiny body that he must have slipped into the water for as I returned the glasses to the rock it had become vacant again, with only the remains of the fish as evidence of their passing.

THE RASP OF THE CORNCRAKE
MAY 1996

A number of years ago the late John Hillaby, author, scientist and long-distance walker, told me he had been camping in Derbyshire when he was wakened quite early in the morning by the sound of two curlews pouring out their beautiful liquid call, a sound that rarely fails to provoke a real delight in the listener. John lay in his tent in a half doze, taking real pleasure from the curlew's call, when he was abruptly brought to his senses by someone in a neighbouring tent shouting, 'Can someone shoot those bloody birds?' One man's delight is another man's annoyance.

I wrote last week of the hardy individuals who are currently walking across Scotland on The Great Outdoors Challenge and I know that several of them will complain about being wakened early in the morning by the repetitive calls of the cuckoo. This harbinger of summer rarely fails to provoke squeals of delight when first heard, and most folk make a mental note of their first cuckoo call of the year, but when it goes on morning after morning it can begin to irritate.

These thoughts came to me after reading a press release from the RSPB about a survey the charity is carrying out of the UK's population of corncrakes, another bird which has been known to drive people almost completely senseless. Some friends of mine were making a television programme about climbing on the Hebridean island of Pabbay last year, and unfortunately for them they had camped in a field close to where a pair of corncrakes were nesting. At first my friends were delighted with the novelty of camping so close to what has become a relatively rare species, but after a few mornings of being wakened by the corncrake's rather monotonous rasping call they were almost ready to do the unthinkable. I'm glad to say they didn't. There are few enough corncrakes surviving in the UK as it is.

The RSPB is asking for the general public's help in identifying the whereabouts of Britain's corncrake population. Since the bird sings mostly at dusk, through the night and early in the morning, the RSPB is asking postmen, milkmen, newspaper deliverers, health visitors, farm workers or anyone else who might be out and about at such hours to be alert.

Corncrakes spend much of their time hidden in tall vegetation and the only real clue to their presence is their song. May and June are the best months to hear them as the birds have just newly arrived from Africa and are eager to set up their territory, find a mate, and nest. The song is easily recognised – a continual rasping, buzzing sound and has basically two notes, 'crake-crake' repeated frequently, sometimes for hours on end, especially, it seems, when you're trying to sleep!

The decline in number and range of corncrakes, as with so many species, reflects the changes in agricultural practices that have taken place in the UK since late last century. The mechanisation of grass cutting in particular, combined with earlier cutting dates has led to a greater mortality and losses of nesting grounds. Mowing of grass tends to take place later in the year in north and west Scotland, and so this area has become, more or less, the corncrake's last stronghold in Scotland.

OF THE HIGH AND LONELY PLACES
MAY 1998

Of all bird songs there can be few as moving and evocative as that of the cock snow bunting. A rare breeder in Scotland, this little bird is a true lover of the high and lonely places, a black and white fleck of beauty to be seen against the harsh wind-scoured tundra.

Perhaps it's the gauntness and solitude of the snow bunting's breeding ground that evokes such a sense of passion in the listener, but I can't think of a birdsong that is more evocative. Last week I spent a couple of days on the high Cairngorms where I laid amongst the rocks just as the first shafts of warm sunshine began to burn off the thin swirling mists that had earlier shrouded the area. In this magical atmosphere I watched this small bird of the high places.

With its jet black mantle and dazzling white wings with ebony primaries the cock snow bunting was as vivid in those surroundings as its song was intense in the early morning stillness. Rising from the screes the bird rapidly beat its white wings until he was fifty feet or so above the ground. Then, fluttering his outstretched wings like a skylark he glided earthwards with an explosive and intense song, continuing for all he was worth as he landed on a rock with wings upstretched.

As he closed his wings the outpouring of song became almost a cry, a moving and powerful anthem, half the voice of some sentient creature proclaiming itself and half the voice of the arctic wastelands.

It had been some time since I spent more than just a few hours on the Cairngorm High Tops. After enjoying trips this year to the hills of Mallorca and Morocco, and having just come home from a couple of weeks on the rain-soaked hills and moors of Sutherland it felt good to be back in this Monadh Ruadh environment. It didn't take long for me to remember why spring and early summer are always so good on the high plateaux.

In a land where the basic elements of rock, air and water so completely predominate, it seems odd to me that there should be any illusion of welcome. Vast wind-scoured slopes and gashes of glens offer little in the way of comfort or ease, and yet up here the untroubled waters and ancient stones cast a spell as soothing as they are dramatic. The high, lonely lochans reflect the mood of the skies which, in turn, dictate the future, ordained by the winds and clouds of Biera.

The experience of being up here is special. Up here, I've learnt the simplicity of being, uncluttered by everyday things, the ascending grace conceded by these vast lands to all who are prepared to ask for it, but while these hills are so powerful in their own way, they are also sensitive and fragile. Our tenuous relationship needs to be nurtured. Along with a small sparrow-like bird, and great granite mountains, we belong to a biotic community and it's only when we view our relationship from that stance that can we begin to benefit from it.

SPRING SONG
APRIL 1999

I'm sitting at the edge of the moor, a small outcrop of rock softening the cold blow of the early morning wind. From the pock-marked flatness below me comes what I can only describe as a cacophony of bird sound, a tumultuous celebration of spring. A thin mist is drifting across from the high tops, but it's the only hint of grey in a landscape that looks as though it's just been washed clean and hung out to dry.

This crackling freshness gives a vibrancy to the morning, an atmosphere enhanced by the piercing bubble and squeak of waders. All my favourites are out this morning, and obviously in fine fettle.

Who can fail to be moved by the bubbling crescendo of the whaup, or curlew? There must be hundreds of them around this spot, and they're all making music as though delighted to feel some hint of warmth from the early sun. I listen to the thin call, rising slowly and then becoming faster until the great climax to the song: a bubbling sound, a liquid trill that is loved by outdoors folk everywhere.

Combine that particular music with the plaintively shrill pee-wee of the lapwing, another song that moves exiles to tears. This is the song of the moors, the song of wide, open skies and the fairm-toons of the north-east, the evocation of Lewis Grassic Gibbon's *Sunset Song*. But what a mis-named bird. How much more evocative and descriptive are the local names of 'peesie' and 'teuchit' or the even more popular 'peewee.' Watch its mad acrobatics, its crazy, abandoned flight, tumbling to earth as though about to crash land, only to swerve at the last possible moment, and soar upwards again, twisting and tilting its wings as though careering through some invisible obstacle course. And all the time squeaking and trumpeting in that uncanny characteristic call.

Add the high-pitched piping of the oystercatcher, the Servants of St Bride, and you get a medley of wader song fit to lift the heart, and this morning my heart is well and truly stirred by the sound of it all.

A few mornings earlier I had listened to a similar sound elsewhere, but the choir had been enlarged by black-headed gulls and whooper swans. From a distance the sound of the swans almost resembled the baying of a pack of hounds, but as they flew closer in smaller groups the music became sweeter, more of a mellow bugling than the honking of geese, a lost and somehow triumphant sound in the stillness of the early hours. What a sight they made as they flew low over the waters, long necks outstretched like Concorde,[1] the long, powerful wings whistling as they cut clean through the air, a steady powerful rhythm that would shortly fly them back to Iceland, Greenland and their northern airts in one long, unbroken flight.

As I wander home for breakfast a robin chortles out its sweet song in the woods, and a wren scolds me for making such a noise. There's a skylark in the field and the sound of it cheers me like no other sound can.

---

1. Some readers will recall Concorde, a supersonic jet that was capable of flying at twice the speed of sound. It crossed the Atlantic in three and a half hours and was in service between 1976 and 2003. The design of the aircraft was long and slim with a slightly drooping nose and looked for all the world like a flying swan. The aircraft was discontinued because of low passenger numbers, possibly because of safety fears. In July 2000 it crashed soon after take-off killing all 109 people on board.

FOX ENCOUNTERS
AUGUST 2001

In over thirty-five years of wandering hills and mountains I've only encountered a hill fox on three occasions. The first was in Morvern where I was walking with Tom Weir. We had sailed into Loch a' Choire in a boat belonging to a mutual friend, Bob Sorrell from Cumbria, and Tom and I climbed the hill just west of Kingairloch village. We were so engrossed in our blethering it was a surprise we saw anything, but as we sat by some rocks to eat our lunch some sixth sense suggested to me that we were being watched.

I looked slowly round and was surprised to see, not twenty yards from where we sat, an old dog fox nonchalantly watching us from the top of a bluff. I quietly nudged Tom to look behind and as we took our cameras from our packs old Reynardine stood up, shook himself, and padded up the hill, as relaxed and unconcerned as you like. It was the highlight of our day.

My second sighting of a hill fox was less formal. I was walking in upper Glen Lyon when I stopped for a breather, and looking back down, noticed a russet blur. It was a fox running up the hill from the roadside. As he approached me, he obviously caught my scent for he drastically changed direction and ran over an intermediate rise. I suspect he had been scavenging near a farm, was disturbed by a car on the road, and ran up the hill. I never saw him again.

The most recent encounter was the strangest of all. Gina and I were camping by Angle Tarn below Bowfell in the Lake District last weekend. We had arrived at the tarn in the late afternoon after a cold day of blustery showers. Our plan was to cook and eat our evening meal then walk it off by climbing Scafell Pike, England's highest mountain, in the evening. It was a grand evening wander and we arrived back at the tent about nine o'clock, had some supper, and settled in for the night, a very wet one as it happened.

At three in the morning, I was abruptly wakened by the sound of things falling over in the porch of the tent, no more than ten inches from my ear. When I pulled down the zip between the inner tent and the porch and shone my torch I immediately realised that our food bag, a large, white net bag with the next morning's breakfast and lunch inside, was missing. Thinking that a sheep had perhaps nosed in I jumped out of my sleeping bag and into the wet, dark night, wearing no more than my boxer shorts. Torch in hand, with the rain teeming down, I saw the thief wasn't a sheep but a fox, who sat no more than twenty yards away tearing at the bag to get at the food inside.

As soon as it saw me, it tried to run off, dragging the bag behind it before giving it up and making good its escape. I retrieved the bag, came back to the tent where Gina shouted at me to turn around. There was the fox, following no more than ten yards behind. With little shyness and a disconcerting lack of fear, it watched me as I threw the food bag into the tent and climbed back in to dry myself. After a few minutes it padded off into the night.

I can only think it was used to stealing from tents. Many people camp at this spot and climb Scafell Pike as we had done, leaving their tent unattended. Possibly our fox was a vixen with a family to feed, or maybe it was a tame fox, possibly handreared and used to human beings. Whatever the reason, our fox encounter made it a night to remember.

PTARMIGAN GRUMBLES
FEBRUARY 2006

For those of us who walk the Scottish hills on a regular basis, the sight of a flock of ptarmigan is not a rare occurrence. Yet I am aware that for so many visitors to Scotland a sighting of this bird of the high Arctic can be the highlight of a holiday.

On several occasions I've chatted to ornithologists from the south who have sweated their way onto the Cairn Gorm plateau and have spent hours watching these plump birds, delighting in their relative rarity. Even familiarity doesn't reduce their appeal. The ptarmigan, like the mountain hare, is an indicator of the changing seasons, metamorphosing from its rather dowdy grey and black summer plumage into its pure white winter coat, and vice versa in the spring. I've also come to appreciate and enjoy its croaky call, like old men in the pub, and often lain in my tent at night listening to their gossips.

For many hillwalkers, the sighting of ptarmigan is a highlight of a walk in the Scottish highlands, but are these sightings becoming less common? Are there fewer ptarmigan in the hills? The British Trust for Ornithology is asking hillwalkers for their help to find out.

The ptarmigan is an arctic relic, confined to mountainous islands of wintry weather. As Britain's only truly resident montane bird, it is cleverly adapted to its mountain habitat. To avoid peregrine, golden eagle and other predators, the ptarmigan relies on camouflage and is the only British bird to moult into a pure white winter plumage. In these snowless days you can't help but think that nature has betrayed the ptarmigan, watching them run across the black gravels of the high plateaux, as bright and conspicuous as a dayglo suit. In fact, the ptarmigan moults its plumage three times during the year to blend with rocks, snow or patches of each, depending on the season. Or at least, that's the idea.

These remarkable birds occur widely across the Scottish highlands and on a few islands of the Hebrides and the Clyde. They normally occur at altitudes over 750m, but in the far north-west they can be found as low as 200m. However, changes to the overall population and distribution of ptarmigan are not well understood. Worryingly, there appears to be some evidence that the ptarmigan's range has contracted.

It is becoming ever more important to understand Scotland's mountains and their wildlife as they face a variety of potential threats including increases in predators such as crows and, of course, climate change. Ptarmigan are thought to be sensitive to these changes. The birds will therefore be a key indicator of the condition of our mountain habitats, which are recognised as a high priority under the UK Biodiversity Action Plan.

Hillwalkers and other hill users will gather information to feed into Project Ptarmigan. Participants will keep an eye out for ptarmigan (and their signs, such as droppings and feathers) as they walk in the bird's range.

You don't need to be a birdwatcher to take part in Project Ptarmigan, as BTO Scotland will issue straightforward guidelines. Encountering a ptarmigan is always a noteworthy experience: all you need to do is to make a note of these wonderful encounters with this charismatic Scottish bird.

HANDS ON HANDA
SEPTEMBER 2007

Blown off the waterlogged hills, we headed for the coast. As we approached Scourie we almost overlooked the single-track road turnoff that leads to the tiny hamlet of Tarbert and the ferry to Handa Island.

If it was going to remain wet and windy we might as well suffer the elements on a coastal walk and since Handa was still on my list of Scottish Things-To-Do-And-See we spent the night on the Scourie campsite and returned to the Tarbert road next morning.

By that time it had rained and blown, blown and rained all night and I guess the bad weather simply blew itself out. By the time I wrestled my old campervan down the winding road to Tarbert the clouds had been torn apart, exposing great expanses of blue sky and, for what seemed like the first time in months, the sun shone hot on my bald head.

Even before we jumped into the tin boat that acts as ferry between Tarbert and Handa I knew it was the wrong time of year to visit the island. The place is a wildlife reserve, looked after by the Scottish Wildlife Trust, and its claim to fame is in its resident seabird population, except that most of the seabirds, and most certainly the puffins, kittiwakes, razorbills, and guillemots, would have left their breeding ledges on the cliffs to winter out at sea.

A number of years ago I visited the island in June although I never set foot on it. We arrived by powerboat and came close enough to the north-west cliffs of the island to be almost deafened by the clamour and cacophony of screaming gulls. We scanned the tiers of bird-haunted ledges on the cliffs through a blizzard of wheeling white fulmars, thousands of them, all riding the air currents on their short and stubby wings. Despite the incredible visual and aural spectacle, the pungent stench from the guano on the cliff ledges effectively stopped us going too close.

We didn't linger that day as we didn't want to upset the nesting birds but I did promise myself I'd return. The fact that it was 'off-season' didn't matter too much. There would still be the bonxies, the great skuas, to see, and with a bit of luck, black-throated divers and of course, the spectacle of the great cliffs of Torridonian sandstone.

The Scottish Wildlife Trust has created a good walk around the western part of the island, a route that takes in all the visual splendours of the reserve. I'm not one to stick to footpaths but on this occasion I was happy to. Wander too far onto the moors and, chances are, you'll be dive bombed by a territorial great skua, a big, heavy bird with little fear of man.

Not far from the start of the walk you'll pass through the remains of a village that once was home to twelve families. Now only a ruckle of stone and a single gable wall are still standing, a poignant memorial to an ancient way of life that is gone forever. The Handa villagers, like those on St Kilda, were ruled by a queen, usually the oldest widow, and a parliament that met every morning to plan the work of the day. Their staple diet was potatoes, fish, seabirds and their eggs but the great potato famine of the mid-nineteenth century forced the families from the island.

Above Puffin Bay you get your first breathtaking view of the great cliffs of Handa, about eighty-five metres in height at this point, and just a little way around the coast a narrow geo bites into the land. Its vertical walls are about a hundred metres in height and the entrance to the geo is virtually blocked by the impressive bulk of the Great Stack of Handa, or Stack an Seabhaig, the hawk's stack.

In season over 9,000 guillemots breed on its ledges. Razorbills lay their single egg on crevices near the top of the Stack and kittiwakes build nests made from grasses cemented together by droppings. Puffins nest in burrows on the cliff tops. The place becomes a raucous bird metropolis with an estimated 180,000 seabirds at any one time. Today it was as silent as the grave, with only a few wheeling fulmars to suggest that this is the greatest seabird breeding site in Scotland.

From the Great Stack the walk follows the cliff tops of the island all the way back to the ferry. The views across Eddrachillis Bay towards the Stoer peninsula are dramatic, with the phallic Old Man of Stoer distinct at the far point. Landward the views are dominated by Foinaven, Arkle, Ben Stack and Quinag and if it's clear you might just make out the dim line of Lewis shimmering on the far horizon.

Before we returned to the mainland we briefly visited the tiny graveyard where the graves are not of island people but of mainlanders who were buried here so they wouldn't be dug up by wolves. Another place, another time, another world.

WHALE WATCHING
AUGUST 2009

We sat above the angry waters of the Minch at the very northern tip of the Isle of Skye. Rubha Hunish is a wild and lonely spot, a rugged peninsula whose wind-ruffled moorland culminates in impressively steep basalt cliffs. The rock climbers in our team gazed at them longingly, but we weren't at Rubha Hunish to climb rock. This was the start of a television walk for BBC Scotland that would take me through the Isle of Skye, a journey on foot that would link two of the most impressive landscapes in Scotland, the Trotternish ridge and the Cuillin. Here at Rubha Hunish, the Trotternish ridge was laid out before us.

We were camping here and, before we turned in, we sat

above the rocks and gazed out to sea for we had been told this was a prime spot for seeing minke whales. I tend to take these suggestions with a pinch of salt, rarely having such luck, but within minutes of settling down someone yelled 'Yar she blows' or words to that effect. Sure enough, about a hundred metres offshore we saw the arched shape and fin of one of these incredible mammals.

It may not have been watching humpback whales off Vancouver Island or kayaking withOrcas off the coast of Alaska but watching minke whales from one of a number of coastal vantage points in the UK can add a thrilling moment to any coastal walk. Indeed, a whole new whale and dolphin-spotting industry appears to be encouraging many folk out to sea to spot these phenomenal beasts for themselves, armed not with harpoons but with cameras.

The common minke whale can be categorised into two or three subspecies: the North Atlantic minke whale, the North Pacific minke whale and the dwarf minke whale. All minkes are part of the marine family that includes the humpback whale, the fin whale, the Bryde's whale and the fabled blue whale.

Common minke whales (the kind you are likely to see from our coasts) are distinguished from other whales by a white band on each flipper. The body is usually black or dark grey above and white underneath. Most of the length of the back, including the dorsal fin and blowholes, appears at once when the whale surfaces to breathe. The whale then breathes several times at short intervals before 'deep-diving' for anything up to twenty minutes. Deep dives are preceded by a pronounced arching of the back and this is what we witnessed from our vantage point on Rubha Hunish.

The larger whales typically leap about three-quarters out of the water, before twisting on their axis prior to re-entry which is believed to protect their internal organs from the shock of their huge bodies hitting the water. Minkes can swim close to shore and often enter bays, inlets and estuaries making them one of our most sighted whales. Popular minke whale viewing areas include the Isle of Man, County Cork in Ireland and the islands of Mull and Skye.

It's often difficult to distinguish one minke whale from another and in most cases they either travel singly or congregate in small pods of two or three whales. It was difficult to say how many we saw; there were about twenty appearances but whether that was all the same whale or a small pod of whales I have no idea.

It's often been said that the biggest wild mammal we can see in the UK is the red deer stag, but an adult minke whale is considerably bigger than that. Minke whales can grow to about 7.8-9m/25-30ft long, and weigh about 6-7.5 tons. Females are about 0.6m/2ft longer than males, as with all baleen whales. The largest minke whale ever recorded was about 10.5 m/35 ft long weighing 9.5 tons.

Thankfully minke whales have not been the target of whalers since a world-wide moratorium on whaling in the late eighties, but Japan, Iceland and Norway have continued hunting for minkes on so-called scientific grounds. These scientific grounds have been criticised by many environmental organisations and it's well known that these countries have ambitions towards resuming large scale whaling operations.

How did the minke whale get its name? One tale suggests that a German whaler by the name of Meineke mistook one of these small whales for a blue whale, to the amusement of his fellow whalers. From then on whalers called them 'Meineke's whale', which eventually became minke or minky.

CHAPTER FOUR

Against the Elements

The old saying: 'there is no such thing as bad weather, only bad clothing', doesn't hold much truck amongst seasoned hillwalkers and mountaineers, all of whom at some point will have had a thorough soaking despite the quality of their gear. Even ultra-expensive, high-tech clothing can fail spectacularly in the face of a genuine Highland rain-fest. The first time I came close to suffering from hypothermia was in the late seventies when my old pal Peter Lumley and I were testing some of the very early Gore-tex fabric waterproofs in the Cairngorms. It would be a couple of years later that WL Gore, the manufacturers, discovered that their waterproofs worked better when the seams were sealed. In those early days, the raindrops percolated through the seams and migrated over the inner face of the fabric. We were as wet inside as we were outside, shivering, and had to pitch camp early so we could dive into sleeping bags and spend a couple of hours brewing up hot drinks. For a while, manufacturers sealed the seams with glue before Gore hit upon the idea of nylon tape.

I think it's a fact of Scottish mountain life that, every so often, the conditions can become so bad that no fabric invented by man will keep the weather out. Those who think up trite and clever phrases about bad weather and bad clothing will never have experienced such a phenomenon, and I'm prepared to make the claim that, very occasionally, the Scottish mountains can be hit by extreme weather that is simply incompatible with human life. In such conditions even the best of gear, the most expensive and thoroughly tested, will not save you, and this is perhaps a good time to remember those who test gear for the various magazines and web sites. Those guys and gals who face horrible conditions to put newly designed gear through its paces, coping quietly but critically with pinched boots, sleeves that are too long or hoods that don't quite cinch tight. Such individuals are often considered to be blessed – think of all that free gear – but they are not blessed. They are self-sacrificing individuals who suffer so we don't have to.

When laying out all the wonderful reasons why hillwalking in Scotland is a marvellous activity, it's difficult to ignore the fact that much of the time the weather is rotten. It's not always seriously bad, of course, but it does pay to be weather observant to such an extent that you become a slave to the weather fore-casts, learning the language of weather fronts, high pressure systems, air mass, barometric pressure, dew point and even the doldrums, albeit that is a nautical term. Most of us are more familiar with the alternative doldrums, the depression that takes hold when we watch the weekend forecast of rain, cloud and wind.

Many years ago, I made the decision to make my own judge-ments about the weather rather than rely solely on what the forecasters told me. I took note of the forecast, set out to wherever I had planned to go, and made the decision to face the weather or not once I reached the foot of the hill. On most occasions if the weather was truly bad, I could take a low level walk somewhere nearby, but it was surprising how often the weather was better than it looked from inside the car. Once outside it never felt quite as bad and, as the following essays illustrate, it often improved as the day went on. I would have missed some great walking experi-ences had I simply turned tail or stayed at home.

Some of these mixed-weather days are the best of all. Early on in my hill-climbing career I was dragged up a very cloud-covered hill in the west highlands. I wasn't enjoying it and questioned the sense in walking up a mountain when I couldn't see anything. The words were barely out of my mouth when a gust of wind tore a huge hole in the cloud, revealing a view of surrounding hills and mountains that took my breath away. It was for all the world like sitting in the darkness of a theatre when the curtain is suddenly parted to reveal a world of light, colour and breathtaking vibrancy. The world as a stage, my companions and I mere players. I'll always remember the advice Tom Weir gave me many years ago when we discussed mountain photography. 'The best shots,' he reckoned, 'are taken at good moments on bad days.'

Scotland's mountain weather can be fickle, but it's those very complexities that create the moods and impressions – the atmospheres – that makes hillwalking in Scotland such a unique experience. In world terms Scottish mountains are not high: only 284 summits rise beyond 914m/3000ft and the highest, Ben Nevis, is only 344m/4409ft above sea level, but because of Scotland's latitude and the often cold and windy weather this northerly position attracts, our comparatively bite-sized hills offer a very real challenge to hillwalkers.

While the majority of the summits can be climbed comfortably and back in a day, mist and rain often reduces visibility and can make navigation extremely complex. In winter conditions, any time between November and April, there is a real threat of avalanches, white-out conditions and full-scale arctic blizzards and only the foolhardy would treat the Scottish hills with anything less than utter respect.

Then there are the days that remain longest in the memory, when the rock is warm to the touch, when the hills are purple and languid in the warm sun, when the lazy call of the cuckoo is symbolic of the heavy, slumbering atmosphere of the day. In conditions like this it's easy to understand what motivates those who escape to the hills. Then there are the days when mists sift and surge, lit by a morning sun, to reveal and expose, hide and conceal. Drifting mists like gently scented breath, as though the very earth was exhaling in the cool of the day. Other days are more ominous, when dark clouds gather and approach like doom-laden Valkyries, heralding fine gauze curtains of drifting rain that threaten and drift ever closer before the first few drops have you reaching for your waterproofs, usually with a curse or two. But even on days like these there is powerful drama to be enjoyed, a visual and sensory experience that demonstrates the raw power of nature, the overriding sensation that we are insignificant against the burgeoning reality of the natural world. Such simple species as us can only do what we can to protect ourselves from the elements but can never stop it; we can forecast it and learn to cope, but we can't prevent it. We can only wonder at its sheer power and immensity and patiently await the arch of colours that signals hope, the rainbow of redemption and maybe the end of the storm.

Appropriate safety precautions must be taken by anyone venturing onto the hills, in any weather conditions. Don't set off without waterproofs and spare clothing. Food, a map, compass, whistle and torch are vital items of equipment. Scottish winter hillwalking is essentially mountaineering: an ice-axe, crampons and specialist winter gear are essential, as is an understanding of snow conditions, including avalanche awareness.

Everyone venturing onto the mountains should be able to navigate. There are numerous courses offered by qualified instructors and centres and learning to navigate can be a lot of fun. When you set off on your hillwalk let someone know where you are going and when you will return. Every year search parties waste countless hours searching in the wrong places. Appreciation of our wonderful mountains is heightened by the peace of mind that comes with the knowledge that, should something go drastically wrong, at least the rescue teams will know where to look for you.

MEALL DUBH, GLENGARRY
DECEMBER 1989

Great plumes of spray were being blown over the Loch Loyne Dam and the white horses on the loch's surface wouldn't have disgraced the Corrievrecken whirlpool. I pulled in, killed the car engine, and felt the wind buffet the vehicle from side to side. When a splatter of rain hit the windscreen I seriously considered going home. With daylight hours in short supply and a weather forecast that warned of 'extreme buffeting' on the high tops, I thought I had chosen my hill quite carefully. Meall Dubh is the highest point in the vast expanse of high moorland that's wedged between Loch Garry and Glen Moriston, a Corbett that I previously climbed on a sunny morning en route to Skye. It's that kind of hill: relatively diminutive, easily climbed but with the big advantage of being a great viewpoint. Or at least it used to be. A seventeen-turbine wind farm now graces the summit slopes, but more of that later.

Bearing in mind Meall Dubh's relative ease of ascent I thought it would be an ideal leg-stretch to help ease out the old year, an opportunity to drift uphill without too much effort and mentally recharge myself for the year ahead. No pressure, no risks, no fight against the short daylight hours. A Sunday stroll, with good views from the top, but it took a fair bit of mental discipline to propel me out of the car and into Gore-tex. A complete head-to-foot covering.

The Allt Garbh-Dhoire, normally a pleasant little burn, was in full spate and I had to follow it high into the spacious bowl of Coire nam Brach before I could cross. Even its minor tributaries were white with swollen meltwater. By now, fairly high on the hill, I was being buffeted about by a mischievous, rather than a deadly wind and, every ten minutes, as regular as clockwork, a rain shower would sweep across the moors in full drenching mode. The showers at least had the good grace to signal their approach with a sudden darkening of the sky behind me.

By now I realised I had scored a tactical if unintentional point. All the way uphill beside the burn I had been squelching over sodden wet ground but, by being forced high into the corrie, I had come close to the broad ridge that runs north from an undistinguished top called Carn Ban to the rocky top of Clach Criche. Compared to the slopes below, the ridge was relatively dry underfoot with the advantage of a following wind that pushed and shoved me along the undulations with great enthusiasm.

Between Clach Criche and the descent before the final climb to the Corbett, a rosary-chain of high-level lochans, still partially frozen, filled the hollows between each undulation. The gusty wind was blowing the water that lay on top of the ice into mini spumes, swirling and blowing like geysers, a sight that I don't think I've seen before on the Scottish hills. As I climbed the final slopes to Meall Dubh, with the wind now becoming a little more menacing than mischievous, I knew that the views I had hoped for would be obscured by the cloud and rain. Away to the north the dim outline of the Glen Shiel hills were enhanced a little by snow streaks and behind me, with the waters of Loch Loyne lapping at their skirts, the big hills of Gleouraich and Spidean Mialach were barely discernible. One view I didn't expect, spoiling any hint of a panorama to the south over Loch Garry, was the view of seventeen wind turbines, barely a few hundred metres from the summit cairn. What crass, insensitive planner allowed permission for such a siting of these hideous things?

I know we need to meet various renewable targets but surely, as a nation that's proud of its glorious landscapes, a nation that relies on tourism, such industrialisation should be kept to brownfield sites, or at least close to the centres of population that require the energy?

Despite the weather I had been enjoying myself so, rather than spoil the day with a rant, I crammed a sandwich into my mouth, had a drink of coffee in the shelter of the huge cairn (the summit is marked by a small pile of stones close to the big cairn), and hightailed it downhill, taking a direct line back to the Allt Garbh-Dhoire.

BEN OSS AND BEINN DUBHCHRAIG, TYNDRUM
APRIL 1992

Torrential rain swept along Strathfillan and the hills were hidden in a mire of mist and cloud. By the time I pulled into the parking area at Dalrigh, just south of Tyndrum, that part of my brain that is logical and reasonable was urging me to stay in the car, turn around and go home. The weather forecast had reckoned on sunny spells with showers, so perhaps this was just a long shower? The sun might come out as I breasted the hill's summit and make it all worthwhile? In any case, what's a bit of rain and wind? I pulled on my waterproofs, shrugged logic aside and went for it! I'd love to be able to report that my intuition was correct, that it ended up a magnificent day after a wet start, but it didn't. It was one of those days that appear to be increasingly frequent in Scotland, when the only view is of a map and compass.

My intention was to climb the Munro pair of Ben Oss and Beinn Dubhcraig, fairly easy hills that rise on the south side of the Cononish glen. Both tend to be overshadowed by the sensual beauty of Beinn Laoigh, but their traverse usually offers some stunning views down the length of Glen Falloch to the Crianlarich hills and Loch Lomond.

From the south Ben Oss, 1028m/3373ft, appears as a fine-pointed peak and Beinn Dubhcraig 977m/3205ft is more rounded but presents a craggy, well-broken face but, from the north-east, the usual approach, Oss falls down in steep slopes above Coire Buidhe while the summit ridge of Beinn Dubhcraig sits over the wide and open Coire Dubhcraig above recent forestry plantations.

Just below the younger conifers, like a form of consolation, remnants of the ancient pine woods of Caledon stand proudly, wind-blown, twisted and gnarled. This Coile Coire Chuilc fills the confluence of the River Cononish and the Allt Gleann Auchreoch.

I could barely see the trees never mind the hills as I crossed the River Fillan by its old bridge. In 1306 a battle took place here between the MacDougalls of Lorn and the forces of Robert the Bruce. Hence the name of the place: Dail-righ, the king's field. As I sloshed my way along beside the railway a curious thought flashed through my mind. Robert the Bruce was allegedly encouraged by the spider to keep trying. Perhaps the Bruce's spirit still lingered here below Beinn Dubhcraig, encouraging hill-goers like me to ignore the lousy weather and just go for it. Or perhaps not . . .

Sodden, boggy footpaths followed the rushing waters of the Allt Coire Dubhcraig through the trees. Three deer fences were crossed before I reached the open hillside and, for the first time, now that I was beyond the shelter of the pines, I became aware of the force of the wind. It was roaring in from the west so I knew it would be worse by the time I breasted the exposed summit ridge and was at its mercy.

Old snow patches made the ascent through the corrie a little more interesting despite the wind and rain and, as I was approaching the ridge, I could hear the wind roaring like a banshee. The summit isn't that far along the ridge so I made a dash for it, stumbling and rocking in the wind, trekking poles flailing dangerously.

It didn't take a lot of thought in deciding to abandon Ben Oss. I'd climbed it twice before, and if I ever decide to add up the Munros I've climbed three times and perhaps go for a triple round I'll simply come back and climb it again. It won't be going anywhere...[1]

In reasonable conditions Ben Oss can be climbed from Dubhcraig by returning along the summit ridge and descending steeply westwards to a col. From there the route follows a wide ridge over a knobbly summit and onwards in a south-west direction to the summit. It's possible to descend immediately north into Glen Cononish but the ground is steep and broken in places so it's probably advisable to return over the knobbly summit and back onto Beinn Dubhcraig, where its north ridge can be followed back down to the lower reaches of Glen Cononish. Either that or do as I did, simply follow your outward route back to Dalrigh.

BROAD CAIRN, GRAMPIAN
OCTOBER 1998

Glen Doll in the Angus Glens can be the starting point for some great high-level sorties into the eastern Cairngorms, including

---

1. I did eventually go back to climb Ben Oss for a third time, and help complete a third round of the Munros.

the Mounth roads that run from Glen Clova to Ballater (the Capel Mounth) and from Glen Doll to Braemar (the Tolmount) as well as the two Munros of Mayar and Driesh. Unfortunately, surrounded by high hills on three sides, Glen Doll is an awkward place to get to. From my home in Badenoch it's probably forty to fifty miles as the eagle flies, but well over double that via Blairgowrie and Kirriemuir. That's why I was so reluctant to turn my back on the rain-soaked hills of the Angus Glens.

On the basis that things always look worse from inside the car, I wrapped myself in waterproofs and set off towards Jock's Road, on the promise that if things didn't improve I'd simply make the most of a low-level walk and go home. But things did improve.

The path that climbs the length of Glen Doll north of the White Water has become known as Jock's Road, although traditionally the route is called the Tolmount. Jock's Road, named after a climber by the name of John Winters, is the steep section that climbs out of Glen Doll opposite the dark crags of Craig Maud. By the time I reached this steeper ground the rain had stopped, the dark clouds had rolled away and sunshine caused steam to rise from the damp rocks. Still swaddled in Gore-tex it caused me to steam gently too.

It was a good place to stop and strip off. Below, the White Water tumbled through a wild and rugged landscape before vanishing into the green choke of conifers that covers much of lower Glen Doll. On the other side of the glen Corrie Kilbo and Corrie Fee opened up beyond the steep and glistening crags of The Dounalt and Craig Rennet. I gave thanks to Jock for his path as we climbed over the lip of Glen Doll onto the grassy plateau beyond. Once beyond the confines of the glen the path passes the rough howff known as Davy's Bourach, built by the Angus gangrel Davy Glen, and follows the ridge that runs to Crow Craigies before dropping into Glen Callater bound for Glen Clunie and Braemar. The sun only shone intermittently now, and a brisk wind sent rain clouds scudding across the wide skies. Huddling below the cairn of Crow Craigies, I ate some lunch before taking a direct line north-east to the obvious rocky summit of Broad Cairn, 998m/3274ft.

From Broad Cairn I descended the rocky slopes to a hideously eroded bulldozed track which, and I have it on the highest authority, was created on the instructions of the Duke of Edinburgh so shooting parties would get quick and easy access to the high plateaux. It's probably one of the worst examples of high-level bulldozed tracks in the country. Fortunately, I didn't have to stay with it for long. Just before I reached Sandy's Hut at the top of Corrie Chash I turned right and, in total contrast, descended one of the most delightful footpaths in the area, down to the pinewoods and the dashing River Esk at Bachnagairn.

It's almost four miles back down the glen to Glen Doll but it's a picturesque walk beside the busy, bustling stream below the curiously named crags of Juanjorge. Lower down you have to cross the river at a ford, so despite enjoying an unexpected rain-free day, I still managed to get my feet wet.

MEALL DUBHAG/GARBHLACH, CAIRNGORMS
JANUARY 2001

I had a distinct feeling of déjà vu as I left the familiarity of the old Foxhunter's Path that climbs from Glen Feshie onto the lonely solitude of the Moine Mhor, the high tableland that billows south from the rocky edge of Loch Einich's deep hollow.

Sudden storms are certainly not unknown in the Cairngorms and it appears we can thank climate change for the recent frequency of such outbursts but, as I climbed up the path from Achlean, the sun shone on me from a blue sky. However, things aren't always what they seem in this part of the Cairngorms, and I could see, from the build-up of storm cloud in the south-west, that the good conditions wouldn't necessarily last.

About twenty-five years ago, on Hogmanay, I climbed up here to bid the old year farewell. Little did I realise how close I would come to my own farewell. A sudden, vicious storm caught me out as I crossed Am Moine Mhor, the great moss, towards the Munro of Mullach Clach a' Blair and it was with more luck than judgement that I managed to navigate my way out of it, on my hands and knees. The wind grew so strong I couldn't stand upright and the spindrift stung my eyes so badly I couldn't open them for more than two or three seconds. At one point I thought I might die from suffocation as wind-driven snow filled my mouth and nose and choked me.

The memory of that day haunts me whenever I return to the Moine Mhor, and today was no different. Great banks of black cloud hovered over Meall Dubhag and the deep slash of Coire Garbhlach, the long, winding corrie that bites its way deeply into this high plateau. The clouds, with accompanying wind-borne snow flurries, heightened my misgivings but there was no real malevolence in any of it. Indeed, as I approached Meall Dubhag, a mere rise in the plateau that was stripped of its Munro status away back in the seventies, my tensions were released as the cloud cover became increasingly ragged, and straying sunbeams lit the rocky depths of Coire Garbhlach with the intensity of floodlights.

This was my first walk of the New Year, a first-footing jaunt into my hills of home. No peak-bagging today, no Munros or Corbetts, just a visit to a magical chunk of Cairngorm landscape, an attempt to re-connect with whatever spirit dwells in this high and lonely place. Back in the forties, V. A. Firsoff wrote: 'To those with attentive ears who listen to the voices of silence they will yet confide wonders, less tangible but no less worthy, which live in human hearts and in the granite heart of the Cairngorm hills ...'

More recently, my good friend Jim Crumley and I climbed onto the Moine Mhor from Coire Garbhlach. After negotiating steep snow slopes we eased ourselves over the corrie edge to gasps of astonishment from Jim: 'You emerge from Coire Garblach to find yourself nowhere', he later wrote in his book, *A High and Lonely Place*. 'Oh, there are points of reference, but between any of these and your stance on the rim of the corrie there is just the rolling, dipping, flattening, climbing, sprawling dimensions of Am Moine Mhor, the Great Moss. You have not climbed to a summit at all, but to a space.'

It was this sensation of spaciousness that I enjoyed as I followed the snow-corniced rim of Coire Garbhlach above vertiginous cliffs of schist and gneiss towards the Cadha na Coin Duibh. I stayed as close to the edge as possible, as close as the snow cornices would allow, gasping at the depths that fell away from the broken, rocky frieze that forms the southern ramparts of this unusual corrie. There is nothing else in the Cairngorms quite like it, and very few hillwalkers take the trouble to come here.

Just below the Cadha na Coin Duibh, where the corrie edge flows to the summit of Meall nan Sleac, I left the rim behind, to descend the track that runs down the length of Coire Caol into the pinewood sanctuary of Glen Feshie. Chaffinches kept me company as I followed a series of paths and tracks alongside the roaring River Feshie, all the way back to Achlean.

LEUM UILLEIM, LOCHABER
MAY 2002

Between the spasmodic bursts of hot sunshine the dark showers were of monsoon quality. The rainfall that made May one of the wettest spring months on record has turned the hill areas of the highlands into a wet and soggy mattress and it feels like months since I've returned home with dry feet, despite the technological advances of waterproof boots.

You would expect the Bank Holiday weekend to provide something in the way of decent weather. In between the showers the weather gods smiled but the weather of the previous days turned what should have been a long, glorious hill-day into a fight against raging rivers and sodden ground. I should have got out when the going was reasonably good but those bouts of sunshine spurred me on until I eventually managed to get myself trapped by raging torrents of brown, peat-stained water.

The plan was simple: I wanted to climb the Corbett of Leum

Uilleim, 909m/2982ft, not by the usual approach from Corrour Station on the West Highland Line but by its back door, from the Blackwater Reservoir and its western neighbour Beinn a' Bhric.

The footpath from Kinlochleven, alongside the River Leven, was flowing with peat-stained water, and even the footpath alongside it was well and truly in spate! Several times I had to make detours to cross the normally placid tributaries that flow into the Leven but, about half a mile short of the Blackwater dam, I was brought up short by brown, raging waters that I simply couldn't cross without the risk of being washed away.

I backtracked a little before climbing steep, wooded slopes onto the hillside above where I managed to circumvent the worst of the flooded stream but, even up here, high above the river and the birch woods that line its course, I slipped and stumbled on ground that felt more like a soaking wet sponge.

After several inelegant slides on my backside I was soaked through, but managed to stumble along to the glen that separates the Glas Bheinn massif with Bein a'Bhric and Leum Uilleim. Realising that I still had to cross the Ciaran Water I stayed high above the glen until past the river's source at Loch Chiarain. Even then I had to wade across the Allt Feith Chiarain, which spewed forth from the north side of the loch.

By this time my feet felt as though they should have been webbed and it was a relief to climb comparatively dry slopes to the big curving ridge of Beinn a' Bhric. A high bealach separates the summit from Leum Uilleim, a short and straightforward climb to one of the best viewpoints in the area.

While Beinn na Lap, Ben Alder, the Glen Coe hills and the nearby Mamores and Grey Corries all looked impressive the scene was dominated by the amount of water that lay on the barren flats of the Rannoch Moor. As though it couldn't soak up any more the Moor lay beneath a patchwork of silver flood, glinting in the sunlight like an inland lake covered in islands. I don't think I've ever seen so much water so far from the sea.

Leum Uilleim is normally climbed from Corrour Station via

the long and easy angled north-east ridge of Beinn a'Bhric, and that's the route I'd recommend in future when weather conditions have been wet. To avoid the floods I took a different route back to Kinlochleven, staying as high as possible above the rivers. I had to wade the Allt Feith Chiarain again but from the bothy at the south end of Loch Chiarain I took the hill path over Meall na Cruaidhe and down to the end of Loch Eilde Mor where I followed a pipeline back down to Kinlochleven. By the time I reached the car my feet looked like pulp.

BYNACK MORE, CAIRNGORMS
SEPTEMBER 2002

Bynack More is my 'bad weather' hill. Lying to the east of the main Cairngorms massif this 1090m/3576ft Munro tends to benefit from the bigger hills' rain shadow and on days when the western Cairngorms are being drenched it's surprising how often Bynack More remains dry.

On windy days it pays to be a little more circumspect. Theoretically, you'd assume that the heavily muscled bulk of Cairn Gorm would protect its smaller neighbour but theory, however sound it may be, doesn't always work in the mountains, as we were to discover.

With the Feshie hills and Braeriach swathed in a dark, ominous layer of cloud, my brother-in-law Raymond Bainbridge and I drove up the length of Glen More and parked near Glenmore Lodge. We began walking through the lovely Pass of Ryvoan in dry and bright conditions and it wasn't until we reached the River Nethy that we noticed the wind.

The track we were on followed the course of one of the Cairngorm 'mounths' or passes, the Lairig an Laoigh, which runs from Abernethy in the north to Braemar in the south. Both this pass, and its parallel neighbour, the Lairig Ghru, were once droving routes resounding to the movement of cattle. Indeed, the Lairig an Laoigh can be translated as the pass of the stirks or calves. It must have been a long haul for the cattle as they climbed up from the comparatively fertile basin of the River Nethy to the scree-girt high ground, which forms the skirt of Bynack More itself.

This grand little hill stands apart from its loftier, more popular neighbours, as though keen to emphasise its individuality and gritty character, despite its inferior height and mass. Bynack More's finest features tend to be more subtle, less glaringly elephantine, than its immediate neighbours, and it exhibits its finest face to the north above the Forest of Abernethy. From here it appears as a fine conical peak, steep slopes rising smoothly to a narrow crest, a direct contrast to the tor-studded whaleback of distant Ben Avon and the leviathan mass of Cairn Gorm.

Bynack More is divided by a large, high-level, grassy depression into two distinct rocky summits. On its western shoulder lies a subsidiary top known as Bynack Beg, the little bynack. The main summit was at one time known as Ben Bynack but the late Rev. W. Forsyth of Abernethy suggests this was a wrong use of the Gaelic. According to this local historian, Bynack derives from Ben-Eag, the hill of the cleft, a nick between the summit rocks, which you can see from Strath Nethy. Other Gaelic scholars suggest the word comes from 'beinneag', little mountain (compared to its neighbours even Bynack More, the big Bynack, is a little mountain) or even from Am Beidhneag, a chimney pot or roof-ridge.

It didn't take us long to realise we were in for a battle. Despite a couple of light showers the cloud level remained above the summits, but it was the wind that was to prove challenging. As we approached the main ridge a couple of violent gusts almost stopped us and by the time we climbed the rocky ridge it was apparent that we would have to take care simply to remain rooted to the ground.

The wind was coming from the south-west so, just as Cairn Gorm protects Bynack More from the worst of the western gales we reckoned we could use the summit ridge of Bynack More to protect us. It worked! We traversed across the slopes above Coire Odhar in relative calm and it was only when we dared pop our heads over the ridge that we felt the full demonic fury of the wind.

The summit cairn was of course fully exposed to the gales so we didn't linger. We tried to take some photographs but it was too blustery so we retreated back into the shelter of our eastern slopes and stopped for lunch. Although we felt rather pleased with ourselves there was a slight disappointment that we had to return by our outward route rather than continuing over A' Choinneach to The Saddle from where we could have climbed Cairn Gorm. The Saddle, above the foot of Loch Avon, confronts one of the wildest views in Scotland, with steep granite slab slopes dropping down to cradle the grey waters of Loch Avon. At the head of the loch rises the improbably square-cut face of The Sticil, like a massive tombstone set amongst the high plateaux that surround it.

A traversing path climbs the steep slopes from The Saddle at the head of Strath Nethy to Ciste Mearaid and from there it's an easy descent either by Cairn Gorm's north ridge to Ryvoan, or by way of the Sron an Aonaich ridge and the Allt Mor footpath back to Glenmore.

BIDEAN NAM BIAN, GLEN COE
APRIL 2005

We're experiencing one of the wettest Aprils on record and the weather showed little sign of changing as we drove down the length of Glen Coe looking for the best option on a day when far-flung views certainly wouldn't be on the agenda.

We settled for an ascent of Stob Coire nan Lochan, with the option of tacking on the Munro of Bidean nam Bian, the highest mountain in the old county of Argyll. All going well we hoped to wander along the Bidean ridge to the hill's other Munro top, Stob Coire Sgreamhach, finishing off with a descent down the length of the marvellously atmospheric Coire Gabhail, known in the tourist guides as the Lost Valley.

The peaks of Glen Coe were new to my son Gregor and

daughter-in-law Sarah, and I was sorry the weather wasn't kinder. Bidean nam Bian is the name of an entire massif, and a complex one at that, with several pointed tops and deep-cut corries. There are a variety of routes to the 1150m/3773ft summit and in winter conditions most of these routes can be considerably challenging. Great rock crags, the Diamond and Church Door Buttresses, add drama and a sense of history to the scene. The first climbs there were put up by some of the great pioneers of rock climbing in Scotland: Norman Collie, Harold Raeburn and JH Bell at the end of the nineteenth century, but we were to see little of the buttresses. As we climbed into the corrie we were enveloped in the cool and damp embrace of wet cloud and, although it wasn't actually raining, were soon sweating inside our waterproofs.

With visibility reduced by the clouds, we could just discern the north-east ridge of Stob Coire nan Lochan rising to our left. As we climbed higher the ridge became narrower and rockier and soon some mild scrambling made us use our hands as well as our feet. There was much more snow about than I had anticipated too, and since we hadn't brought any ice axes with us I became pretty convinced the summit of Stob Coire nan Lochan would be as far as we could go.

However, the ridge that connects with Bidean looked fairly clear of snow so we set off optimistically, enjoying the romp despite the damp conditions. There were patches of wet slushy snow around, but as we climbed the steep ridge onto Bidean the snow cover increased dramatically. It was decision time. The ridge was steep and narrow and a simple slip, without an ice axe to arrest the fall, would have meant a long slide into the blackness of the corrie depths where vertiginous crags lurked. The summit of Bidean nam Bian would be there another day, so we backtracked to Stob Coire nan Lochan and followed the hill's north ridge to Aonach Dubh before sliding down wet snow patches into Coire an Lochan.

By this time we were wet through but the drifting mists on the black crags and the raging waterfalls held our attention and made it a pleasant descent. We stopped for a final brew above a little howff, a natural shelter that I used as a youngster when I came here to climb, and I suspect I bored Sarah and Gregor with my reminiscences. It was on that west face of Aonach Dubh that I learned to rock climb. Over three decades ago, skinny, nervous and unsure, I was shown the ropes by a bunch of more experienced youths from the Lomond Mountaineering Club. There was little difference in age between us, but light years' difference in experience and attitude. I learned much from them but, more importantly, in climb after climb, I learned to love this place, its crag and its burn, and its little howff. It's always good to return.

MEALL FUAR-MHONAIDH, INVERNESS-SHIRE
MARCH 2006

Early on Sunday morning Drumnadrochit looked like a ghost town. A bank of mist lay across the village and dirty piles of old snow lay alongside the main road. To be fair, paradise itself would look grim under such conditions and I asked myself, more than once, what I was doing here. Surely I would have been better staying in bed on such a morning?

The narrow road that runs to Bunloit climbs steeply above Drumnadrochit, each narrow turn slippery with fresh snow. If there was any more in the course of the day, chances were I wouldn't get back out again. Sometimes you have to make such decisions before you set foot on your hill and constant drips from the trees suggested it was already turning milder. Further snow wasn't forecast. It was worth the risk.

I was heading for Meall Fuar-mhonaidh, a 699m/2293ft hill that I hadn't climbed before. A few years ago I passed it when walking the Great Glen Way, down the length of Loch Ness, and liked the way it appeared to dominate the landscape on the north side of the loch. Despite its commanding position it's not a big hill and I knew there was a path all the way from the car park at the end of the Bunloit road to the summit. The route begins gently and follows a succession of paths through birch woods.

It was gurgling wet underfoot, where there wasn't any old snow, and I was thankful to reach the ridge where hard snow covered everything, including the wet and eroded footpath.

Meall Fuar-mhonaidh, the rounded cold hill, is the high point on a long and narrow ridge that parallels the narrow slash of Loch Ness. It runs on a north-east to south-west line, so views from the hill are apparently very good, from the Moray Firth to Ben Nevis down the length of Glen Albyn, or the Great Glen. Not that I saw very much today. Thick mist still shrouded the hill although every so often the light would change, turning from murky grey to milky blue, as though I was about to burst clear of the cloud into sunshine and blue skies. I found myself becoming quite excited at the prospect, more than half expecting to find the summit clear with only the tops of the highland hills surfacing above the cloud temperature inversion. It wasn't to be. I moved uphill slowly, creeping up the steeper snow-covered slopes, cutting slivers of steps with my ice axes, comfortable in my silent, grey world.

A cairn soon loomed into sight, sooner than I expected. This couldn't be the summit surely? I checked my new OS map application on my iPhone – the GPS signal suggested I was still a good distance from the true summit so I took a bearing, passed another false cairn, traversed a small dip and eventually stomped up to the real summit.

Mist still hung heavily all around, a windless mist, cold and clammy. I thought how appropriate the name of the hill was and recalled some lines from a poem I'd discovered a few days earlier.[2]

> It's February! Wyvis sulks in cloud.
> Meall Fuar Mhonaidh, clear-headed in the gale
> unfolds South, West and East; ecstatic peaks

2. The poem was written by Anne MacLeod and was commissioned by Mary Scanlon, a former MSP for Highlands and Islands, in 2005, as part of a Holyrood Link project, through which poets and MSPs were partnered and explored areas of mutual interest.

surging through cold years towards the waves
where all our history began: a lyric feast
Glorious, small. Unfettered.

I was glad I hadn't stayed in bed ...

BEN VRACKIE AND KILLICRANKIE, PERTHSHIRE
JULY 2007

Pitlochry, normally bustling with people, was uncharacteristic-
ally empty. Only a handful of brave souls braved the lashing
rain, their golf umbrellas adding a touch of colour to a dismal,
monochrome scene.

The forecast had almost persuaded me to stay at home but I
can think of fewer things worse than a Saturday spent indoors
so went to the north Perthshire town to walk some of its forty-
one miles of low level tracks and paths, one of the finest path
networks in the country. The various routes cover an area of
some eighteen square miles with most of the walking routes
radiating from the Garry and Tummel rivers. With all the rain
that had fallen during the week my guess was that the linns and
waterfalls would be spectacular.

It was only as I drove into Pitlochry that I caught a momentary
glimpse of Ben Vrackie, 836m/2759ft, through the low clouds.
It was enough of a temptation to consider the combination of a
low-level riverside walk with an ascent of Pitlochry's own little
Corbett. I knew Perthshire Council had been improving the
Ben Vrackie footpath, the kind of path that makes navigation
virtually superfluous, and the route north from the mountain
drops kindly down to the deeply wooded cleft of the Pass of
Killicrankie. From there a footpath runs alongside the Tummel
and the Garry back to Pitlochry. I guessed it would be about
twelve miles.

The starting point for the ascent of Ben Vrackie is a new
car park just beyond the village of Moulin, but I left my car in
Pitlochry on the basis that the mile or so uphill would be easier

at the beginning rather than the end of the walk. Moulin itself boasts a fine old inn which serves marvellous bar meals but it was too early in the day for that. I followed the signs through the dripping Creag Chuinnlean woods and onto the open moor above.

Even at this low elevation it was misty, but I recalled the words of mountaineer John Mackenzie, Earl of Cromartie, who, in one of my Wilderness Walks programmes, urged me not to become frustrated when mist obliterated the far-flung views. Instead, he said, just concentrate on the micro views, the plants, the lichens, the rock formations and the movement of the cloud on the breeze. It was good advice, a paradigm shift that brings you closer to the landscape you're walking through. Probably for the first time on Ben Vrackie I really recognised its mish-mashed geological structure, the schists, the quartzites, the epidiorites that have given its name as the 'speckled' or 'dappled' hill.

Beyond the bealach between Creag Bhreac and Meall na h-Aodainn Moire, the new path crosses the dammed eastern end of Loch a' Choire and climbs the slopes east of Ben Vrackie's south-west crags. It's a steep climb but worth it for the views from the summit, which, on a clear day, include the triple-peaked Beinn a Ghlo, the great rounded massif of the Drumochter hills, the unmistakable cone of Schiehallion and down the superb, wooded trench of the Tummel.

The easiest way to descend to Killicrankie is to return to the bealach between Creag Bhreac and Meall na h-Aodainn Moire and follow the path that runs north from there but I wanted to enjoy this rock-dappled landscape as long as I could. In thick mist I navigated round to the outlying Meall an Daimh, enjoying the suitably mournful call of golden plover, before dropping down mixed heather and rock slopes to Killicrankie where I followed the trail alongside the spectacularly flooded River Garry. The Soldier's Leap here is only about eighteen feet wide but the short and rocky run-up would have made it a difficult leap even for Bob Beamon. Stray beams of sunlight lit the scene as I wandered through the historic Pass of Killicrankie, site of the 1689 battle between Government forces and Claverhouse's Jacobite rebels, back to Pitlochry where the tourists had once again been tempted out by the odd burst of sunshine.

MEALL AN FHUDAIR, STIRLINGSHIRE
MARCH 2008

With a clutch of good Munros easily accessible nearby, not many hillwalkers make the effort of visiting lonely Meall an Fhudair. This 'gunpowder hill' may lack the curves and peaks of some of the nearby big shots, like Beinn More and Stobinian, or Cruach Ardrain or even Ben Lomond, but there's a quiet wildness about Meall an Fhudair, a sense of space and remoteness that comes from its position, centred in the great wedge of rocky knolls and outcrops between Glen Falloch and Glen Fyne.

I went there on a day of rain and snow showers, when the mists rose and fell like a stage curtain and the ground was so waterlogged that the biggest danger to life and limb was from drowning. I must confess to a sense of quiet and rather smug satisfaction when my map and compass work took me directly to the windbreak cairn in the midst of a thick snow flurry.

My day had started late, and I had to change my plans for a big Munro round. By the time I reached Glen Falloch it was past midday and, at this time of the year, that doesn't leave much in the way of daylight for climbing a small mountain, never mind a clutch of Munros. So, I hastily changed tack, knowing that a good hydro track zigzagged up from the road before contouring round the south-east slopes of Meall an Fhudair. I knew from a previous visit that I could access the summit from a knobbly ridge that runs west from a neighbouring peak called Troisgeach but, because of the shortage of time, thought I'd take a more direct line.

Because the ground was so wet, with patches of soft, slobbery snow filling the contours between the rocky outcrops, I wanted to stay on the hydro-road for as long as I could. After climbing from the roadside near Glenfalloch Farm, the road met a higher road that eventually made its way into the mouth of Glen Arnan, and the high pass that links Glen Falloch with Glen Fyne, before petering out. Rather than climb to the north to reach the summit of Troisgeach I took a bearing on the summit of Meall an Fhudair and set off on a long meandering line that was to carry me over outcrops, around semi-frozen lochans, over knolls and across bubbling streams. All the time I faithfully stuck to the task, eying the magnetic needle of the compass to the bearing, looking ahead for features on my line of vision to walk to.

This is where GPS units come into their own. I'm afraid I'm not one for using a GPS to plot my course for the day, or trace where I've been when I get home, but as far as I'm concerned a GPS has one, and only one, useful feature: its ability to give a grid reference.[3] If I know exactly where I am at any given moment, thanks to the satellite signals that communicate with the GPS unit, I can find my way easily using traditional map and compass navigation. Indeed, with a map and compass, and the knowledge of using them, and a GPS to get regular grid reference information, there's no reason for anyone getting lost on the hills again. Just make sure the batteries in the GPS unit don't run out.

As I climbed, the weather played peek-a-boo, clearing occasionally to offer breathtaking views south across Beinn Damhain towards Ben Vorlich, Ben Vane and Ben Ime, or west towards the long bulk of Beinn Bhuidhe. It wasn't until I reached the summit and cowered down behind the windbreak for a coffee, that I realised what a huge, wild area this is. Once the snow flurries cleared I was blessed with a couple of minutes of clarity, and to the north recognised the big Munros of Ben Lui, Ben Oss and Beinn Dubhcraig, rising steeply from the lochan-splattered moorland. When I stood up and peeked over the wall of the windbreak, way below me in the south-west lay the silvery waters of Loch Fyne at Cairndow.

---

3. I never did become an enthusiast for GPS units but for the past dozen years or so I've relied almost exclusively on the OS maps downloaded to my mobile phone. I still carry the relevant map though, just in case those damned batteries run out.

I more or less retraced my steps into the Lairig Arnan with a pink glow permeating through the cloud from the south-west, but as soon as I hit the hydro road the heavens opened and when I eventually reached my old campervan on the A82 I was soaked through. The light had gone, I was wet and cold, but the sense of satisfaction that came from a successful exercise in navigation lingered with me all night long.

CHAPTER FIVE

Slow Adventure

I've always been intrigued by the use of the word 'adventure'. It tends to be associated with exciting, fast-paced, high-adrenaline sports, activities that often have the word 'extreme' prefixing them, suggesting a high element of danger: extreme rock-climbing, extreme fell-running, base jumping, slacklining, pursuits that call for a high level of skill, ability and commitment.

The word has also been used to package and commercialise less-extreme activities. 'Adventure trekking' is a good example, a package aimed at the cash-rich but time-poor, those who are happy to pay someone else to organise a journey where the element of risk, or adventure, is diminished to such an extent that it is virtually non-existent. Likewise, the term 'micro-adventure' has been popularised in recent times and covers activities like bike rides, overnight camping trips or walks down the local canal. Micro it may be but adventure it is not. It seems there may be an element of truth in the suggestion: 'one man's adventure is another man's walk in the park'.

Bearing that in mind, a new term is gaining traction and I have a growing sympathy with it. 'Slow adventure' is about easing down, immersing yourself in a place, in its traditions and community. It's about surrendering to the forces of nature as you reflect, reconnect and come closer to the natural world. It is, in many ways, a state of mindfulness brought on by time and passage, moving through a landscape at a pace and in a way that allows you to 'connect' with that landscape and everything in it.

Needless to say, just as the fast-paced, high-adrenaline adventure market has been packaged for a certain sector of the outdoor market, so the concept of slow adventure has also proven to be highly marketable. Just as the Norwegian word 'Hygge' and the rather cringeworthy Scottish term 'Coorie' have been used to describe some kind of cosy contentment so 'slow adventure' has been adopted by a number of outdoor activity providers to suggest a relaxed 'return to the womb' kind of experience.

The term was coined by Pete Varley, an academic at the West of Scotland Campus of the University of the Highlands and Islands. Pete, a keen mountain biker and kayaker, wrote a fascinating paper on the subject, a paper that was very much aimed at marketing the concept through tourism outlets. It was originally intended as something of an antidote to the 'thrill and rush' tourism that we see today in popular spots like the Fairy Pools on Skye or on the NC500, where people arrive at a chosen destination, take a quick selfie, and hasten off to the next 'bucket list' destination without delay.

I'm slightly uncomfortable with the commercial emphasis of slow adventure in Pete's paper, but I do understand that his academic work is aimed predominantly at the Scottish tourism market. However, there is absolutely no reason why the concept of slow adventure can't be adopted by individuals. Some of us have been practicing its core values for years.

Pre-trip research can inform you about the history and culture of the area you're visiting. You may plan to pick berries or edible fungi to add to your diet and you will inevitably spend time looking at wildlife and the scenery, and in the course of your journey or passage you have every opportunity of 'connecting' with the landscape.

I first recognised this concept of 'connection' from the writing of Colin Fletcher, a Welsh-American who wrote a number of books on the subject of lightweight backpacking.[1] For me, Colin

---

1. I can heartily recommend the late Colin Fletcher's book, *The Complete Walker*, to anyone interested in the philosophy of multi-day backpacking. It was first published in New York by Knopf in 1968 and there have been three new editions since. The book has sold several million copies worldwide. Colin Fletcher, in my opinion the finest outdoor writer in the world, passed away on 12th June 2007.

Fletcher vocalised the joys and insights that many of us experience so that, as we read his words, we could empathise. We were familiar with the unadulterated joy of peeling off socks at the end of a long, hot day, or luxuriating in a warm sleeping bag or enjoying the pleasure of that first mug of tea, but Fletcher articulated these basic delights in such a profound way that they became almost spiritual, almost religious. But Colin Fletcher, in the accepted sense, was not a religious man.

'I suppose you could say that going out into this older world is rather like going to church. I know that it is in my case, anyway,' he wrote. 'For me, praying is no good: my god, if I have one, is a kind of space-age Pan, and It is not interested in what happens to me personally. But by walking out alone into wilderness I can elude the pressures of the pounding modern world, and in the sanctity of silence and solitude – the solitude seems to be a vital part of it – I can, after a while, begin to see and to hear and to think and in the end to feel with a new and exciting accuracy. And that, it seems to me, is just the kind of vision you should be hoping to find when you go to church.'

I can say amen to that, but the real value of slow adventure, whether we are walking, riding a bike or paddling a kayak is, as Colin Fletcher suggests, to make us think. How can we connect with the landscape or the community we are passing through in a more satisfactory way, and how can we hang on to this connection once we are back in our nine-to-five routine in the towns and cities? How can we best benefit the local environment and communities we pass through, and can we absorb the benefits we experience in these places as part of our own psyche? Interestingly Pete Varley emphasises the Scandinavian concept of 'friluftsliv', the philosophy and practice of living and being outdoors, gently co-existing with nature, a way of life that has fascinated me for many, many years.

As I get older, I've become increasingly attracted to this notion of slow adventure. I wrote in my last book, *Come By The Hills*, that I no longer find the summit cairn the priority on hillwalking trips and I like the idea of slowing down the journey to allow a deeper game to be played. I'm attracted to the idea of travelling through a landscape and experiencing all its time frames and seasons, immersing myself in its culture and history but, if I'm being truly honest, I suspect it's growing older that has slowed me down. That's okay, sometimes we need a kick-in-the-pants to slow us down and the ageing body is as effective a means as any.

I've searched through some of my old diaries and newspaper columns to find examples of those days that fall into this category of slow adventure. Those days when the sun shines and you can't find any good reason to hurry. Those days when you are happy to simply follow your nose, with no fixed destination, aimlessly wandering at will. Then there are the days when you walk with a companion and are so busy blethering it doesn't really matter where you go – occasionally it's the company that's important, not the place.

I think exploration falls into this category of slow adventure too, avoiding the guidebook routes, studying maps to work out alternative routes that may be longer, but which allow you to spend more time in the one area, enjoying and appreciating its sense of place. Hills and mountains are so varied when tackled from alternative routes that the whole character of the mountain changes. The views are different, and the feel of the hill can differ so much that what might have been regarded as comparatively dull is given new life. Tackling a hill under the pale light of the moon can change its whole character and ambience.

I recall walking with Hamish Brown many years ago, a man who was a huge influence in my outdoor career. I asked him what the motivation was to become the first person to climb all of Scotland's three-thousand-foot mountains, the Munros, in one continuous journey? His answer was simple. His everyday life was moving so fast he wanted to get off it for a while. That was over forty years ago, and life is infinitely faster today.

Getting off that treadmill for a time, even a day, has immense value for all of us, and that's why I hope this new concept of slow adventure is one we can all embrace from time to time, to experience its unarguable benefits.

MULLWHARCHAR, DUMFRIES AND GALLOWAY
OCTOBER 1988

I left my car in the parking area near the head of Glen Trool, a lovely spot in the heart of Galloway. The nearby Bruce's Stone monument celebrates a clash with English forces in 1307 when Robert the Bruce was beginning his campaign for the Scottish throne. This was an area he knew well and the broken hillsides and scattered woodlands were ideal for his style of guerilla warfare.

I was heading for Mullwharchar, the 692m/2283ft summit where geologists wanted to drill the hard granite rock a few years ago to test its suitability for the disposal of radioactive waste from Windscale, just across the Solway Firth.[2] So far nothing has come of it, although the Galloway hills have been threatened, like so many other hill areas, with large scale wind farm development.

I'm particularly fond of this corner of Scotland and always feel there's something otherworldly about Galloway's hills. The tops stand aloof, like islands, from the serried waves of forestry plantations, and the place names evoke hobgoblin plots of doom and disaster: Dungeon Hill, the Range of the Awful Hand, the Murder Hole, The Wolf Slock... There's a Tolkienesque mindset at work here: Mullwharchar, Craigmawhannal and Craigmasheenie, Rig of the Jarkness, Curleywee, Lump of the Eglin, Shalloch on Minnoch and Cairnsmore of Carsphairn. I know of no other place in Scotland that can boast such an incredible string of extraordinary place names.

---

2. The proposal to dump nuclear waste on Mullwharchar was rejected by Kyle and Carrick District Council on 24th October 1978 after considerable local protest.

I had climbed Mullwharchar before, via a long round of Galloway hills that took in the Rhinns of Kells, Meikle Millyea, Corserine, Mullwharchar itself and the Merrick. This time the intended route was considerably more straightforward, by way of Loch Valley, the Murder Hole, Loch Arron and the curious landscape that surrounds Loch Enoch in the very heart of Galloway. I wanted to take my time. I wanted to linger in these astonishing surroundings.

The waters of Loch Enoch lie in a high granite basin which caresses the 1600-foot contour and the ragged shorelines are surrounded on three sides by high hills: Dungeon Hill, Mullwharchar and the Merrick. To its south the land falls away in a series of craggy terraces and each terrace holds another loch: Loch Arron, Loch Neldricken and Loch Valley. Beyond them lie Long Loch of Glenhead and the Round Loch of Glenhead, a real rosary of lakes. It's said that the silver sand of Loch Enoch's beaches was once collected for sharpening knives.

This is a strange landscape. Bluffs and granite pavements are scattered abroad on the tussocky moorland. Boulders lie everywhere, glacial erratics scattered around at random after being swept along by the ice floes of eons ago. I couldn't see more than twenty or thirty metres in front of me, but the high-pitched calls of young feral goats sounded like the cries of children, the lost children of the mist. It was an eerie sound, but it wasn't long before I came across the depression that held the grey waters of Loch Enoch itself.

From the ragged east shores of the loch a path climbs rough slopes all the way to the summit cairn. Beyond it to the north-east the ground falls away precipitously – the cliffs of the Tauchers! I was lucky this time with the views. Close by rose the hills of the Range of the Awful Hand with their highest point, the Merrick, still cloud-capped, while the Rhinns of Kells and their highest point, Corserine, were flooded in sunshine.

Cloud continued to shroud the Merrick so I avoided it on my descent, skirting Loch Enoch by its western shores and crossing some very boggy ground to a forestry plantation where a forest

ride took me to the ford across the wonderfully named Gloon
Burn. A forest track then descended past Culsharg Bothy and
the Buchan Burn back to Loch Trool and the car park.

CARN LIATH AND CULARDOCH, CAIRNGORMS
MARCH 1992

The thrawn Grampian uplands were dusted with fresh snow,
shrugging aside the advances of spring like a spurned lover. The
cloud was low on the hill and the birds were silent. There were
few signs of activity at the Keiloch sawmill as I strode past, only
the keeper's Labradors broke the silence, barking their welcome
from their caged kennels.

The overnight temperature had dropped to well below zero,
but the weather forecast had promised great things, but perhaps
not for these eastern Grampians! Winter lingers longer here
than anywhere else in Scotland and someone once described
the Corbetts of Carn Liath and Culardoch to me as the 'arctic
side of the Cairngorms'. It wasn't until I climbed out of the
pinewoods above Invercauld that spring finally started to assert
itself. Shimmering mists began to evaporate from the moors and
through the shifting haze I could just discern the snow-crusted
cliffs of Beinn a' Bhuird's eastern corries. A buzzard mewed
above me, and a curlew attempted its spring song, choking a
little on its familiar bubbly climax. Perhaps there was a promise
to the day after all.

There's a redemptive quality to these high, open moors. The
vastness of space, the open sky, the venerable pine trees that
impart an air of timelessness to the entire scene, the poignant
beauty of Glen Feardar, once well populated... It all makes
our brief flicker of life rather insignificant, and we soak up such
atmospheres as though it was the very elixir of life.

I reached the summit of Carn Liath, 861m/2841ft, via its
broad south ridge. An old drystone wall led me almost all
the way to the top, a little rocky outcrop topped with a few
stones. Curiously, two outliers were crowned by larger cairns

so I climbed them as well, before trotting down to the Bealach Dearg, the high point of the ancient right of way I had followed earlier. A locked hut sits close to the crest of the pass, a through-route that has been used by armies, drovers and hill gangrels since time immemorial.

Culardoch, 900m/2970ft, is a mere stone's throw from the summit of the pass and makes a dramatic viewpoint, positioned as it is between two of our finest mountains. The north is dominated by the great mass of Beinn Avon, its white summit crowned by its 'Cairngorm Pimples', the granite tors that are so peculiar to these high Grampian hills, while the prospect to the south belongs to 'dark Lochnagar', belying the words of its own song as its mantle of snow sparkled in the strengthening sun.

I was hot by the time I jogged down the south ridge of Culardoch and picked up a grouse-shooters' path that returned me to the right of way and my outward route back to Invercauld. But it was early yet, winter had at last yielded to the promise of spring, and a grouse-butt made a good backrest. With the day's work behind me I had time to fester in the sun for a while and dream of warmer days.

CARN BHAC, CAIRNGORMS
APRIL 1993

John Farquharson of Inverey, popularly remembered as the Black Colonel, must have been a great character. It's said that he summoned his servants by firing his pistol at a shield that hung on the wall, giving out a bell-like tone.

On one occasion, after the Battle of Killicrankie, he just escaped being burnt to death in his castle when government dragoons set fire to it. He escaped, completely naked, and fled up Glen Ey, leaping across the river to escape his enemies. He later hid on a ledge in a deep chasm of the river for several days, just a few feet above the boiling, foaming waters. The ledge is remembered as the Colonel's Bed and is signposted from the Glen Ey track.

Today, it's almost inconceivable that this peaceful glen was the scene of such violence. A long and sinuous valley that runs south from Inverey near Braemar, its river is fed by the peaty drainage of a ring of Munros, including An Socach, Beinn Iutharn Mhor and Carn Bhac. The bubbling call of the curlew, or the shrieks of peewits are probably the loudest sounds you'll hear.

On past expeditions to this area I've always cycled the five miles of glen to the ruins of Altanour Lodge, its crumbling walls shielded from the winter blasts by its stand of larch and spruce, but over the years I've realised that a bike doesn't allow you to connect with the land. You can only do that on foot, and the five-mile walk to Altanour breaks you in gently, in pleasant preparation for the climbs ahead.

I settled in the heather with a flask of coffee just beyond the ruins and checked the possibilities for the day. The hills that circle the head of Glen Ey offer all kind of opportunities for high-level wandering along wind-clipped ridges, but such pleasant roller-coasting loses much of its charm when you can't see anything because of low cloud. Neither was I dependent of having to return to Altanour to pick up a bike, so a good circular route to and from Inverey was on the cards.

I settled for an ascent of Carn Bhac, 946m/3104ft, a triple-topped hill whose highest point is unnamed on the OS 1:50,000 map. Heather slopes beside the Alltan Odhar offered an easy approach towards the head of Coire Odhar from where it was a straightforward climb onto Carn Bhac's stony summit.

A big, cheery group from the Forfar and District Hillwalking Club were enjoying their lunch as I arrived. It looked as though the whole town had come to Carn Bhac for the day, but five minutes later I was in solitude again, studying compass bearings that would take me around the head of the steep-sided Coire Bhearnaist onto a long ridge that looked rather interesting on the map.

What a marvellous ridge this was! Narrow and steep-sided in the heart of a wild and tumbled quarter that lies between Glen Ey and upper Glen Tilt, it runs out in a north-east direction towards Carn Damhaireach (the map refers to it as the Top of the Battery). Up here, still below the cloud level, I sat and watched a huge herd of deer move across the opposite hillside like a cloud shadow. Wheatears flirted with me, leading me along the narrow ridgeline, and the calls of whaups rose from the glens below.

All too soon it was time to descend steep, heather-covered slopes into Glen Connie where a bulldozed track took me back alongside the Allt Connie and its crashing waterfalls to Inverey, once the scene of battling dragoons but today a quiet and peaceful upper Deeside hamlet.

FUAR THOLL, WESTER ROSS
MARCH 1994

I smelt summer as soon as I stepped out of the car. The scent was that of warm earth and new grass, the faintly sweet coconut perfume of early bracken growth. It was Easter weekend, the clocks were going forward and it was officially summertime!

I was celebrating the change of season at Achnashellach, that rhododendron-clad corner of the highlands with its unmanned railway station, Victorian hotel and the legendary Gerry's Hostel, but I had come to Achnashellach for Fuar Tholl.

Presiding over the Achnashellach Forest like some prehistoric watchtower, the 907m/2976ft Fuar Tholl, or cold hole, is one of the most impressive hills in the land. Its three tops are guarded by steep cliffs of Torridonian sandstone, soaring skyward from the lower pine-clad levels of Coire Lair. Corrie-bitten and savage in its splendour I have climbed Fuar Tholl twice before but never had a view from its summit. Perhaps the advent of official summer might bring me a change of fortune.

The track that climbs out of Achnashellach and into Coire Lair is a delight. I crossed the railway, pleased that Network Rail hadn't seen fit to ban pedestrians as they've tried to do in dozens of other crossings throughout the nation, followed the forestry track through the woods before dropping down to the old stalkers' path that follows the deep gorge of the River Lair. What a fabulous start to a walk, with pine trees sheltering the path that climbs over sandstone slabs, crinkled and creaked with streaks of quartzite that glint and sparkle in the sun.

As you surmount the lip of Coire Lair it's worth pausing to take in the scale of things. Two Munros are the normal attention-grabbers here, Sgorr Ruadh and the long, curving ridge of Beinn Liath Mhor. The classic Coire Lair Horseshoe walk gathers both in, the two Munros linked by a high pass, and stronger walkers often add Fuar Tholl as a kind of afterthought. Indeed, I had previously treated the mountain in such a disrespectful way myself, but promised to make up for it today. I would spend the entire day on it.

Despite the legitimacy of official summertime, and my earlier intimations of seasonal weather, a cold east wind blew across the face of the corrie and chilled me to the bone. It was, I had to remind myself, still only March, and the easterly breeze wouldn't let me forget it. I wrapped up, crossed the river and followed the stalkers' path west towards the Bhealaich Mhoir, the high, slabby, lochan-infested saddle that connects Fuar Tholl with its northern neighbour, Sgorr Ruadh.

As you climb towards this saddle the vertiginous defences of crag-girt Fuar Tholl betray a weakness – between the eastern buttress and the massive cliffs of the Mainreachan Buttress a deep corrie offers a line of approach. Its slopes are certainly steep but after a climb over grass and steep scree you emerge onto a ridge that's only a short distance west of the mountain's summit. For such an impressively craggy mountain it's a fairly simple ascent.

As I sweated my way up the scree the clouds descended, and swirling mists gave me only sporadic views of the terraced sandstone cliffs towering above me. For the third time cloud had robbed me of the views from the summit but I didn't mind too much; indeed the mists added to the dark atmosphere of the place as I crossed over the summit ridge to Creag Mainrichean, the top of the Mainreachan Buttress, whose sheer crags could be seen in dramatic profile as I descended the steep and rocky ground towards the Bhealaich Mhoir.

By the time I reached the saddle, cloud shrouded everything and I opted for the path that runs down Coire Lair back to the start. After a cold and misty day, summertime was waiting for me in Achnashellach.

BEN TEE, GLEN GARRY
MARCH 1999

Ben Tee, the fairy hill, is seen to best advantage from Glen Garry where its conical shape makes a picturesque backdrop to the woods and the loch. At 901m/2973ft it falls just short of Munro height so it's relatively unfrequented. Despite its position, in the cleft formed by Glen Garry and the Great Glen, it makes it a superb viewpoint with the hills of Knoydart and Glen Shiel laid out before you and the whole trench of the Great Glen, leading to Fort Augustus and Loch Ness, stretching away to the east.

I described Ben Tee in this column about eight years ago and on that occasion climbed the hill from the south, via the glorious Kilfinnan Falls. This time I wanted to tackle it from the north, from Glen Garry, a longer route of about a dozen miles following a network of forestry tracks that emanate from the little farming community at Greenfield. Following a couple of weeks in which more snow had fallen on Scotland than in the previous ten years put together I loaded the car with boots, ice axe and crampons, snowshoes and touring skis, equipped for any eventuality.

I had a dreamy notion of Nordic skiing along the forest tracks until I reached the footpath that runs up to the high pass of the Bealach Easain between Ben Hee and the sharp nose of Meall a'Choire Ghlais. At that point I would exchange the skis for snowshoes and plod up the deep snow to the summit, but I hadn't realised how much damage an overnight thaw can do.

An old Scots folk song suggests: 'The snaws they melt the soonest when the wind begins to sing...' Especially if those winds come from the south-west. Instead of snow-covered forestry tracks the route from the bridge over the narrows of Loch Garry was covered in a kind of glazed slush and the mountain itself had been largely stripped of snow. With only a few white streaks standing out against the dark of the heather, I decided to lighten my load to just trekking poles with an ice axe strapped to my pack. I doubted if I'd have to use it.

Forestry tracks tend to offer good approaches but, unfortunately, my ancient OS map didn't show the complete network of forest tracks that exist now in this part of Glen Garry. At the first junction I took what I thought was the most obvious route only to discover it petered out about a mile later. Fortunately, I had a GPS with me. A quick check gave me a grid reference that showed if I continued for a couple of hundred metres I'd come across the Allt Ladaidh. A footpath, on the river's west bank, would take me to the path I should have been on. It was a mistake worth making. The footpath climbed through woods, alongside a river that was roaring and cascading with brown, peaty snowmelt. Icicles, large as organ pipes, hung from the river's banks and the pawprints of a fox led me all the way to the track I should have been on.

From this point a broader track continued up the east bank of the Alt Ladaidh to the ruins of some shielings and a path junction. One went west and then south to Clunes on Loch Lochy-side while the other headed south over the Bealach Easain to Kilfinnan. From this vantage point Ben Tee rises on uncompromisingly steep slopes to its conical summit. As soon as possible I left the very faint path and took to the heather, making slow progress on slushy snow. By linking up some of the longer snow patches, the surface of which was firm enough to allow me to kick steps, I managed to move a bit faster, with shifting mists swirling in the bealach below and in Coire Ghlas opposite.

It was early afternoon by the time I reached Ben Tee's big summit cairn. Across the great gulf of the Bealach Easain below me the sharp nose of Meall a' Choire Ghlais was fringed with snow, looking for all the world like a classic alpine ridge.

The last time I was here I climbed it before striding round the big horseshoe ridge that encloses Choire Ghlais, taking in the Munro of Sron a' Choire Ghlais, 935m/3085ft, a summit that's usually linked with its close neighbour Meall na Teanga. Today I simply slid and slithered back down Ben Tee's slopes to the old shielings and along increasingly slushy forestry tracks to the car.

BEINN BHREAC, CAIRNGORMS
MARCH 2002

Braemar sparkled in the sun and the hills that rose beyond the serpentine Dee looked as if they had just been whitewashed. Spring snow had fallen at the end of one of the finest spells of winter weather I can remember. Dry days and more than the expected quota of sunshine have given me some great days out and it looked like I was set for another.

In the months running up to the creation of the Cairngorms National Park much has been written about these mountains, their arctic landscape, their high-level plateaux, their sculpted corries and deep trenches, but I wanted a long hillwalk that would link two of the area's finest glens, Glen Derry and Glen Quoich, with a traverse of one of the Cairngorms' least visited Munros, Beinn Bhreac.

Glen Derry rarely disappoints. Ancient pines solidly anchored and generous in their shelter make Glen Derry an oasis of peace in the wind-blown turmoil of the winter hills. From old Derry Lodge, all the way along the reworked footpath to the bridge over the River Derry, you walk in the footsteps of old. Drovers once made their way down here with their herds of black kye. Armies probably marched between Mar and Abernethy by the same route. More recently, pines were felled higher up the glen and floated downstream to the Dee. Today, the National Trust for Scotland is trying to encourage regeneration of the progeny of those felled pines.

Beyond the footbridge I left the track and climbed steadily

up the western arm of Coire an Fhir Bhogha. The sun shone and the high tops sparkled, so I wanted to tease out the route to make the most of the day. I also had a notion that it might be rather atmospheric to wander down Glen Quoich in the gathering dark of evening, the 'thin' time of the Ancient Celts when the barriers between our world and the 'otherworld' are at their most transparent.

Across the deep trench of Glen Derry, below the summit of Derry Cairngorm, lay the deep-set bowl of Coire an Lochain Uaine, one of five 'green lochans' in the Cairngorms. It was below this hanging corrie that the stalker-turned-poacher Uilleam Rynuie, or William Smith of Rynuie, built his little howff where he could gaze down Glen Derry and 'be on guard against the Earl of Fife's foresters'.

It would have been good to tease the day out even more by climbing Beinn Bhreac's close neighbour, Beinn a'Chaorainn, but the high plateau between the two tops, the Moine Bhealadh, was covered in the worst of all snow conditions, a crust that doesn't quite take your weight. You end up fighting the stuff, either willing yourself three stones lighter to stay on top, or crashing through the crust up to your calves with each step. I didn't want that sort of frustration to spoil the peace of my day.

Beinn Bhreac, 931m/3054ft, has two cairned summits, like two billowing breasts, whose eastern slopes fall sharply away into deep, dark corners that eventually widen out into the cleft of the dark glen – Gleann Dubh. The crusted snow made the descent awkward, although the gloomy confines of the glen had protected it from the melting rays of the sun. Snow bridges criss-crossed the river but crossing them would have been no more than a lottery. Instead, I avoided the river as much as possible.

The light was fading and the first stars were flickering as I wandered down the track that parallels the Quoich Water. By the time I reached the Linn of Qouich by Allanaquoich it was pitch-black and my head-torch cast a pool of light into the foaming waters of the Punch Bowl. Taking ten minutes here,

I emptied the remains of my flask and prepared for the final four-mile trek along the road to Linn of Dee and my waiting car. Only the owls kept me company.

NA GRUAGAICHEAN, THE MAMORES
DECEMBER 2003

I had been giving a talk in Kinlochleven as part of the opening week of the new Ice Factor, the world's biggest indoor ice-climbing wall and the latest event in the renaissance of this former aluminium smelter village. With the new ice-climbing facility in place, and with the West Highland Way bringing thousands of backpackers to the village, Kinlochleven looks set to become the adventure capital of the West Highlands.

Man-made facilities apart, the area's finest resource is the jumble of high hills that cluster together above the village, some of them served by a network of stalkers' paths, many of which climb high into the mountain corries and onto the connecting ridges.

After my Ice Factor gig I stayed the night in the Mamore Lodge Hotel, situated almost a thousand feet above the waters of Loch Leven.[3] Next morning, stuffed full of a good west highland breakfast I decided to make the most of the elevated position. It had been some years since I traversed the twin tops of Na Gruagaichean, one of the most imposing peaks on the nine-mile long Mamores ridge, the high corrie-bitten wall that forms the natural barrier between Glen Nevis in the north and Loch Leven in the south.

In the Scottish Mountaineering Club guide to the Central Highlands, author Peter Hodgkiss suggests few hills of comparable stature are so little climbed except with others. While Na Gruagaichean is certainly impressive from Kinlochleven, Peter suggests: 'Its grace of form and the complexity of its twin tops are only revealed when approaching along the main ridge.' A

---

3. The last time I passed the Mamore Lodge Hotel it had closed down

stalkers' path reaches the main Mamores ridge less than a mile north-west of the summit, and starts, very conveniently, about half a mile north-east of Mamore Lodge.

My plan for the day was deliberately unambitious. With a lot of low cloud about and icy conditions underfoot, conditions could potentially make the traverse of Na Gruagaichean's two tops rather awkward.

The climb up through Coire na Ba was straightforward but, higher, great snow fields covered the stalkers' path. That wasn't much help! Instead, I took a direct line up steep snow slopes to reach the main ridge in about ninety minutes. Hard snow and *névé* covered the rocky ground and I kicked steps up the ridge's twists and turns towards the north-west summit. Visibility was poor, but I was aware of a cornice edge close by. Fragile and potentially lethal, I kept my distance but at the same time welcomed its presence as a navigational aid. With it on my left I was going in the right direction!

Stopping at the first summit I strapped on my crampons in preparation for the steep two-hundred-foot descent into the narrow gap that lies between the hill's two tops. In the event, the terrain was more awkward than difficult with soft snow hiding deep gaps between the rocks. From the gap, another steep climb took me to the higher of the two, at 1056m/3485ft. Feeling rather pleased with myself and encouraged by the relatively windless conditions, I decided to retrace my steps to the low point on the ridge and continue over the neighbouring Munros of Stob Coire a'Chairn and Am Bodach.

All went well until it began to sleet. By the time I reached the summit of Stob Coire a'Chairn it was snowing blizzard-style and the wind was knocking me about like a punch-drunk boxer. Rather than push into its blinding fury my self-preservation instincts took control and I turned tail and stumbled away as fast as possible, always difficult in crampons, back to the low point of the ridge where the stalkers' path dropped into Coire na Ba. Lower down, the snow turned to torrential rain and by the time I limped back into the Mamore Lodge car park I was

1. A snow covered ridge on Beinn Liath Mhor

2. Ben Tee above an autumnal Loch Oich

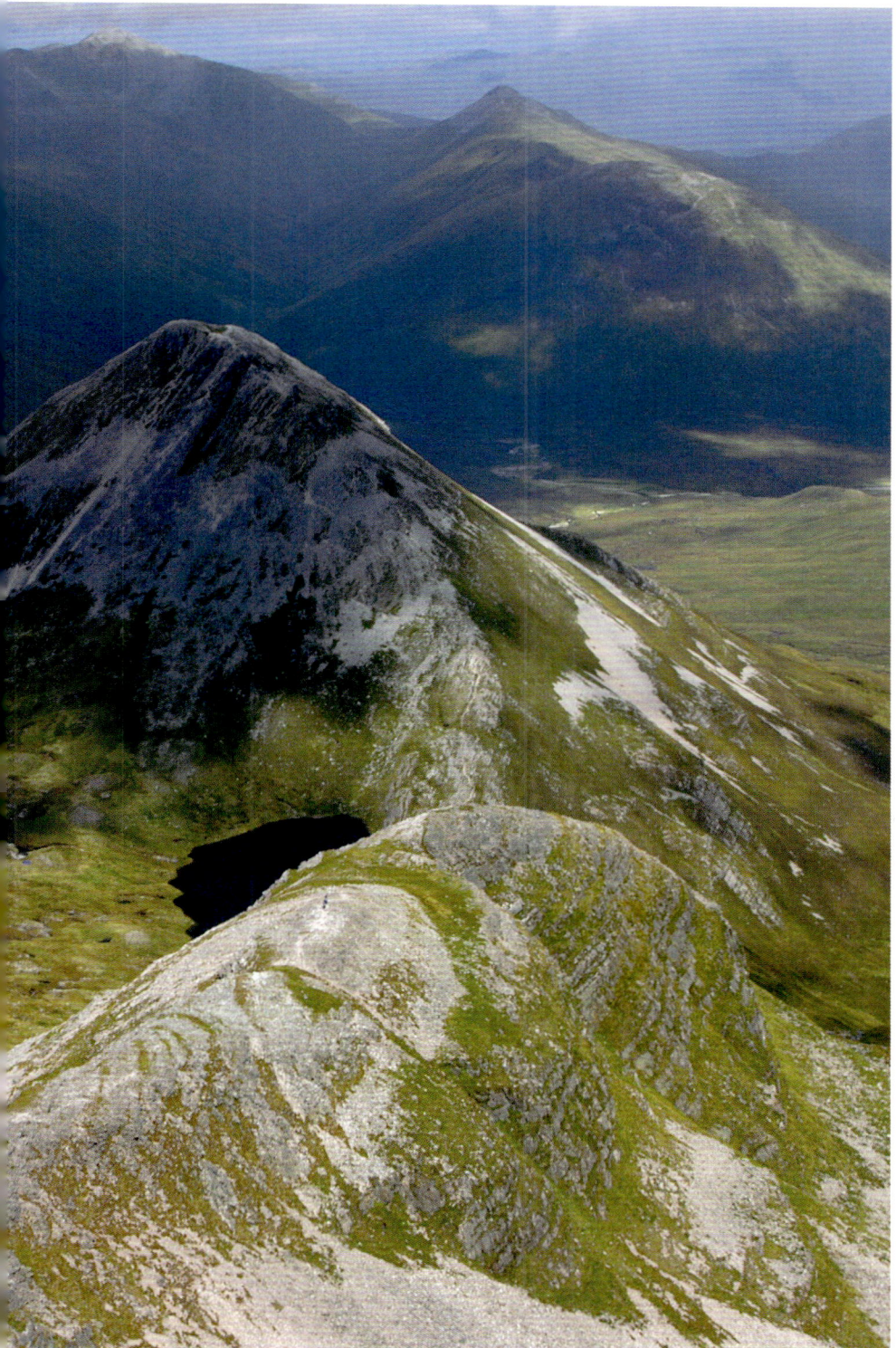

3. Binnein Beag in the Mamores

4. Coastal scenery at Hallaig, Isle of Raasay

5. Evening light on the mountains of Letterewe

6. Evening light on the Strathfarrer ridge

7. Following the wall over Black Shoulder on Cairnsmore of Carsphairn

8. Fuar Tholl

9. Hallaig, the scene of Sorley MacLean's great poem on Raasay

10. Loch Hourn and Barrisdale Bay

11. Leaving Glen Bruar on the ancient Minigaig route

12. Liathach from Loch Clair

13. Looking towards An Teallach from A'Mhaighdean

14. On Ladhar Bheinn above Loch Hourn

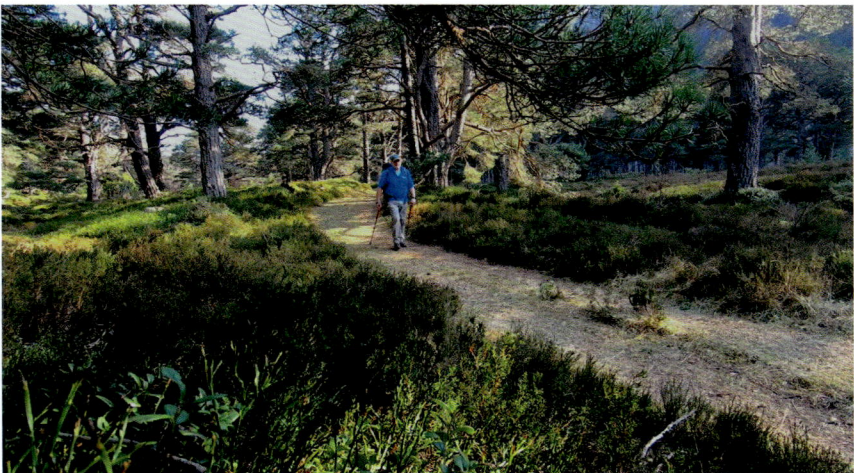

15. Rejuvenated Glen Feshie. Trees grow from a luxuriant carpet of mixed vegetation

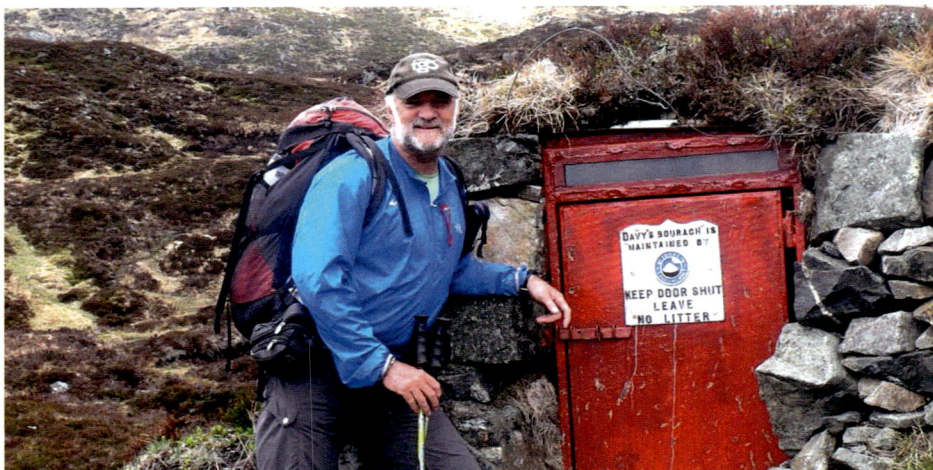

16. The author outside Davy's Bourach on Jock's Road

17. The Carn Mor Dearg Arete on the Tranter Round

18. The dispossessed scratched their messages on the windows of Croick Church

19. The path rises into Coire Lair with Fuar Tholl dominating

20. The ptarmigan, a bird of the high places that could be a casualty
of climate change

21. The Skye Cuillin

22. The summit of Beinn Macdui, the UK's second highest

23. The summit view from A'Mhaighdean

drenched and more aware than ever of how quickly conditions can change on Scotland's winter hills.

SGAIRNEACH MHOR, DRUMOCHTER
APRIL 2005

It was to be a lazy Saturday, the morning given to pottering about, attending to those little domestic tasks that had been put aside for another day when, in the evening, I had to give a talk to the Munro Society in Birnam in Perthshire. That left me with an afternoon to climb a hill, to make the most of the unseasonably warm sunshine and clear weather.

The obvious choice was somewhere along the A9 and with its easy high-level access from Drumochter Pass I plumped for Sgairneach Mhor, the big stony hillside, 991m/32351ft. Despite its name, Sgearnaich Mhor doesn't have a lot of rock on its slopes although its big north-facing corrie, Coire Creagach, does boast a few mini-crags. Indeed, it's that big corrie that gives this hill its character, a huge wind-scoured bite out of the hillside that always looks quite dramatic in winter when big snow cornices hang over the corrie lip.

I remember ski touring over this hill with a couple of friends, John Love and Bob Telfer. Thick mist covered the summit slopes, and we were convinced we had skied past the summit cairn. Following our ski tracks back, we peered through the mist in search of the cairn, when Bob suddenly vanished from view. He had skied over the cornice.

Shocked, John and I peered over the edge to see him, legs and skis spreadeagled, hanging on a few feet below. Fortunately, he hadn't skied over the edge at the corrie's steepest point. If he had, the outcome wouldn't have been so happy. John, being the remarkably forthright guy he is, told me later that the first thought to cross his mind was: 'Damn, I think Bob's got the car keys!'

It was a far cry from winter when I left the A9 and took the recently resurfaced path between the two porcine hills of Drumochter, the Boar of Badenoch and the Sow of Atholl.

Already I was stripped to a tee shirt and the early afternoon sun shone from a cloudless sky. It was hard to believe it was still only mid-April. A good track runs through the glacial moraines between the hills, a track that gives easy access to the north-eastern slopes of the well-rounded Sgairneach Mhor.

The Dalnaspidal deer forest boasts four Munros: Sgairneach Mhor, Beinn Udlamain, A'Mharconaich, and Geal Charn, an area once known as the Druim Uachdair, the ridge of the upper ground. Tackling the four in one outing isn't a difficult proposition, but the logistics of the approach does mean a walk along the A9, either at the beginning of the day, or at the end, depending on where you park. A Sustrans cycle track that runs adjacent to the road means you don't have to actually walk close to the traffic.

After seeing to my chores in the morning I was still in a pottering mood. Knowing I wouldn't have time to wander round all four Munros, I was happy to climb one, and make my way back to the car via Coire Dhomhain, the long, rising glen that separates Sgearnaich Mhor from the other Drumochter Munros.

I found an easy river crossing before the long climb up Sgearnaich Mhor's grassy north-east ridge. Moving easily, feeling relaxed in the sun, I cosseted myself by adjusting my walking stride to those pottering rhythms of the morning and, in no time at all, I was wandering along the lip of Coire Creagach, recalling Bob's little ski trip.

Cornices still hung over the edge, and great swathes of snow still lay in the corrie below. A pair of ravens kept me company, calling to each other as they performed show-off acrobatics. A wheatear bobbed on the summit trig point as I approached, its white rump feathers gleaming in the sun, my first sighting of the season. To the south, Schiehallion stood proud, and the jumble of the Cairn Mairg and Lawers hills were still swathed in white. Beyond lay the celestial twins of Stobinian and Ben More and, further north, through the haze, rose the Wall of Rannoch hills, the Glen Coe hills and, closer at hand, the snow-streaked Ben Alder massif.

There wasn't a sigh or a breath of wind – the stillness of the high places. I listened to try and capture a sound, any sound, but couldn't, other than the faint pulse of the blood coursing through my own veins. Such silence is rare on a mountain top, and after a quick bite I lay back in the sun, closed my eyes, and instantly fell asleep.

On the long descent down the path in Coire Dhomhain the world felt like a good place. Meadow pipits and skylark sang their sweet songs and high above me a great herd of deer moved across the hillside, grazing contentedly in the warmth of the afternoon sun.

BEINN MACDUI, INVERNESS-SHIRE
DECEMBER 2007

I've lived in the shadow of the Cairngorms for thirty years and am passionate about these hills. I love their brooding heights, their deep trenches and chasms, their high plateaux and wind-scoured corries and the fact that I don't have to travel very far to climb amongst them. So, as a seasonal treat, I set off last Sunday in the company of Neil Birnie from Wilderness Scotland towards Creag an Leth Choin at the head of Lurcher's Gully. Our plan was simple – we didn't have one, but simply set off to wander aimlessly, free as a cloud.

As luck and the weather gods would have it, it was a day in a million. A shallow covering of snow made the hills sparkle and the sun shone from a cloudless sky. It was bitterly cold, but we hardly noticed as we tramped up the ridge towards Lurcher's Meadow, then over the boulders to Creag an Leth-Con's narrow summit that steeply overlooks the deep cleft of the Lairig Ghru pass. From horizon to horizon the world was sparkling white. Away in the west Ben Nevis lifted its rounded head above the long ridge of neighbouring Aonach Mor and, beyond the Great Glen, the hills of the northern highlands appeared as a snowy jumble rolling to the far horizon.

Creag an Leth-Con, or Lurcher's Crag, is neither a Munro nor a Corbett but it does offer marvellous views up and down the length of the Lairig Ghru. It's a great summit for a half-day walk – through the Chalamain Gap from the ski road, up Lurcher's Crag's north slopes and back to the ski road via Lurcher's Gully, an ideal Christmas Day appetiser if you happen to be in the Aviemore area for the holidays.

As so often happens when you head for the hills without a plan one soon begins to formulate, almost unconsciously, without intent or design. With a glorious winter day before us it would have been a pity not to head for Beinn Macdui, Scotland's second highest mountain, and check out the oft-stated assertion that on a clear day you can see both Morven in Caithness in the north and the Lammermuir Hills in the south. With Morven clearly in view from Lurcher's we were intrigued to see if we could add the Lammermuirs to our line of sight.

We could! This must have been the clearest view I've had on all the dozens of times I've stood on Macdui's 1309m/4295ft summit. Away beyond Largo Law and the Lomond Hills of Fife we could clearly see the Pentlands and away to the left a thin line of blue hills were positively identified by Neil as the Lammermuirs.

By the time we had a spot of lunch the weather began to show faint signs of change. Long, ragged strips of cloud appeared in the sky and a mischievous wind began to blow great spumes of spindrift across the plateau. We crossed Macdui's north top and stumbled down snow-covered boulders to the snow- and ice-covered Feith Buidhe that in turn tumbled over the precipice to an ice-shrouded Loch Avon deep below us.

The wind had already stripped Beinn Meadhoin of snow and the setting winter sun was beginning to turn the slopes pink, a premature Alpenglow that intensified as we crossed the slopes at the head of Coire Dhomhain and down the Fiacaill Coire Cais back to the car park. As we set off on our separate journeys home I couldn't resist stopping by Loch Morlich to photograph one of the finest sunsets I've seen for years. Red and pink clouds from a blazing, fiery sky were reflected on the frozen surface of the loch. It was the perfect end to a thoroughly pleasant day.

CAIRNSMORE OF CARSPHAIRN, DUMFRIES & GALLOWAY
NOVEMBER 2010

The Green Well of Scotland is a rather grandiose name for a stretch of the Water of Deugh, a lively burn that flows from the conifer-covered hills of the Carsphairn Forest in north Galloway. After a night of torrential rain it was livelier than usual, foaming, bubbling and brown with peat. I was rounding off a visit to Galloway, an area that tends to be as remote from my highland home as a visit to Sutherland would be for Borderers, and after a couple of very wet days all I wanted was a casual stroll up a hill before the long drive north. The ascent of Cairnsmore of Carsphairn, one of Galloway's Corbetts, looked ideal.

On a previous visit, many years ago, I climbed this hill from Knockgray Farm, just east of the village of Carsphairn, so this time I planned an even simpler route via the hill track that climbs to the hill's big south-west-facing corrie from the Green Well of Scotland, a name that has always intrigued me. Kayakers tend to associate it with a lively stretch of the Water of Deugh, but other writers describe it as a 'neat and attractive rocky gorge flanked by ash and beech'. Yet again, I've heard it described as a pool in the Water of Deugh just below an old hump-backed bridge, close to what is now the A713 Castle Douglas to Dalmellington road. Apparently, a local counterfeiter by the name of Dodds once made coins from a local ore and eventually threw his master's dies[4] into the pool to hide them from the excisemen.

Close to the Water of Deugh a gate gives access to a track that makes its way past some cowsheds to an old footbridge over a tributary of the Water of Deugh, the Benloch Burn. Under normal conditions, I'm told, this is a trickle of water that can be crossed easily, but after a weekend of heavy rain it was swollen

---

4. Die (n): A shaped block of metal or other hard material used to cut or form metal in a drop forge, press, or similar device, according to Collins Dictionary. This gives us 'the die is cast' when something is finalised.

to double its width, and running fast. The footbridge that once spanned the burn had been washed away in a previous storm and, after walking less than half a mile, the in-spate burn effectively stopped me dead in my tracks.

Loath to chuck it and go home after such a short walk, I checked upstream to see if there was an easier crossing. There wasn't, so there was only one thing to do, off with the boots and socks and wade. My trekking poles offered good support in the fast-flowing water, and although it reached my knees it wasn't particularly cold, although it was a tad unpleasant first thing on a late November morning.

Beyond the Benloch Burn, the track climbed steadily across the flanks of Willieanna and Dunool, high above the Polsue Burn, before coming to an abrupt halt beside a drystone wall. After a bright start the cloud had gradually lowered and it was clear that, within a matter of minutes, I would be following a map and compass, although I soon discovered that the drystone wall made a good navigational aid virtually all the way to the summit.

Cairnsmore of Carsphairn, at 797m/2614ft, is the highest of Galloway's Cairnsmores. An old rhyme makes the point:

> There's Cairnsmore of Fleet,
> And Cairnsmore of Dee;
> But Cairnsmore of Carsphairn
> Is the highest of the three.

Sadly, I didn't see much from the summit trig point other than a mesmeric drift of cloud. I should have been able to gaze to the north-east to the rounded tops of the Lowthers, or south towards the Rhinns of Kells and the Merrick. Instead, I took a compass bearing on a point marked on the map as Black Shoulder and descended from there to a little pass before climbing steadily again to the cairn on Dunool. From there it was an easy descent to another pass just north of Willieanna, but, despite being intrigued by the name (could this little hill be named after a courting couple – Willie and Anna?), I drifted onto an old sheep trod, back to the hill track of earlier, and another wade across the Benloch Burn. It didn't feel so cold this time, maybe because I was going home.

CHAPTER SIX

Before the Hikers

When BBC Scotland asked me to walk a Pilgrims' Trail for our annual Christmas television programme, my producers came up with a cracker of a route, a journey that partly fulfilled the 'spiritual significance' aspect of pilgrimage and partly fulfilled my own definition of a pilgrimage as a 'journey of discovery'.

The route began on Iona, a centre of Irish monasticism for four hundred years and the island from where St Columba, or Columcille, set out to bring Christianity to the Picts of Alba. I was keen to learn more of the ancient Scotland that Columba was determined to evangelise, but also wanted to challenge my own perceptions about 'wild land' at a time when many were suggesting that Scotland's wild land areas were being 'industrialised' by renewable energy projects. I confess to mixed feelings about onshore wind farms, but I was also aware that I rarely saw windfarms on my hillwalking jaunts and was mildly irritated by social media comments about Scotland being 'trashed' and 'destroyed' by windfarm development. So, how genuinely wild is our wild land? I hoped a 250-mile walk, from the Argyll coast to the North Sea, might give me a deeper understanding.

One thing that became evident was that 'industry' is not new to the highlands. In the first few days I visited silica sand mines at Lochaline on the Sound of Mull, the Lurga lead mines in Gleann Dubh, which date from 1730, and more lead mines above Strontian where the mineral 'strontianite' was discovered. From Glengarry I followed an old cattle drovers' road from Tomdoun to Cluanie, a route that originally forded two rivers that were

subsequently dammed and flooded for hydroelectric purposes
in 1957 to form Lochs Cluanie and Loyne.

Over the next week or so we were faced with more evidence
of Scotland's widespread hydroelectric industry as we crossed
from Glen Affric, via the Munro of Toll Creagach, to the big
dam at the head of Loch Mullardoch. Beyond Glen Cannich I
walked through remote landscapes between the head of Glen
Strathfarrar (the only Strath in Scotland that's also a glen) and
Loch Monar. A wild camp and a campfire on the stony shoreline of Monar was highly atmospheric and memorable. Next
day I crossed into the head of lovely Strathconon where the
River Conon and a series of forestry paths and tracks took me
to the Blackwater River, the heavily forested Rogie Falls and
more hydroelectric schemes. The Blackwater River rises high
on the slopes of Beinn Dearg, some thirty miles away and runs
into Loch Vaich to contribute to the huge Glascarnoch hydro
scheme, complete with tunnels, power stations and dams.

Soon Ben Wyvis became the third Munro of the pilgrimage
and, rather surprisingly, our first real view of windfarm activity.
The Loch Luichart scheme is massive, and badly sited in my
opinion. Thankfully, plans for a thirty-four-turbine scheme in
nearby Glen Morie were rejected by the Scottish Government in
2014. I dropped down to the shores of lovely Loch Glass from
Wyvis and crossed a high ridge to the shores of Loch Morie, an
area that was new to me and that surprised me with its atmosphere of remoteness and natural beauty. It would have been a
disaster to spoil it with a large windfarm.

From Glen Morie we followed more old byways to Strath
Ruisdale and Strath Rory, passing the remains of a Pictish Fort
before quiet roads led us east towards the Tarbat Peninsula and
our destination, Portmahomack. Here lay the big surprise of the
pilgrimage, the remains of the only Pictish monastic settlement
ever found in Scotland. The leader of the archeological team,
Professor Martin Carver of York University, told me the site was
just as important as Iona, and a place Columcille may well have

visited, possibly after visiting Inverness where he tried to convert the pagan King Bridei in 565. The founder of the Portmahomack monastery was more likely to be St Colman, who succeeded Aiden and Finan as Bishop of Lindisfarne.

Here, on the edge of this Easter Ross village, lay the remains of the first Pictish monastery to be excavated, providing an unprecedented window on the early monasticism that was inspired by the Columban mission to Scotland in the late sixth century. This shook me to the core. Not just another early religious site, this was a European centre of industry, a manufacturing and distribution base of illuminated books and church vessels like tin bowls and candle holders for the rapidly increasing number of monasteries throughout western Europe. This was the Amazon of the eighth and ninth centuries until it was raided, probably by Vikings, sometime in the ninth century. This place alone puts paid to the theory that the Scottish highlands are being despoiled by new found industrialisation. History shows us something remarkably different.

The Tarbat Discovery Centre displays many of the artefacts uncovered during the excavations and is worth a visit. When we completed filming, I took time to wander around the Centre and sit outside the church to ponder all the trails and tracks I had followed from Iona, and the broad spectrum of people who had trod them before me: saints, monks, soldiers, Jacobites, princes and cattle drovers and, in more recent times, the miners, hydro and forestry workers, crofters and farmers as well as the hikers and backpackers of today. Industrialisation in the highlands is not new, and ongoing run-of-river hydro schemes are changing the face of many glens again.

If there is one thing my walk across Scotland magnified it was the constant echo of times long gone, the voices and impressions of the past that still linger along the byways, in the glens and straths and onto the hills and mountains themselves. The walk also increased my awareness of the cultures, traditions and enforced clearances that have shaped the Scottish Highlands and the people who live here now. This is no wilderness, but a landscape shaped, used, loved and developed by people over a long period of time. I hope some of the walks that follow will allow you to tread in the footsteps of some of them, and perhaps see the place not as an 'empty land', but, as they saw it, a place where people lived, worked, and reared their children, the place they called home.

THE GAICK PASS, PERTHSHIRE/INVERNESS-SHIRE
APRIL 1984

It was a sombre morning. The air was still, although strong winds were forecast, and clouds lay low on the hills. The grey cloudline seemed to hold a heavy weight and I could almost feel its pressure above me, as though something was about to burst. Thankfully, the snows were almost gone and only ice patches remained on the track that ran above the swollen Edendon Water. The bare hills of the Dalnacardoch Forest were hushed and only the river and the occasional grumbling of grouse broke the silence. It may have been some kind of omen, for I was heading for the steep-sided trench of the Gaick Pass, once described by the great writer/naturalist Seton Gordon as the most supernatural place in Scotland.

Beyond the boarded-up Sronphadruig Lodge, a dilapidated place made even more forlorn by the deer fence surrounding it, I crossed a small heather-covered rise and dropped to the waters of Loch an Duin. On either side of the loch rose the twin portals of Gaick, An Dun and Creag an Loch, two hills that fall just short of the three-thousand foot contour. I sensed their presence, but could barely see a hundred feet above the waters of the loch.

Loch an Duin fills this narrow glen, and its hill slopes rise sheer on either side. There is barely room for a footpath, but the stony shoreline does the job. A sandpiper-haunted place in summer, the waters lay still like glass and mists hung from the hillsides like torn shrouds. Somewhere in the distance I could hear an aeroplane but it seemed strangely removed from reality, a drone from another world.

Beyond the loch I was into the heart of Gaick, a broad strath surrounded by some of the steepest hills in the country. Deep-cut glens burrow into the hills: 'Black Gaick of the wind whistling crooked glens, ever enticing her admirers to their destruction' was the warning of one eighteenth century Gaelic writer. This is the home of the Leannan Sith, the faery sweetheart, her fatal attraction luring hunters and travellers. It was here in 1958 that Colonel Jimmy Dennis was reported to have seen a tiny elf-like creature. Later a local keeper told him he had seen the Sprite o' Gaick.

The district's link with the supernatural may have been forged as long ago as the late fourteenth century when Walter Comyn of Ruthven, in a mood of cruel sensuousness, decreed that all the women between the ages of twelve and thirty in his employ should work in the fields naked. On the day in question Walter's horse turned up foaming at the mouth with his torn-off leg trailing from one of the stirrups. The rest of his body was later discovered at a place called Leum na Feinne in Gaick with two golden eagles feasting gluttonously on it. Comyn's gory end was attributed to witchcraft.

It was a more recent event that sealed Gaick's evil reputation. In January 1800 Captain John McPherson of Balachroan, known as the Black Officer (he was a recruiting officer for the army) and three companions were killed when an avalanche destroyed the bothy in which they slept. The annihilation, so sudden and complete, was put down to supernatural causes. A memorial stone marks the spot near Gaick Lodge.

Beyond Gaick it's an easy, if long, walk down the length of Glen Tromie, once described as Gleann Tromaidh nan siantan, the glen of the stormy blasts. The place lived up to its reputation. With the ever-increasing wind behind me and darkness overtaking I managed to make good time, but weary legs and a tarmac road don't make a good match. With the ghouls of Gaick well behind me I had a greater fear ahead. I had arranged for my wife to pick me up at Tromie Bridge, and I couldn't be late for that!

BEN VENUE, TROSSACHS
DECEMBER 1986

Away to the west, streaks of yellow light lit up the darkening sky of the Trossachs and Loch Katrine stretched through the rough and tumbled landscape. In the north-west the Crianlarich hills bowed before the higher tops of Stob Binnein and Ben More and, further east, the Ben Lawers range all but dwarfed its neighbouring Tarmachans. The twin tops of Stuc a'Chroin and Beinn Vorlich stood clear, their highest slopes swathed in early snow.

It was getting late in the afternoon with darkness probably less than an hour away, yet we lingered, eager to tease out every moment from our eyrie on the summit of Ben Venue, one of the finest viewpoints in the southern highlands.

Ben Venue is the Hill of the Caves and, with its twin tops, its western outliers and craggy countenance, it lords over the rugged landscape of the legend-rich Trossachs. There are whispers of the past in every notch and cranny of these hills. The slopes that tumble from the summit of Ben Venue towards the shores of Loch Katrine are breached by the Bealach nam Bo, the Pass of the Cattle, an ancient trade route for stolen cattle, driven back from the lowlands to the MacGregor lands at Glengyle. And below the Bealach nan Bo lies the knobbly Coire na Urisgean, the corrie of the goblins.

Sir Walter Scott, who found so much inspiration here, depicted the goblin's corrie as a retreat for Ellen Douglas and her father after they had withdrawn from Roderick Dhu's stronghold on Eilean Molach. An even older account suggests this corrie was the meeting place for all the goblins in Scotland. According to *Scenery of the Southern Confines of Perthshire*, published in 1806, 'the solemn meetings of the order were regularly held in this cave of Benvenew'.

Most folk climb Ben Venue from Ledard Farm on the B829 Aberfoyle to Inversnaid road. We left a car behind the Loch Achray Hotel and drove around to Ledard, over the Duke's Pass and through Aberfoyle. That would allow us to traverse the hill, dropping down from the summit through the steep birch-clad slopes to reach the pub by opening time!

A good track runs past Ledard farm and passes a little pool and waterfall where Sir Walter Scott apparently liked to come to work on his notes for Rob Roy and Waverley. A footbridge crosses the Ledard Burn but we weren't to keep our feet dry for long. In its lower stretches, this path can be extremely boggy, but we found it did improve considerably as we climbed higher. With the trees left behind we climbed northwards onto the eastern slopes of one of Venue's outliers, Beinn Bhreac. Here, a wide bealach introduced us to the craggy slopes of Ben Venue itself and, even at this point, the first views of the day began to impress themselves on us.

On steeper ground now, the footpath begins to switchback, weaving its way between rocky outcrops to reach the first, and highest, of Ben Venue's two summits. The view, across Loch Katrine to the Loch Lomond hills and the peaks of the Arrochar Alps, was outstanding.

The path now winds its way through the summit outcrops and, shortly after, reaches Venue's twin top (only a few metres separate the two tops). With the view opening eastwards, out along the silvery lengths of Loch Achray and Loch Venachar to the Mentieth Hills, it was hard to understand the thinking behind the hill's original name. In an old Statistical Account, the hill is recorded as a' Bheinn Mheanbh, the small peak. With the growing darkness dimming the distant views it was hard to see anything closer at hand that made this hill look diminutive in comparison.

THE ARGYLL STONE, CAIRNGORMS
DECEMBER 1989

The waters of Loch an Eilean were flat calm and the stillness of the air almost eerie. Strands of limpid mist hung over the forest as though the earth itself was breathing and a laggard sun eased itself over the brow of Cairn Gorm, softening the dark shadows between the trees where the heather was laced with delicately frosted spiders' webs.

Not wanting to destroy such intricate artwork, I retraced my steps back to the broad track that follows the shores of Loch an Eilean, Scotland's loveliest loch, set deep in the heart of the Caledonian pine forest of Rothiemurchus, near Aviemore.

Few mountain ranges can boast such delightful approaches as the Cairngorms. In both Speyside in the north and Deeside in the south, the skirts of the mountains are covered in magnificent pine forests, ancient and venerable and full of interest. Isn't it odd that most visitors to the Cairngorm tops choose a high-level car park and a corrie full of ski-lift paraphernalia as their starting point?

Tempted as I was to spend a day in the soft light of the forest, I wanted to get up high. It's not often you get such a perfect day in December.

Protecting Loch an Eilean and its close neighbour Loch Gamhna from the southerly gales, a long ridge drops down from the high plateaux of the Moine Mhor. Linking the high tops of Sgor Gaoith and Sgoran Dubh Mor, the ridge continues north before swelling into a broad whaleback above Rothiemurchus. This final rise on the ridge is noted for its two granite warts, or tors, the Clach Choutsaich, Coutt's Stone, and the Argyll Stone, a larger and more impressive tor than can easily be seen from certain parts of Strathspey below.

The ridge can be reached from the track that runs southwest from Loch Gamhna towards Inshriach Forest. Leaving the path that runs up alongside the bubbling burn of the Allt Coire Follais I was convinced I was in for a real thrash through knee-deep heather, but I was so engrossed with the wide views that were opening up that the summit ridge arrived before I knew it.

The stone, the Clach Mhic Cailein is apparently named after the Earl of Argyll who is said to have passed this way after of the Battle of Glen Livet in 1594 where he was defeated by the Earl of Huntly. No doubt the clansmen followed the route of the ancient Rathad nam Meirleach, the caterans' road through Abernethy Forest and Glenmore. That would have certainly brought them past Loch an Eilean but for the life of me I can't imagine why they wanted to climb onto the Creag Dhubh ridge above Rothiemurchus, unless they wanted to reach high ground to see if they were being pursued.

Local tradition suggests MacCailein Mor, the Duke, wanted to stop and rest at the first spot from which he could see the mountains of Argyll. This is a reasonable thought, except you can't actually see very far west from the Argyll Stone, although the views of the adjacent high tops of the Cairngorms are spectacular. From further along the Sgorans ridge, particularly from Sgor Gaoith, you can certainly see the hills of the west.

THE CURSE OF CLUNY
FEBRUARY 1992

Wrapped in waterproofs I left the parking area beside the old General Wade bridge at Garvamore, at the foot of the Corrieyairack Pass, and followed the south bank of the Spey for a mile or so before climbing through a narrow defile in the crags to reach the rocky summit of Creag Chathalain. I was in search of a cave, a living reminder of an ancient tale known as the Curse of Cluny.

In the sixteenth century, Cluny, Chief of Clan MacPherson, betrothed his eldest daughter to one of the High Kings of Ulster. The groom's party made its way across the sea to Scotland and Badenoch with a huge entourage of knights and nobles. One of them was a young warrior by the name of Cathalon.

During the wedding feast, Cathalon fell in love with the bride's younger sister and she him, but the young couple believed Cluny would never offer the hand of his youngest daughter to any man other than an independent chief. They decided to elope.

True to his word, Cathalon returned in early winter and the young lovers set off towards the wilds of the Corrieyairack, their plan being to flee through the Great Glen to the west coast, where they could catch a boat back to the Antrim coast. Sadly, the young lady couldn't travel very fast as by this time she had become heavy with Cathalon's child. Nightfall caught them only a few miles up the glen, where they sheltered in a cave in a hill that became known, even today, as Creag Chathalain.

In the gloomy afternoon light I didn't search too fervently for the cave, but stayed on a relatively high shelf of land that was shared by two adjoining tops, Meall a' Chaorainn and Meall Liath-Chloich. From the latter I dropped down to the infant Spey and crossed it by a bridge just below the bothy at Melgarve. Just east of the bothy, a little below the Corrieyairack road, lies an ancient standing stone. When Cluny discovered that his youngest daughter had run off, he ordered his soldiers to give chase and return with the heart of the Ulsterman, and local opinion has it that this is his burial place.

The weather deteriorated and the glen was swathed in a blanket of fresh snow. The lovers' footprints were found and, about two miles from the cave, they were overtaken. Despite a brave fight, Cathalon was overcome. He was put to the sword and his heart cruelly carved from his body to be taken back to Cluny as a trophy. However, as they buried the body the soldiers discovered papers in the young man's pouch proving that young Cathalon was no mere 'duine uasal' or simple laird. He was the rightful heir to the High King of Ulster, a true and legitimate thane. To this day no-one knows why he kept this fact secret, although it could be that he wanted someone who loved him for his own sake, and not because he was of royal lineage.

When Cluny was told, he expressed great sorrow, but was privately delighted that his youngest daughter hadn't been carried off by a commoner. He ordered a giant standing stone to be placed over the burial place in due respect of Cathalon's rank.

It was good to pass some time leaning against that stone on its level stretch of ground close to the River Spey, recalling its antiquity and purpose. There isn't much left of it, but it remains as a reminder of the consequences of hasty vengeance, the swift retribution that for many years has been known as the Curse of Cluny.

THE MINIGAIG
MAY 1992

After a cloudy morning the sun broke through and flooded the broad slopes with its warm radiance. The land stretched away under an infinity of domed sky, with every feature delicately etched, and ridge followed ridge, a landscape of rolling moors and shadowed glens.

The route ahead was no more than a suggestion really, sporadically marked by tiny cairns across a landscape that refused to conform to any accepted pattern. Ahead lay the faint tracings of the old Minigaig road. To the north and to the west, the peaks and tops had sunk and dwindled into a distant mass and the great plateau spread itself aimlessly, a lofty tableland patched in the black and white of peat hags and late-lying snow.

Two ancient routes link Perthshire's Blair Atholl with Kingussie in Badenoch. The Minigaig replaced the older Comyn's Road some time before the seventeenth century. It seems probable that Comyn's Road fell into disuse because the Minigaig was more direct and slightly shorter. Seventeenth-century maps show it as the sole route across the Grampians.

Until General Wade built his new road over Drumochter Pass the main route through the wild and remote Grampians was this high-level bridleway that crosses the wedge of high, broken land between the Pass of Drumochter in the west and Glen Tilt, Glen Geldie and Glen Feshie in the east.

Earlier in the day I left Blair and made my way by various paths and tracks into Glen Bruar where, at the far end of the glen, the land rears suddenly and a rough path zigzags up the slopes towards the Minigaig Pass. But this is like no normal pass that rises to a summit and then immediately descends. For no less than three miles this vast upland of hillocks and brows rolls in serried knolls that appear to stretch into infinity. I was captivated.

Standing for a long time, staring at the still and silent spread of it, inimical under the shadows of the sun, I recalled the supernatural tales of the sithens, the fairy knolls, and remembered the ill-fame of the place. Like nearby Gaick, the Minigaig has a particularly bad reputation, having claimed many victims on its storm-swept plateau. I recalled the words of a modern guidebook: 'The Minigaig . . . is perhaps the bleakest and most featureless terrain crossed by any major hill track.'

Today the Minigaig was smiling, and I pushed on, eager to drop into Coire Bhran and make my way into upper Glen Truim, over the Beinn Bhuidhe ridge and down to Kingussie for a pint.

This old right of way certainly takes you through some wild country and, if you plan to walk it in a long, single day, make sure you're fit. I've walked the Minigaig in winter several times and camped overnight and would suggest two days with an overnight bivouac high on the Pass or below Coire Bhran. I can't think of a better way to spend a summer night, high on the hill with the ghosts of the drovers and soldiers who passed this way in times gone past.

BORERAIG AND SUISINISH
AUGUST 1997

Although the highlands and islands are littered with the remains of former villages and townships, few exude such an air of sadness and desolation as Boreraig and Suisinish, the lost villages of Skye.

A ten-mile walk visits both by following the shorelines of Loch Eishhort and Loch Slapin. Although the remains of Suisinish are in the most scenic location, with the rocky ramparts of Bla' Bheinn and Clach Glas frowning down on them, to my mind the most atmospheric is Boreraig.

So, what will you find there? Well, a three-mile track begins near the old ruined church of Cill Chriosd on the Broadford to Elgol road in Strath Suardal and runs past an old marble quarry before the bare and empty moorland above Loch Eishort. Soon it drops into the peaty glen of the Allt na Pairte where you might be brought up short by the view of green, corrugated fields, pressed into a bright crescent, dotted here and there with the old walls and gable ends of former homes.

Despite the ruins, and bracken fronds that have swallowed the fields of barley and oats, and scrubby sycamores that choke the burn, there is a lushness about the place. Look closely and you might recognise the remains of runrigs and lazybeds that tilt towards the rocky shoreline.

A single standing stone in the centre of the village bears testament to the antiquity of the place as a centre of habitation, but it's many a year since children laughed here or old men told their tales. Those are the things you'll see at Boreraig today but, if you have a mind for it, settle down beside one of the gable walls and let your imagination drift back to the middle of the nineteenth century when clan chiefs realised they had become landowners and landlords. Some continued to have the interest of their clansfolk at heart, but many became convinced that some kind of land reform was necessary and that the land could generate more profit than crofter rent. There was a demand for wool and flockmasters from the borders were looking for new areas to graze. The highlands and islands were ripe for their hardy cheviots and blackface, and the landlords could take much higher rents from the shepherds.

In this area of Skye, Lord MacDonald decided that his people could make a better life for themselves abroad, and he could earn more money from sheep. So, the people were displaced.

The first group of villagers were sent to Campbelltown from where they set sail for the new world on the Government ship *Hercules*. Many of them died from smallpox. The news got back to Skye and, as you can imagine, the remaining villages were reluctant to follow. Lord MacDonald's factor and his henchmen decided force would be necessary. The people were burned from their homes and, in a final act of humiliation, the factor doused the flames of the burning cottages with stoups of the precious milk from which the villagers made their butter and crowdie. One old man, aged eighty-six years, was forced to leave the land that he had paid rents on for sixty-five of them.

A rough path picks its way west for a couple of miles, through the no-man's-land between Beinn Bhuidhe and Carn Dearg on one side, and the salt water of Loch Eishort on the other. Soon the green fields of Suisinish come into view.

Suisinish smiles a little more than Boreraig. In a spectacular setting above Rubha Suisnish, where Lochs Eishort and Slapin meet, a leaning plateau of pasture contrasts with the blue of the sea, as delightful a situation as you'll find in this scenically blessed isle. But, beyond the fields, away from the steep cliffs and their salt-laden updraughts, the husks of former homes cast a shadow across the sparkling seas and verdant smiles.

A track, built by the Board of Agriculture earlier this century in a token attempt at encouraging the re-crofting of Suisnish, now follows the shore of Loch Slapin, north to the bay of Camus Malag where, across the head of the loch, Bla Bheinn and Clach Glas rise majestically.

It's become almost trendy to deny the highland clearances, to suggest the landlords really had the welfare of the people at heart, and that may be true in some areas, but here in Skye the records tell a different story. I hope these ruins at Boreraig and Suisinish are preserved as a reminder of man's inhumanity to man.

CREAG AN TUIRC, STIRLINGSHIRE
JANUARY 2002

For most hillwalkers in Scotland this coming year will be notable for two events. New legislation will give the public a legal right of responsible access to all land and inland water, and the first of our national parks will be created in the Trossachs and Loch Lomond area.

In celebration, I spent a bit of time in the Trossachs last week and, in particular, enjoyed a short walk high above Balquhidder Kirk, an ideal little outing for post-Hogmanay hangovers.

I had intended walking through the marvellous Kirkton Glen to Glen Dochart, but spent too much time noseying around

Balquhidder church instead. For anyone with even a passing interest in the history of this area this church is fascinating. The present building, built by David Carnegie of Stronvar, was opened in September 1855, but it shares its environs with a building of greater antiquity. A ruined church bears the date 1631 and was built by David Murray, Lord Scone, whose initials appear above the doorway. It's built partly on top of the pre-Reformation church and its bell, donated by its erstwhile minister the Rev. Robert Kirk (who was convinced of the existence of faeries and elves and wrote a book about them) was used until 1895.

The pre-Reformation church dates from the thirteenth century, or possibly earlier. Some of its foundations can be seen near Rob Roy's grave in the kirkyard and was known as Eaglais Beag, or Little Church. It's thought it may have been built over the grave of St Angus. Indeed, his cell was believed to have stood in the field below the church. Old foundations were removed from there in about 1860. A large stone, the St Angus Stone, believed to have lain over his grave, now leans against the north wall inside the present church. It's thought that it dates between AD 750 and 850.

Much of this Balquhidder area is historically associated with the Balquhidder Fergussons, the MacGregors and the Stewarts of Glenbuckie and, high above the Balquhidder kirk, on a rocky bluff, is the gathering place of Clan MacLaren. In those far-off days, each clan had a place to which they were summoned by the Fiery Cross, the burning emblem that was traditionally carried by runners around the clan district calling the men to battle. Like the MacGregors, the MacLarens knew turbulent times. They were staunch supporters of the Jacobite cause and even after Culloden continued to bear arms and wear the white cockade, in direct opposition to London's rule.

This Creag an Tuirc, the Crag of the Boar, is a superb view-point that's well worth visiting. A relatively short walk, it is well signposted, and the quality of the view is out of all proportion to the minimal effort required to climb up. It's worth spending some time on the summit for the view is wonderful. The fifteen-mile length of the Balquhidder glen stretches into the far distance, and from each side a series of overlapping mountain slopes, shade upon shade, drop down into the long slit that cradles Loch Voil and beyond it, Loch Doine. Beyond lies Inverlochlarig, where Rob Roy died and, a little bit closer, between the two lochs, lies the house of Monachyle Tuarach, where Rob and his wife Mary MacGregor of Comar (called Helen by Sir Walter Scott!) settled into married life.

As you gaze on the scene, it's worth considering that this landscape of lochs and craggy mountain bluffs inspired the likes of Scott, Wordsworth and Hogg. They recognised a good view when they saw one.

CARN CHUINNEAG, EASTER ROSS
JULY 2005

When the flockmasters arrived in Glen Calvie in Easter Ross the eighteen families who had lived in the glen for generations were moved to make way for sheep.

Some of those smallholders and tenants, with nowhere else to go, fell on the mercy of the local church at Croick and, with the help of the minister, set up booths and shelters in the church grounds. To enter the church itself was thought to be verging on sacrilege for they had been told theirs was 'the wicked generation' and their predicament was a direct form of divine chastisement. In their desperation, some of them scratched messages of despair on the church window, messages that just over 150 years later offer a poignant reminder of one of the most shameful periods in Scottish history.

As I wandered up the length of Glen Calvie towards the double-breasted Corbett of Carn Chuinneag I was reminded of the curiously cyclic nature of highland history. The folk of Glen Calvie were cleared to make way for sheep, but now commercial sheep farming has all but disappeared from the district as estate owners reforest the lower slopes to provide winter shelter for deer. As I ate my lunch by the summit cairn I gazed down towards the oil rigs in the Cromarty Firth and, above them, on the hills above Dingwall, counted over two dozen giant wind turbines.

Carn Chuinneag looms high over the southern confines of Glen Calvie and I have to say the estate has done a marvellous job in reforesting the entire length of the glen. Lower down, the Caledonian pines are a delight and, beyond the Lodge, as the glen narrows, the riverside is lined with birch and rowan. The ground vegetation is lush, a direct testament to the removal of sheep, and the bird-loud two-and-a-half-mile walk up the glen from the River Carron was an absolute delight.

Although it's not a high hill, Carn Chuinneag is certainly taller than any of its immediate neighbours in the high plateaux of the Easter Ross deer forests. As I climbed higher, I became more aware of the bare wildness of this corner of Scotland. The long ridges and plateaux fell away below me, and I began to see familiar landmarks, particularly across the rolling tops of the Freevater and Inverlael Forest to the west.

Beinn Dearg, the flat-topped Seana Bhraigh rising above Strath Mulzie and the Wester Ross and Sutherland coastal fringe of Coigach, Cul Mor and Cul Beag, Suilven, Canisp and the higher hills of Assynt all began to appear. Behind me rose the northern trio of Ben Hope, Ben Loyal and Ben Klibreck. Beyond them lay the Pentland Firth. Although the waters of the North Sea were perfectly clear in the east, the curvature of the earth robbed me of views to the Minch that I knew was there, just beyond the outlines of Suilven and its neighbours.

Swopping the views of the hill's west top with those of the higher east top involved a short descent to a wind-scoured bealach, and another climb to the rocky summit and trig point at 838m/2749ft. Ben Wyvis lay close at hand, lording it above the curiously land-locked Cromarty Firth. Only a narrow opening at Nigg gives access to the Moray Firth, and Nigg of course, is today an important centre for the maintenance of North Sea oil rigs. I hadn't realised that a climb up an Easter Ross Corbett would give me a lesson in highland history, and perhaps a glimpse of the future too.

CARN MOR, MORAY
MARCH 2011

An old right of way runs from Bellabeg in Strathdon over the Ladder Hills to Glen Livet. As the route climbs out of Glen Nochty it passes an old house that goes by the odd name of Duffdefiance. History has it that a local character by the name of Lucky Thain once squatted in it and refused to move even when the laird, a gentleman by the name of Duff, came and tried to make him move on.

Another good cross-country route, the Steplar, runs from Glenlivet to the Cabrach for about thirteen miles, crossing Thiefsbush Hill and Dead Wife's Hillock. What tales lie behind such names?

I gazed down on this storied landscape and wondered. From my lofty perch on Carn Mor, the highest of the Ladder Hills that form a high boundary line between Donside and Glenlivet, I looked down on the greens and browns of the Braes of Glen Livet, an unseasonably pastoral scene marred only by the thirty-odd spinning giants of a distant windfarm, as out-of-place in this setting as graffiti daubed across a Constable.

Beyond the Braes lay Scotland's whisky mountain, Ben Rhinnes and its close neighbour, Corryhabbie Hill, whose southern and eastern flanks ease into some of the most under-valued (by hillwalkers) country in Scotland, the wonderfully rolling hills of upper Glenlivet and Glen Fiddich, names well known to those who enjoy the occasional nippy sweetie.

In the late eighteenth and early nineteenth centuries, this area hid numerous illicit whisky stills operated by local people. To evade Government regulations many of them were secreted in secluded parts of the Braes and the illegal whisky smuggled south and east using remote hill tracks. I had followed one of these old 'whisky roads' earlier in the day climbing from the Well of Lecht, on the A939 Tomintoul to Cockbridge road, onto the slopes of Carn Dulack.

The car park at the Well of Lecht is a convenient start and

finish point for the ascent of Carn Mor, 804m/2639ft and its Corbett neighbour, Carn Ealasaid, 792m/2600ft. In the 1730s iron was mined here and the ore taken by pack-horse to Nethybridge for smelting. In 1841 the mine was re-opened to produce manganese ore and the present building built as a crushing plant, driven by a water wheel. Today, the building is an empty shell.

The comparatively unfamiliar Ladder Hills attracted me simply because the weather forecasts reckoned the eastern Grampians would see more sun than anywhere else. They were right. While the high tops of the Cairngorms appeared as a lumpen mass of hodden grey, the lower, rounded, snow-covered tops of the Ladder Hills sparkled brightly in the sun. The temperature was hovering around freezing point when I left the car but higher up the hill the strong north-westerly wind reduced the wind chill factor to an uncomfortable level.

I traversed the hillside above the old mine building, following what remains of the old whisky track through heather patched with snow. As the old road crossed over the ridge of Carn Dulack to begin its long descent to Glenlivet, I left it and followed a line of fence posts around the head of the glen and onto the peat-hagged bealach between Carn Liath and Monadh an t-Sluich Leith. Beyond the latter's snow covered, dome-like summit, a narrowing ridge descends to another col before climbing stead-ily to Carn Mor and its trig point summit.

In the strengthening wind this wasn't the place to linger so, after a few moments contemplating the place-names and the history of the glen, I retraced my steps over Monadh an t-Sluich Leith before climbing to the summit of Carn Liath. From here old argo-cat tracks led me back down to the Well of Lecht.

HALLAIG, RAASAY
SEPTEMBER 2012

I'd never visited Raasay before and as the ferry ploughed its way through wind-torn waves from Sconser in Skye I settled down to read through the lines of Sorley MacLean's great poem, 'Hallaig'. Somhairle MacGill-Eain was, arguably, the greatest of Gaeldom's bards. Born at Ostaig on the Isle of Raasay in 1911 his upbringing was rooted in the richness of Gaelic culture. 'Hallaig' is one of his best-known poems and I've always been attracted by its underlying themes of nature. Indeed, while much of MacLean's work dwells on the brutality of war and modern exploitation he often uses landscape as a kind of symbolism. His work doesn't offer much in the way of light reading, and a Gaelic-speaking friend of mine once suggested that reading the poetry of Sorley MacLean can feel like a physical work-out.

In contrast, the walk to Hallaig, situated on the sheltered east coast of Raasay, is fairly easy. Despite the stormy sea crossing and the threat of wind-blasted rain, the truncated cone of Dun Caan, at 443 m/1453ft the highest point on the island, offered a degree of shelter from the westerly gales. From time to time the sun broke through the clouds and illuminated the golden bracken of the slopes with uncanny brilliance. Beyond the green swell of the sea lay the mainland mountains of Wester Ross.

I left the car at the end of the public road at North Fearns, where a simple wooden signpost pointed the way to Hallaig. In1919 some crofting families were evicted from Acarsaid Thioram on the island of Rona and came to this part of Raasay where they tried to take land to live on. They were arrested but later released following a public outcry. They returned to Raasay and became known as the Rona Raiders. Following this, the British government took ownership of both Rona and Raasay and the population of the former went into severe decline as most crofters followed the Raiders and moved to the larger island.

Beyond the road end a lovely green track runs along the top of the cliffs. This is the original road built to access the crofting township of Hallaig. Grass and moss have grown over the ancient cobbles just as bracken now dominates the fields that once grew oats or barley. As the path curves its way around the lower slopes of Beinn na Leac it rises slightly below a dark cliff below which, with a view out across Hallaig Bay, lies a tasteful memorial cairn to Raasay's most famous son, Sorley MacLean. It also carries the words of 'Hallaig', in both Gaelic and English.

> Time, the deer, is in the wood of Hallaig.
> The window is nailed and boarded
> Through which I saw the West . . .

Beyond the cairn, through ancient woodland, I came across the first of the old buildings, roofless and bare. Through the wood of Hallaig, a large copse of small, stunted birches, a bubbling stream hinted at life in an otherwise empty landscape, populated only by the ghosts of those evicted or forced to emigrate.

On the hill beyond the wood, more shells of buildings lay scattered, monuments in themselves, recalling the hard lives of those who once lived, worked and died here. I sat amongst the cold stones and wondered if those crofters were as thrilled by the blend of sea and mountains as I. What, for them, lay beyond the blue-tinted mountains that formed the horizon across the sea? What does the next twist of history hold for a place like Hallaig?

Sorley MacLean's poetic vision transformed the trees of the wood of Hallaig into people – the native rowan, the hazels and the birch became groups of young women, suggestive perhaps of the earth's regenerative power from which all life springs. Perhaps the poet's vision of a populated Hallaig is better than reality ever was?

Promising myself that I must return here, perhaps to bivvy down within the protective walls of some old blackhouse, I followed the track back through stark woods and along the green trail with the mountains of Skye teasing me through curtains of windswept rain. This may not have been the hardest of walks, but it surely is one of the most evocative.

CHAPTER SEVEN

Water, Water, Everywhere

It's something we're not short of in Scotland, a land where droughts are rare, where a rain shower is always waiting to tap you on the shoulder and where the landscape occasionally feels like a giant, soggy sponge. Perhaps the German/American poet Charles Bukowski was thinking of Scotland when he wrote: 'We ain't got no money honey but we got rain'. Not sure about the economics of that but our excess of rain can certainly be harnessed to our advantage.

Let me give you an example. The area around Loch Quoich, just west of Glen Garry, has the distinction of being one of the wettest places in Scotland. In December 1954, 25cm/10 inches of rain fell in a twenty-two hour period and the annual average is in the region of 4.5m/15ft. It's not surprising that the North of Scotland Hydro-Electric Board harnessed the waters of Loch Quoich for its Glen Garry hydroelectricity project and, in doing so, changed what was a seven-mile natural loch into a ten-mile-long reservoir. By raising the water a hundred feet they drowned the former village of Kinlochquoich and doubled the maximum breadth of the loch. The scheme was completed in 1962 and, since then, hydro has been considered as one of Scotland's most important and reliable generators of power. Now, mixed with wind power, both onshore and offshore, and the advent of wave and tidal power, the future of renewable energy is exciting. Perhaps we ain't got money, honey, but we're self-reliant on clean energy.

Aesthetically, it's easy to consider the massive amount of Scotland's rainfall as a negative, particularly as you battle into a rain-soaked gale on a mountain top, but anyone who has spent any length of time in dry, barren countries of the world will realise that it's not a bad thing to have a steady supply of moisture. Drought is one of the major problems on the planet. Just have a look at the finest landscapes we have and invariably there will be water in it somewhere: cascading streams, glistening crags, reflective lochs and, of course, waterfalls, the tumbling cascades that have captured the imagination of writers and poets for generations. Sir Walter Scott once remarked that 'any poet, however poor his attainments, can describe a waterfall'. Indeed, he described at least one himself, the Grey Mare's Tail that drops down from Loch Skeen in Moffatdale in Dumfries and Galloway. 'White as the snowy charger's tail, drives down the pass to Moffatdale'. Norman Nicholson refers to his 'chain of water, the pull of the earth's centre' whilst others anthropomorphise, describing cascades and cataracts as 'the voice of the mountain'. In his wonderfully adjectival poem 'Inversnaid', Gerard Manley Hopkins describes the course of the Inversnaid Burn in tumultuous, fast-moving terms: 'His rollrock highroad roaring down, In coop and in comb the fleece of his foam, Flutes and low to the lake falls home'. It's a much-loved poem that ends with that most famous of environmental pleas: 'Where would the world be, once bereft, of wet and wildness? Let them be left. O let them be left, wildness and wet; Long live the weeds and the wilderness yet'.

I'm totally with the poets when it comes to the glories of waterfalls but I'd add a little corollary to that: the sound of running water is worth more than all the poet's words. So often I've pitched my tent close to a mountain stream, the sound of which has gently nursed me to sleep. I adore the musical orchestrations of a highland burn: the base notes of the deeper-running water set off by the tinkling melodies of the faster-moving upper levels. Audibly there are few things more impressive that the surge, roar and absolute power of a waterfall in spate. And we have no shortage of them in Scotland.

I've mentioned a few in the essays that follow, but there are literally hundreds of them, maybe even thousands. When the weather is foul on the high tops, when the rain is battering the peaks, you can be sure that lower down there will be a waterfall waiting to grab your attention and impress you almost as much as a mountain-top view does.

Scotland is one of the most beautiful countries in the world, and water, whether it be waterfalls, rivers or lochs, plays a major role in that. Nature is the world's great artist and water is one of her finest brushes. Take a look at how a sunset, and its glowing, radiant colours, are reproduced on the still waters of a West Highland sea loch. Or look down from the high tops on Loch Avon, Loch Etchachan or Loch Einich, surely the jewels of the Cairngorms, or gaze on the perfect mix of sea loch and mountain from almost any mountain top on the west coast. It's water that makes Scotland's scenery so vibrant and sparkling. Water is the element that elevates a pretty scene into a magnificent one, creating emotions that can reduce us to tears of joy and wonder.

Best of all are mountain springs, the spot where the water gushes, or in some cases seeps, out of the earth itself. The birthplaces of our streams and rivers is where the water is at its most pure before anything gets a chance to pollute it or taint it in any way. Such places are sacred.

Over the years I've probably drunk from thousands of mountain springs. I don't like to pass one without stopping, and cupping my hands, taking a deep draught of it. Pure and sweet, it's the wine of the land. I've also discovered these springs are where certain types of vegetation flourish. Cresses, mosses and lichens thrive in these spots, nurtured by the pure, unpolluted water. Because so many of these sources tend to be high in the hills they are also places of intense beauty and it's refreshing not only to drink the water, but just to sit beside the flow and enjoy its ethereal, tinkling sound, taking time to wonder about the spring's secrets. How is it possible for so much life and vigour and beauty to be sustained in what are often open, exposed and wild surroundings?

We refer to springs as water sources but the real source, of course, lies in the clouds above, the clouds that bring the rain, the mist, the snows in winter, and the gentle, persistent percolation of moisture through rock and soil to emerge as bubbling streams through the earth's crust. The river's story doesn't actually begin where it is born. Rather, the spring, amid its austere and desolate surroundings gives life from a source outside of itself, life of eternal duration far beyond its own tiny boundaries. It might come as a surprise that the hidden springs, high on the hills, are an intimate, quiet, gentle expression of the eternal elements of the universe, the rain, the storms, the snow and the clouds, elements that are, conversely, often violent and life threatening.

Here, compressed into a mere life-giving stream, lies a tiny fragment of the titanic forces of wind and weather that encircle the planet to determine its climate. These are the elemental sources of energy derived from sun, moon, stars and all the awesome arrangements ordained during the creation of the cosmos. It's a lot to consider, when taking a drink of water from a mountain stream.

CALLANDER CRAIGS, STIRLINGSHIRE
NOVEMBER 1987

I wanted to see the effect a week's rain and melted snow had on one of my favourite waterfalls: the Bracklinn Falls near Callander. This is a wonderful spot, a dramatic cleave in the landscape through which the River Keltie roars over a succession of huge sandstone blocks that form a rough natural staircase. The colouring is rich, with a profusion of mountain ash, oak and beech. A fiercely theatrical spot, which so obviously inspired the bard of the Trossachs himself. Sir Walter Scott, never one to miss a good scene, brought the Bracklinn Falls into his great story, *The Lady of the Lake*.

> As Bracklinn's chasm, so black and steep,
> Receives her roaring linn,
> As the dark caverns of the deep,

Suck the wild whirlpool in,
So did the deep and darksome pass,
Devour the battle's mingled mass.

No exaggeration there. The walk to Bracklinn Falls can be combined with a longer walk over the Callander Craigs, which rise in wooded splendour to the north-east of Callander. This has been a popular route with locals and visitors to this highland border town for generations and the paths are well signposted and easy to follow.

The highest point of the Craigs, Beacon Crag or as it is locally known, Willoughby's Craig, rises to a height of 335m/1100ft. Its ascent, while steep and rough in places, is not too difficult. When we parked our old campervan in the car park beside the River Teith I was vaguely aware that the access road to the Callander Craigs path sounded something like Taliban. I was close, and as soon as the sign marked Tulapin Crescent appeared I knew we were going in the right direction.

Another signpost pointed out: 'To the Crags and Woodland Walk', and within minutes we were climbing steeply through mixed woodlands of oaks, chestnuts, beeches and firs, mixing with the twentieth-century conifers, with occasional glimpses across the serried roofs of Callander to the distant Gargunnock Hills and Campsie Fells.

The path climbs gently at first, below the wide, green canopy, and then more steeply up a series of natural steps. Here and there we had to use our hands to negotiate steeper, rockier sections but soon the path levelled off as it wound its way through some young birches and pines to the summit. The view that opens up as you reach the summit cairn is wide-ranging for such a lowly viewpoint. Look west along the length of silvery Loch Vennachar, its head seemingly choked by the high hills of the Trossachs. To the right you can peer into the very bosom of Ben Ledi, that great wild north-east corrie, and to the east your gaze carries you along the broad strath to Stirling, the Ochils and beyond to the dim outline of the Pentlands near Edinburgh.

An impressive cairn decorates the summit mound. It was built in 1887 to commemorate Queen Victoria's Silver Jubilee, and from it we squelched down the muddy path, squiggled our way through the birch scrub and eventually reached the tarmac in Glen Artney. A short descent led to a faded signpost, which points to a footpath that leads to the Red Well, a mineral spring, close to the road. This is a semi-circular stonebuilt wall with a central plaque embedded in a large stone. Below it a pipe supplies the red ore-coloured water.

Within minutes we reached another car park, from where another footpath took us to the Bracklinn Falls where, according to legend, Sir Walter Scott rode his horse over a rickety bridge for a wager. It's well worth a visit, especially after a period of heavy rain when the falls are at their most spectacular. On our return we followed the road into Callander and passed an hotel called Arden House that looked vaguely familiar: was this not the house in fictional Tannochbrae, the home of the original *Doctor Findlay's Casebook*? I think it was.

BRUAR FALLS, PERTHSHIRE
MARCH 1988

The natural miracle of hydrodynamics is best observed after a period of heavy rain when our moors and mountains harness all the fallen moisture, soak it up like a gargantuan sponge then, by unseen energies, force it up though the surface of the ground in the form of bubbling streams. The Bruar Water, just north of Blair Atholl, feeds from the great, soggy plateaux and moors of upper Atholl and initially flows down the empty miles of Glen Bruar before, chameleon-like, changing character completely.

As the ground falls away the waters become agitated and turbulent, before crashing and thundering down the deep gorge that cradles its bed. At the foot of the gorge the water roars over a series of falls and cascades before finally surging through a natural arch in the rock and into the pools below.

What makes Bruar so spectacular is the simple combination

of rock, water and trees, basic elements that offer grandeur on a magnificent scale, but in the late eighteenth century this narrow glen was virtually devoid of trees. One visitor to the falls, William Gilpin, commented: 'One of them indeed is a grand fall, but it is so naked in its accompaniments that it is of little value.'

Another visitor, in 1787, was Robert Burns. He wasn't all that impressed either and soon after wrote 'The Humble Petition of Bruar Water to the Noble Duke of Atholl'. This eleven-verse poem contains the lines, 'Would then my noble master please, To grant my highest wishes? He'll shade my banks wi' tow'ring trees, And bonnie spreading bushes.' The Duke of Atholl acquiesced and the first trees were planted in 1797. Sadly, the Bard died before the plantations grew but others have left their impressions in words and pictures: William Wordsworth, William Turner, Queen Victoria and thousands of appreciative visitors from home and abroad.

When storm-force winds literally blew us off the Atholl hills last week we thought we'd console ourselves with a low-level walk just off the A9 near Blair Atholl. The Falls of Bruar more than made up for our disappointment. We only walked for a few minutes before hearing the water's roar. Gazing down on the peat-brown waters as they gushed under the Lower Bridge, the power and vitality of the water was almost frightening. As the thundering cataract gouged its way through the tight, narrow gorge, surging, rumbling and roaring over the waterworn rocks of the river bed I could almost swear I felt the old stone bridge vibrate.

Beyond the stone arch the footpath climbs steadily uphill to the Upper Bridge which forms a man-made arch across the top of the gorge. Looking down on the river from this high vantage point was no less spectacular than the Lower Bridge and it was easy to understand how, over the aeons, the river has been able to carve its deep recess into the very bedrock of the land.

From the Upper Bridge the path climbs away from the bridge before sweeping round to begin its long descent back to the Lower Bridge. There are numerous deviations you can make here from the main path into Baluain Wood where another footpath runs north into Glen Banvie and the ancient Comyn's Road makes its way to upper Glen Bruar but we weren't tempted. The continuing roar of the wind in the trees above was enough to keep us to lower ground, at least for today.

LOCH OF THE LOWES, PERTHSHIRE
MAY 1996

The town of Dunkeld, in highland Perthshire, has a certain charm, probably due to its antiquity, to which was added a bit of a buzz in the morning, as we hiked up the suitably named Brae Street. Views of the town and river opened up behind us; even on non-mountain walks we like to get a bit of height.

Dunkeld is thought by some to mean the fort of the Culdees, while others believe it to mean the hill of the Caledonians. Whatever the origins of the name it was certainly an early seat of Scottish sovereignty and Celtic Christianity. Dunkeld Cathedral dates from the thirteenth century, was destroyed by the Reformers in 1560 and was repaired and re-roofed by Stewart of Ladywell in 1600. It was restored again in 1815, then in 1908.

We didn't linger too long on the tarmac streets. We had planned a circular walk around the town through a fine, varied landscape of woodland, farmland and forest. With the last of the houses behind us we followed signs to the Fungarth Pass before coming across a sign to the Loch of the Lowes. A number of years ago I presented a radio programme from here about ospreys and, being spring, I realised the Lowes' ospreys would probably be nesting. It was too good an opportunity to miss so we dumped the Fungarth Pass idea and headed down a wider track to the road. A quarter of a mile later we were at the Nature Reserve.

The Loch of the Lowes is a reserve of the Scottish Wildlife Trust and shelters a variety of birds, plants and animals. Ospreys regularly nest in a pine tree on the shores of the loch and a hide close by gives the public an opportunity to watch them at relatively close quarters. We were in luck. The ospreys returned to Loch of the Lowes at the end of March and eggs were laid at the beginning of April, including the fiftieth egg laid by this particular female. Most ospreys lay thirty eggs on average. On 18th May the first chick was hatched. At the time of our visit the SWT[1] team were anxiously awaiting the second hatching.

Living as we do in Badenoch, we've become familiar with the sight of ospreys, one of the great reintroduction stories of the twentieth century. These fish-eagles were severely persecuted in the early years of last century and actually became extinct in Scotland. It was only the sterling work by a group of enthusiasts that ensured the osprey's return in 1954, nesting in the pinewoods near Loch Garten on Speyside.

The ospreys are magnificent birds and to see one dive-bomb into a loch and then heave itself back into the air on waterlogged wings with a fish in its talons is one of the most memorable sights of the highlands.

There are, of course, plenty of other things to see at Loch of the Lowes. Red squirrels are still present, and great spotted woodpeckers can be seen from the osprey viewing windows, while fallow and roe deer are often seen from the hide. Other than the osprey season, the other good time to visit here is early winter when the wildfowl population peaks. As many as three thousand greylag geese roost on the loch as well as goldeneye, mallard, goosander, wigeon, teal, tufted duck and great crested grebes.

LOCH DUBH, MONAH LIATH
DECEMBER 1999

We've had snow outside the house for over a fortnight now and, while the blizzards seem to be in abeyance for the moment, freezing cold temperatures clutch the land in a vice-like grip. Because of the vagaries of this astonishing spell of weather I haven't

---

1. Scottish Wildlife Trust

travelled very far, but I'm luckier than most. I can see a Munro
from my bedroom window (indeed, I climbed Meall Cuaich last
week) and there are a handful of Munros within a few miles of
my home village. Curiously, we haven't had nearly as much snow
here in Newtonmore as other areas so I can still wander the local
hills without having to fight through waist-deep drifts.

For a change I thought I'd visit a high-level loch. Loch Dubh,
the black loch, sits in a cradle of high hills below the summit
slopes of Carn Dearg and Carn Ban in the Monadh Liath. The
main thrust of these hills extends east from the Corrieyairack
Pass along the north side of the River Spey. They are high
rounded hills, broken by steep-sided glens, and form the water-
shed between the Spey and the remote headwaters of the Tarff,
the Findhorn and the Dulnain rivers. There is a spaciousness
here that allows you to walk for miles above the two-thousand-
foot contour and rarely see another soul. You are more likely to
see wildlife here than in most popular hill areas, and you can
thrill to a silence broken only by the melancholy sound of golden
plover over the high-lifted moorland. Golden eagle and peregrine
falcon hunt here, and you have a better chance of seeing the
arctic dotterel than you would in the neighbouring Cairngorms.
Ptarmigan are common and you'll trip over more mountain hares
on the slopes of A' Chailleach than you could ever imagine. The
wide undulating plateau of the range's summit is made up of peat
and fringe-moss on loose stony debris, a cover which holds snow
well, making it an ideal playground for ski tourers.

There wasn't quite enough snow for skis today, although I
could have done with snowshoes up higher, where the snows
had drifted. From the road end in Glen Banchor I made my way
through the broad glen past the old farmhouse at Glenballoch.
I remember old Archie Anderson who lived here until about
twenty years ago. He was always keen to come out of the house
and have a blether with passing walkers, but I suspect he was
quite happy eventually to move from this lonely spot to a house
in the village with central heating and a television signal.

A rough footpath continues west from here past new

plantations of deciduous trees and then along the banks of the River Calder. I was surprised to hear stags roaring, an unusual sound for December. I would have thought their annual mating would have been finished by now, but perhaps they were complaining of the cold when it was cold enough to silence the hill streams and even the river beside me. Only a narrow channel in the middle was free of ice.

Near Dalballoch the path pulls away from the river and follows a narrower stream into Gleann Lochan, a glen that narrows significantly as you climb higher into the high corrie that once gave it birth. On a day like today, with icicles hanging from the cliffs and snow everywhere, it's not difficult to imagine the great glacier that scoured out this glen, grinding its way south from the high plateau. The origin of that glacier would have been in what we now know as Coire nan Laogh and the classic corrie lochan that fills the floor of it is one of my favourite spots in the Monadh Liath.

From the far shore of Loch Dubh an array of small cliffs rises steeply, the gullies packed with snow and the cliffs shining blackly. I've camped up here often enough, always in summer, and watched golden eagles. I've heard the call of black-throated divers from the loch too. Today the place was silent, not even a murmur of streams. I was heading for a high bealach to the south Carn Dearg and from there steep slopes would drop me down into Gleann Ballach. In no time I was picking my way across the icy covering of the Allt Ballach where I disturbed a herd of about fifty stags and red deer hinds. Like me, the deer didn't want to spend any more time than necessary on the high tops in this unusual arctic blast of December weather. Unlike them, I had a warm home to return to.

THE FALLS OF GLOMACH, WESTER ROSS
DECEMBER 2004

It's difficult to suggest the best time of year to visit the Falls of Glomach, the impressive cataract that tempts hundreds of walkers every year into a wild and remote corner of Kintail. I have a suspicion that this fag end of the year is as good as any, before the ground becomes too soggy again from winter's snow. Last time I saw the Falls of Glomach was on a long walk to Cape Wrath the summer before last. The weather eventually put paid to my ambitions of walking between Fort William and Scotland's farthest north-western point but all that excess of rain swelled the Falls into epic proportions. Not only did the raging torrent look impressive, you could literally feel the thunder and power of it. The ground shook below my feet and the air was cool with the icy draught of the golden-brown waters. I was impressed by the sheer spectacle of power and potent energy.

The downside was that even the most diminutive of streams had swollen to such a degree that every crossing became a nightmare. Some rivers were simply impassable. Indeed, as I left the awesome display of the Falls of Glomach behind, I had great difficulty in getting out from below the chasm that contains the falls. Every side-stream had become a raging torrent and I eventually escaped with very wet feet and a new respect for fast-running water.

The Falls of Glomach route is well signposted from Inchnacroe in Strath Croe. A footpath links with the old Forestry Commission car park at Dorusduain before heading north through the Dorusduain Wood to the confluence of the Allt Mam an Tuirc and the Allt an Leoid Ghaineamhaich. A bridge crosses the latter stream and a good footpath winds its way up the hillside before climbing gradually to the 518m/1700ft Bealach na Sroine. Those uninterested in aquatic displays could always leave the path hereabouts and climb over the Meal Dubh shoulder of A'Ghlas-bheinn, and on towards the summit of the Munro, but the Falls of Glomach, said to be the second highest falls in the country, are well worth a look, especially after wet weather when the feeder streams are swollen and the Falls are consequently a greater spectacle.

The top of the waterfall lies about a mile beyond the Bealach na Sroine and involves a descent of about 600 feet. As you drop down from the pass you'll notice the sprawling strath of Gleann Gaorsaic and its various streams and burns that feed the main river, water courses that drain the slopes of big mountains like Beinn Fhada and the magnificently sculpted Sgurr nan Ceathreamhnan. All that water harnessed into a narrow steam and then directed into a narrow, rocky cleft where it plunges for some 183m/400ft, twice the height of Niagara, into a deep, black chasm. You'll probably see the spray and hear the thunder long before you see the waterfall itself.

Alternatives to the grind back up to the Bealach na Sroine include continuing down the length of the Allt a'Ghlomaich to the bridge over the River Elchaig. From the north side of the river a Land Rover track runs west to the end of the public road in Gleann Elchaig, but of course you have to arrange for a pick-up. It's also a steep and potentially difficult descent down the side of the Allt a' Ghlomaich, especially after heavy rain. Alternatively, from the top of the Falls, head east, then south through Gleann Gaorsaic to the Bealach an Sgairne where a footpath will take you back to Dorusduain.

LOCHAN NAN CAT, PERTHSHIRE
MARCH 2005

The track that runs up to Lochan nan Cait or Cat, below Ben Lawers is not old. It was bulldozed in relatively recent times to service the little hydro dam high in the glen, but drop closer to the Lawers Burn and you'll come across a much older track, cobbled and worn, a byway that once heard the clatter of cart wheels carrying the roofings for the summer shielings and freshly cut peats for the winter fires.

Follow this old *rathad* into the corrie of the cat, a classic hanging-valley, complete with its high-level mountain tarn, Lochan nan Cat. The Lawers Burn issues from the lochan and legend has it that an outlawed MacGregor once hid in a cave behind a waterfall of the burn. His pursuers tracked him down with a bloodhound, but the fugitive managed to kill the hound with an arrow and make good his escape.

This deep and craggy Coire nan Cat has been defined by two long ridges that emanate from the square-topped summit of Ben Lawers, the highest mountain in the southern highlands. The imposing summit of Lawers is only 17ft short of the 4000-foot mark and the views, needless to say, are extensive: from coast to coast on a good day and, according to some accounts, from Ben Wyvis north of Inverness to the Lothian hills in the south. An old book, *In Famed Breadalbane*, claims that a native of the district, one Malcolm Ferguson, paid for the erection of a giant cairn of stones so that it could be said his favourite hill reached 1219m/4000ft. No less than thirty men and two stonemasons were set to work one day in 1878 and doubtless they were delighted with their attempt to recreate the forces of nature. There's little left of the tall cairn today.

There's little left of the shielings either, although you can still find their foundation stones in odd little circular clusters, usually where the grass is greenest. Here too lie the remnants of drystone walls, marking out the in-byes, tilting up steep slopes on the boundaries of ancient steadings. The cutting of peat was the probably the reason for these high-level shelters, and for the cobbled track, or perhaps the womenfolk came up to these high pastures in the summer months to look after the small, dark-haired kye, the cattle of the highlands.

It had been my intention to climb the hills that form the back-drop to Lochan nan Cat, the guitar-shaped stretch of dark water that mirrors the peaks and crags above it. From the upper corrie steep, grassy slopes etch out a devious route through the crags to the Bealach Dubh from where it's an easy climb to the summit of An Stuc, a hill of contrasting characters. While the south ridge of An Stuc, 1118m/3668ft, is straightforward enough the north-east ridge is steep, crumbly and rocky and I soon found myself using my hands as much as my feet, often down-climbing rather than walking. The rest of the route is simple enough – an easy climb to the summit of Meall Garbh, 1118m/3668ft, a long, winding descent to another high bealach and then a long and easy ridge walk to Meall Greigh,1001m/3284ft.

It was a day of squally showers and a fierce hail-laden wind battered me along the Meall Garbh ridge, but it was so cold I decided to descend before reaching Meall Greigh, down beside a long, flower-filled ravine to a hollow in the hillside where half a dozen stone circles were all that was left of a small village of shielings. I lay down here amongst the stones and dried off in the sun, allowing my imagination to hear the distant peel of laughter, or a wail of sorrow blowing in the breeze, the amorphous shadows of things, events, long since passed.

THE EAS A' CHUAL ALUINN, SUTHERLAND
NOVEMBER 2008

Ben Nevis and the Eas a' Chual Aluinn waterfall have two things in common. They both boast the title of 'highest'. Ben Nevis is the highest mountain in the UK and the Eas a' Chual Aluinn is the highest waterfall, but neither are the best examples of their type.

The Ben is certainly a wonderful mountain, but I can think of several others I'd place above it in terms of grandeur and spectacle and while the Eas a' Chual Aluinn may be the tallest free-falling waterfall in Britain at 209m/685ft I can think of others that look more dramatic. The Falls of Glomach in Kintail comes immediately to mind, or the Steall Falls in upper Glen Nevis, or the Grey Mare's Tail that tumbles down the hill from Loch Skeen in the Moffat hills. But perhaps I'm being a little unfair to Sutherland's big waterfall. I've walked up to it twice recently, the first time as part of a new long-distance walking route I've been hiking between Lochinver and Tongue – the Sutherland Trail – with a television crew who have been filming the route for the BBC. On both occasions the waterfall has been less than spectacular, the braided cataract no more than a dribble, thanks to the gloriously dry weather the north-west of Scotland has been enjoying this summer. I suspect I've been unlucky and, since my last visit, there's certainly been much more rainfall to increase the waterfall's discharge, so the Eas a' Chual Aluinn, or the 'splendid waterfall of Coull', is probably back to its dramatic best.

There are those who would claim that the best vantage point to view the falls is from the head of Loch Glencoul, and during the summer months a cruise boat sails up the loch every day from Kylesku, but it's infinitely more satisfying to hike up to the falls yourself, either from the well-worn track that climbs up from Loch na Gainmhich on the A894 Kylesku to Inchnadamph road, or via a longer route from Inchnadamph, a dramatically wild walk that nevertheless follows good paths through some of the most spectacular landscapes in the highlands. You'll need two cars for this trip: one to take you back to Inchnadamph at the end. Alternatively, there is another good path that crosses the western shoulder of Glas Bheinn that would return you to the start, but it would make quite a tough day of some fifteen miles or so.

Inchnadamph has a long and varied history stretching back many thousands of years and we now know that early humans used the limestone caves of Traligill and Allt nan Uamh. Later, Inchnadamph became the heart of medieval Assynt, and fragments of a Celtic cross suggest an early Christian presence here. The ancient castle and burial vault of the MacLeods of Assynt can also be seen, and remains of flourishing pre-clearance settlements can be seen in the glen of the Tralligill River.

A good stalkers' path leaves the glen opposite a footbridge over the Allt Poll an Droighinn to make its way steadily into a high and wide mountain corrie that cradles two lochs, Loch Fleodach Coire and Loch Bealach na h-Uidhe. The route takes a long traversing climb above the second of these lochs before crossing over the Bealach na h-Uidhe itself, a stony place with phenomenal views north and east to Arkle, Foinaven, Meal Horn, Meallan Liath Coire Mhic Dhughaill and Beinn Hee, the great hills of the north.

On the north side of the pass the stalkers' path takes a

devious, curving line, easing out the contours and wriggling between small, sparkling lochans before reaching a junction of paths above the waterfall. Someone has scrawled 'To the Fall' on a large rock and a line of untidy cairns shows the way to the top of the Leitir Dhubh, the precipice over which the waters fall.

To see the falls properly you have to cautiously cross the stream just above the lip and walk a little way to some grassy terraces that offer better views of the 'tresses' of the falls themselves, but be careful. Some years ago, a woman fell to her death here. Her husband, an insurance broker who had just doubled the value of her life policy, was tried and found 'not proven' but committed suicide two years later. As you gaze down on the falls it's almost impossible to imagine that the course of the cascade is four times higher than Niagara!

From the path junction the route now climbs again in a north-west direction, past the spectacular Loch Bealach a'Bhuirich and down through the bealach of the same name to Loch na Gainmhich by the A894. Just before you follow the shoreline back to the road take a quick peek down into the quartzite gorge at the north end of the loch. This waterfall, known locally as the Wailing Widow Fall, often looks just as dramatic as the Eas a' Chual Aluinn and is, in its own way, just as hidden.

LOCH AVON, CAIRNGORMS
MAY 2009

It's taken me years to come to terms with the notion that if I set out for a day on the hills but don't climb a summit, it isn't necessarily a failure. Peak-bagging is addictive and it's not easy to break the habit, but the redemptive qualities of doing so can transform your whole outlook on hillwalking.

I learned this simple lesson a number of years ago from the writings of a wonderful poet by the name of Nan Shepherd. Through her writings about the Cairngorms I realised that the important thing wasn't reaching a particular high point but simply 'being there'. She suggested that people want sensation from the mountain: the startling view, the towering pinnacle, and she described these sensations as sips of beer and tea instead of milk. While there is nothing wrong with the sensational, and even less wrong with sips of beer, the lesson she taught me was that so often the mountain gives itself most completely when you have no particular destination.

Appreciation of 'being there' opens the mind to all sorts of things, including a refound awareness of what lies around you. By eliminating the necessity of reaching a certain peak you find yourself with more time to look around, to contemplate, to wonder ...

We went into the Cairngorms with this desultory notion of merely wandering around to see what we could discover. What we ended up with was a great walk, and that's why I'm writing it here, in the hope that you too might enjoy it as we did. In actual fact the aimlessness of it all was rather spoiled by the showery weather, which made idle contemplation a rather cold and wind-swept experience. Instead, we wrapped ourselves in waterproofs and kept on the move, flitting through the mists that came with the showers, delighting in the glimpses of sunshine that lit up the world that opened up around us with all the drama of a curtain going up on an elaborate and colourful stage set.

We followed the refurbished footpath from the ski grounds car park in Coire Cas into the upper reaches of Coire an t-Sneachda where the crumbly Goat Track carried us up beside the granite cliffs to the cloud-covered col just east of Cairn Lochan.

Below us, the wide, green swathe of Coire Domhain, bubbling with springs and whirling streams, dropped over the edge of the plateau into the upper confines of the Loch Avon basin. We ambled rather aimlessly down the steep path beside the Allt Coire Domhain, swathed in clinging mists that formed droplets on my beard, eager to descend below the cloud level to get our first glimpse of the aquamarine fringe of Loch Avon, deep in its mountain setting.

Our patience was rewarded. A gust of wind and a pierce of light and the cloud was gone. The most spectacular corner of the

Cairngorms opened below us: gleaming white cascades poured down the granite slabs beyond the Hell's Lum crags and below the glistening crags of Carn Etchachan and the sheer rock faces of the Sticil, a chaos of giant boulders filled the corrie floor. Beyond it lay the dark blue waters of Loch Avon, its yellow beaches giving way to aquamarine shallows like those of a Caribbean inlet.

Eager now to stay below the cloud level we followed the path on the Cairn Gorm side of Loch Avon, stopping every few minutes to gorge on sweet blueberries or the shinier, less sweet crowberries. Approaching the eastern end of the loch, we climbed higher towards The Saddle, birthplace of the Garbh Allt, which eventually matures into the River Nethy.

With little inclination for the boggy, rain-soaked upper reaches of Strath Nethy we climbed north instead, up easy-angled slope to the dramatically named Margaret's coffin, or Ciste Mhearaid, and the first pylons of the Cairn Gorm ski grounds. The long nose of the Sron an Aonaich carried us back to our starting point.

LOCH ERROCHTY, PERTHSHIRE
JUNE 2009

I sat with my back against the gable wall of a ruined farmhouse, looking across the blue waters of Loch Errochty to the nearby hills of the Dalnacardoch Forest. Curlews were warbling from the mud flats at the end of the loch and, on the water, a great raft of black-headed gulls screeched incessantly. Beyond the old lazybeds, below the farmhouse, peewits dived and fluttered in that mad, acrobatic way of theirs and from somewhere nearby a cuckoo called.

I had walked over the hill on a fine old track from the Trinafour road, my only company the odd scraggly-looking blackface, for this was sheep country. Indeed, the building that sheltered me from the breeze was once probably a sheep farm and, as I walked along the south shore of Loch Errochty, earlier

in the day, I passed a number of sheep pens, all in various stages
of disintegration. I wondered how many farmsteads and shielings were now hidden from sight, below the blue waters of the
loch that looks so natural in its fold in the hills between Beinn
a' Chuallaich and Sron Chon, for Loch Errochty is a man-made
reservoir, created in 1957 as part of Phase Two of the Tummel
hydroelectric power scheme.

A dam was built at the head of Glen Errochty to capture the
waters of Allt Sléibh and the Allt Ruighe nan Saorach, which
both rise in the high ground to the west of the head of the loch.
Other small streams flow directly off Beinn a' Chuallaich, which
rises just to the south. It was hard to believe that I was looking at
an industrial landscape. Here at the western end of the loch, far
removed from its concrete dam above Trinafour, there was still
a great sense of wildness. The loch appears as an integral and
natural part of this mountainous landscape that rises between
Loch Ericht and Glen Garry in highland Perthshire.

The hill that rose behind me was another clue to the legacy
of sheep farming in the area. Beinn a' Chuallaich is the hill of
herding, and is a Corbett. It had been my intention to simply
climb it from Drumglas on Dunalastair Water but I noticed
on the map a hill track that ran over the hill's Meall na Moine
outlier and down to Loch Errochty. From the old farmstead at
Ruighe nan Saorach, on the shores of the loch, another track ran
over the hill and back to Drumglas offering a fine hill circuit of
eleven or twelve miles or so, just the job for a fine early summer's
Sunday.

Beinn a' Chuallaich, which rises above the Perthshire village
of Kinloch Rannoch, falls just short of the three-thousand-foot
mark and lacks any real individual feature that would make it
special. As part of a longer circuit, it would offer a fine vantage
point to Schiehallion in the south, and out along Loch Rannoch,
the old road to the isles, to the hills of the west.

I left the car by the roadside above the forest and found the
track that eased its way north over the Meall na Moine and
down to Loch Errochty's shoreline. It was like stepping back

in time. A vintage tractor-type-vehicle stood by the old sheep pens, its tyres embedded in the earth, grass and bracken fronds growing into its engine. No doubt it has stood there since the late fifties when these sheep farms were abandoned in favour of flooding the glen. All the way along the shoreline track, the signs of man's past occupation were evident: old bridges across the streams, ruckles of stones that betrayed the whereabouts of the old shielings, lichen-tinged drystone walls that tilted uphill from the shore, and the ruined farmsteads. It was only when I climbed high above the old buildings at Ruighe nan Saorach that I could escape the feeling that this was a landscape that had been emptied and abandoned in our incessant need for energy. I wonder what the next chapter holds for areas like this?

It didn't take long to climb south to Beinn a'Chullaich and from its tall summit cairn I returned to the broad footpath that offered an easy descent route, down to Drumglass by the twinkling music of the burns running down to Dunalastair Water. Only a couple of miles on the quiet road were left to complete a grand hill circuit that gave me a little glimpse of times gone by.

ROGIE FALLS, INVERNESS-SHIRE
APRIL 2010

Our plan had been to climb towards Coire Lair from Achnashellach, but as we drove along the A890 from Achnasheen we were met by torrential rain, gale-force winds and low cloud. Since Achnashellach is reputedly one of the wettest places in Scotland, with an annual rainfall in excess of 4.00m/13ft (surprisingly this pales into insignificance alongside the wettest place in the UK – Sprinkling Tarn in the Lake District with 6.53m/22ft recorded in 1954), we decided to turn around and go elsewhere.

The 'we' I refer to is me and my son's dog, Affric. This grandog of mine is a three-year-old Labrador with a mind that's totally dominated by the need to find dead things to eat. The smellier and more rotten the dead thing the better. For this reason, we generally return home from our trips together with all the car windows open. So, instead of the delights of Coire Lair we returned to the east, past Garve and down to the attractively named Alltan Dubh, the Blackwater River. The Forestry Commission has waymarked some footpaths that visit the Falls of Rogie so we took advantage of the forest's shelter from the wind and rain to visit the rain-swollen river and waterfalls.

Affric vanished within minutes of us leaving the car park and eventually reappeared dragging the leg of a dead roe deer. Judging by the smell the beast had been dead for some time, but Affric was aquiver with excitement. I think he expected me to congratulate him on his putrid find.

The Falls of Rogie area is part of the Forestry Commission's Torr Achilty Forest, which covers some 13,000 acres of Easter Ross. The Blackwater River rises high on the slopes of Beinn Dearg, some 65 kilometres away and runs down into Loch Vaich where it contributes to the huge Glascarnoch hydro scheme. A series of tunnels carries the waters from Loch Vaich to Loch Glascarnoch, and down to Mossford Power Station on Loch Luichart. The Blackwater River itself flows out of Loch Garve and eventually meets up with the River Conan just south-east of Contin.

The Forestry Commission has created a number of forest trails, all of which visit the rather impressive falls and salmon ladder. The route we chose took a nice meandering line through mixed woodland of birch, rowan, hazel, oak and alder. This is the type of woodland I enjoy, the narrow path twisting and turning between rocks that could be up to eight hundred million years old. This whole area is made of Moine Schists, formed when huge forces of heat and pressure built up deep within the earth's core, folding and changing the surface of the land.

The path soon drops to the river, flowing softly and rather stately at this point, but it doesn't take long for things to change. Within a quarter of a mile it takes on a new urgency as it approaches the chasm over which the waters tumble. The name Rogie means a splashing, foaming river although the falls themselves aren't high. When the river's in spate, as it was today, it's pretty impressive. The spectacle is improved by a suspension bridge that has been slung across the river just downstream of the falls. Ideal for photography.

The suspension bridge gives access to the east bank of the river where another track climbs up through the forest to meet up with a broad forest ride. If you go to the left the track will take you to Garve while Contin lies just less than two miles in the opposite direction. That's the route we took, high above the river with distant views of the Strath Conon hills. Eventually we dropped down to Contin where a riverside trail took us back towards Rogie Falls and Creag an Fhithich, the Raven's Crag, where I spent a pleasant ten minutes looking over the gorge and considering the multiple uses of this Blackwater River: as a clear flight path through the craggy landscape for ducks and water birds, as a source of power for hydroelectric use and as a watercourse for Atlantic salmon returning to their spawning grounds every year via the salmon ladder beside the falls. As I contemplated the views Affric was violently sick.

CHAPTER EIGHT

Mountain Folk

Life has a curious cyclic quality and, from my eyrie of advancing age, I occasionally reflect on my teenage years as an athlete and the hours spent in physical training, eating properly, stretching muscles and treating my body as a well-oiled machine. When my passion for track and field athletics began to wane and was replaced by a growing enthusiasm for climbing, among the things that fascinated and attracted me to the outdoor life were the climbers themselves. They were less disciplined than track-and-field athletes but still focussed; they didn't work out in gymnasiums but outdoors in magnificently wild places; they smoked, boozed and didn't obsess about calories but were strong and fit. What attracted me most was their rebellious and unconforming nature. There was something of James Dean's *Rebel Without a Cause* about them.

To a young lad, easing his way out of the controlled, disciplined and highly organised world of competitive athletics, climbers were a breed apart. My good friend, the climber and writer Jim Perrin summed it up, 'they had a sense of the metaphysical dimension, the spiritual travail of risky freedom, that's played out in the climbing, lived through in the life. They knew that richness and defiance.' Put simply, the mountaineers enjoyed a sense of freedom and I wanted to be part of that liberal, anarchic hill-going culture.

In time it became clear this newly cherished culture was as reactionary and illiberal as any kind of community where competition and winning creates a success-based hierarchy. The climbing world had its own heroes and villains, trends and paranoias, and was essentially as competitive as any sport can be, it was just less obvious. There were no bugles or drums, and certainly no trophies or medals.

In the thirty or forty years since, the popularity of climbing walls and entry to the grossly commercial world of Olympic competition has promoted the competitive status of climbing into an international sport. The circle has closed. Today's competition climbers are athletes, as disciplined, diet-obsessed and dominated by the rulebook as I was in my days as a long jumper and sprinter. Some climbers rarely venture outside, on real rock, but are content to swarm up artificial walls, as obsessed in achievement as I was as an athlete. Today's climbing rebels now have a cause – an Olympic medal.

Hillwalkers obsess in their own way: about the height of hills, what hills are summits or tops and how many they can climb in a day. Fashion and the latest fads and 'colourways' dominate the outdoor magazines just as the summit selfies dominate the Facebook and Twitter pages, the new brand markers of success when, for many, the hills have become a sporting arena rather than a place of quiet contemplation. Before anyone accuses me of being a curmudgeonly old greybeard I should point out that I've done all that myself. Indeed, I'm probably as fixated on social media as anyone. I obsessed on Munros and Corbetts (Munroist 913) and I like to wear the trendy gear. I've been there, done that and have the latest Patagonia hat to prove it. What I don't particularly enjoy is the competition, but perhaps I've just had enough of that in my life.

Thankfully, there is still a strong element of the 'metaphysical dimension' in the broad world of mountaineering and long may it continue. Despite maturing into a curmudgeonly old greybeard I still love to meet up with mountain folk. I enjoy blethering about the hills, comparing experiences and routes, gossiping about who has done this and that, discussing places I haven't visited and hearing recommendations about places to go. Indeed, I've been richly blessed throughout my working life in the outdoor industry and a large part of that blessing has been meeting mountain folk from all nationalities and walks of life. These folk have enriched my life and the majority of my closest friends are among them: mountaineers and climbers, mountain photographers, film makers, writers and artists. Some are household names, some less well known, but all are bound in close community, in kinship, by our common love of wild places. By the very nature of our chosen activity, such folk tend to be strong individuals and are big on self-reliance, sharing a sense of responsibility for the environment and for the planet. As if to emphasise that self-reliance, many of us have sacrificed normal careers and lifestyles to spend more time doing those things we love most. Perhaps it's not surprising there is such a strong camaraderie and, although I tend to hike alone, that sense of community, the awareness of belonging, is very important to me.

Over the years I've enjoyed the company of regular hiking companions, including my good wife it has to be said, but generally speaking I'm happy to be on my own. I can walk at my own pace and don't have to change plans to suit others. Sure, I know that going solo to the hills doesn't suit everyone and most folk prefer company, some even prefer to walk with a large group of people, to have a good day out with mates, and that's absolutely fine, but for a number of reasons I choose to walk alone. I walk much slower than I used to, and don't like to hold people up, but I also like to stop and stare and enjoy the wonder of the moment, and what a wonderful concept that is. Plato referred to 'wonder' as the origin of philosophy: a sensing of the mysteries that surround us and within us, a reflection on the deeper meanings of simple concepts and experiences, like resting on a mountain top or leaning against an age-wrinkled pine tree in the forest. And that's an experience best enjoyed alone.

One of the real joys of being a mountain writer is meeting and occasionally interviewing other members of the community, folk with a good story to tell. Sometimes they are well known, more times they are not, but all contribute to the great store of knowledge that has been created about the mountain environment and the people who climb. My job has been to add to that expanding archive, through books, television programmes, magazine and newspaper articles and, as I've looked back through my various newspaper columns and chosen stories about people I've known in the outdoor world, I've realised what a disparate bunch they are. From all walks of life, they have had different ambitions and desires. I could probably have written a complete book about the wonderful individuals I've met over the years, but I've had to choose just ten. Amongst them is mention of the best hillwalking companion I ever had.

ALISON HARGREAVES
AUGUST 1995

It was nine years ago, almost to the day. Julie Tullis, a mountaineer, wife and mother from Kent, died on the stormbound slopes of K2 after becoming the first British woman to climb the notorious Himalayan peak. According to her companion, veteran mountaineer Kurt Diemberger, Julie had become obsessed by this, the second highest mountain in the world.

Julie's husband Terry, who runs a small outdoor gear shop in Bowles in Kent, has always been philosophical about Julie's death and takes an enormous pride in her mountaineering achievements. His experience in coming to terms with the 'other love' in her life is absorbing, and offers an interesting insight into lives where the normal values of family are set aside for more immediate ambitions.

Like Julie Tullis, Alison Hargreaves reached the summit of K2 and, like Julie, she died on the descent. I don't believe Alison Hargreaves shared Julie's obsession with K2. In talking to her at some length only a few months ago I was aware of a burning ambition for success, but that success wasn't limited to one mountain. She simply wanted to be one of the great climbers in the world, irrespective of sex. Alison believed wholeheartedly that, in terms of endurance and coping with the thin air of altitude, women could climb on equal terms with men. I believe she was correct.

What about her children, the question that seeks to lay on her an irresponsibility, a denial of the maternal instinct? The politically correct thing to say is that fathers can go off adventuring and return as heroes while mothers run up the charge of abandoning their children, but while examining this issue it's important to bear something in mind. Alison loved her children with a drive and a passion, and her emotional words when she dedicated her Everest climb to them had a deeper and much more meaningful symbolism. Her children were part of the reason she climbed: she wanted to be successful for them, and for them to be proud of her achievements.[1]

On a more pragmatic level, she realised that success on the world's highest mountains would bring a level of affluence that few mountaineers achieve. She was using her God-given talents and abilities, the thing that she was best at, to earn a living. Working as a team with her husband Jim, Alison climbed commercially, realising that sponsorship would help allow her to continue to climb at a high standard in the greater ranges of the world while, at the same time, helping to provide a good standard of living for her family. In this she was no different from women golfers, athletes or other sportswomen who go abroad for lengthy periods of time.

The glaring difference, of course, is that mountaineering is dangerous. A mountain like K2 is highly dangerous, and it's hard for people to understand what makes mountaineers take such risks, but part of the skill is to minimise that risk as much as possible. Mountaineers are not nutters with a death wish, far from it. Most embrace life with a passion. They love life and live it to the full and much of that vibrancy stems from their love of mountains and wild places. Alison Hargreaves loved life. She was happy, vivacious, vibrant with life. She was a wonderful ambassador for the sport of mountaineering, and a mother her children can be proud of.

---

1. Alison's 31-year-old son, Tom Ballard, died on Nanga Parbat in March 2019. He was the first mountaineer to climb the six major Alpine north faces solo in a single winter season.

BENNY ROTHMAN
FEBRUARY 1995

This week I spent a fascinating evening with an eighty-three-year-old rambler by the name of Benny Rothman. Sixty-three years ago Benny organised a mass trespass on Kinder Scout in the English Peak District in protest against forbidden access to the high rolling moorlands.

Benny knew what he was about when he organised the event. He knew the police would be out in force and that the gamekeepers would be armed with staffs and sticks. He also knew the police would be waiting for him at the railway station in Manchester to stop him turning up at the event in Hayfield, so he cycled there instead.

The event took place and the ramblers were peaceful but Benny, and some others, were arrested and charged with 'riotous assembly'. To this day it is generally believed that these were trumped up charges because an example had to made. Benny served four months in Derby gaol.

In the years that followed, the will of the ramblers prevailed and large areas of common land were opened up for the enjoyment of all, rather than just the privileged few, but many areas in England and Wales are still forbidden to walkers.[2]

Listening to Benny's story I realised that there are many chilling similarities between the Britain of 1932 and today. The country was in depression, there was high unemployment and many working-class people found solace in the fresh air and freedom of the wild places. Here in Scotland, where the numbers were lower and the wild land bigger, there were fewer problems

---

2. The situation changed radically in Scotland on the creation of the Scottish Parliament in 1999. In 2003 the Land Reform (Scotland) Act was passed and included legislation that created a freedom to roam in Scotland. I think it's fair to suggest that without the creation of the Scottish Parliament Scotland would never have had National Parks or such world-beating access legislation; the landowning members of the House of Lords would have seen to that.

but, down south, particularly in the Peak District, surrounded as it is by the huge conurbations of Lancashire and Yorkshire, people were aware that they could be prosecuted for trespass. They were willing to risk that.

Now sixty-three years after that Kinder Trespass, a new piece of legislation, the Criminal Justice Act, makes it a criminal offence for a person to 'disrupt any lawful outdoor activity', to use 'abusive or insulting words to a landowner' or for a camper, when asked to move on by a landowner, to refuse to do so. Walkers can become criminals for going into the countryside as a group to protest what they believe to be unfair or unjust. In essence, the circle has fully turned, and protesters can once again face a gaol sentence, just as Benny Rothman did all those years ago.

So I thought, but Benny corrected me. He reminded me that the police had to trump up charges to jail him for, even in those dark days of the Depression, trespass wasn't a criminal offence. This Tory landowner-loving government, however, has done what even its predecessors didn't dare, and have made 'aggravated trespass', as outlined above, a criminal offence. Things are now worse than they were sixty-three years ago.

The landowners' representative body claim they wouldn't use the new powers against walkers, but several individual landowners have said they would. The Law Society of Scotland have said the new law could be used against walkers, and the Ramblers' Association solicitor Gerry Pearlman has said that walkers and ramblers now face a very real threat indeed.

Here in Scotland, hillwalkers must be careful not to disrupt a deer stalk, for it could be construed as disrupting a lawful activity, with prosecution and a possible gaol sentence following. Even if the walker disrupts the stalk accidentally, the onus is then on him to prove it was an accident – very difficult if there are signs warning of deer stalking by the roadside. It's a pernicious situation, and all walkers can really hope for at the moment is a change of Government as soon as possible.

CHRIS TOWNSEND
SEPTEMBER 1996

On a cold but sunny day last week, 118 days after setting out from Ben More on the Isle of Mull, Grantown on Spey author and photographer Chris Townsend strode to the summit of Ben Hope in Sutherland to become the first person to walk all the Munros, and their tops, in one continuous expedition.

And what an expedition it was, over 1700 miles of it, but amazingly this wasn't Chris's longest. In recent years he's hiked the Pacific Crest Trail and the Continental Divide in the USA, each over 2000 miles, but the American walks pale into insignificance when you consider that, on this walk, he climbed an astonishing 550,000 feet. Almost nineteen Everests!

In 1891, when Sir Hugh Munro published his Munros Tables, he divided the summits in his list, without explaining the criteria on which he based his definitions, into Separate Mountains and Subsidiary Tops, writing that 'the exact number cannot be determined, owing to the impossibility of deciding what should be considered distinct mountains'. Today, the revised list contains 277 Munros and 240 Tops, a total of 517 summits in all, and although there have been about fifteen continuous rounds of the Munros, no-one has ever walked all the Munros and the Tops in one trip.

Chris Brasher, who supplied Brasher Boots for the trip, and I joined Chris for his last Munro, and were impressed that, even after 118 days, he showed little sign of accumulated fatigue.

'I found that after about ten days my body would slow down and would begin to tire, so generally I would take a rest day every ten days or so, depending on the weather. I think it makes sense to rest when the weather is bad,' Chris told me. Those rest days were important, not only to restore strength but to read his way through some three hundred books. 'I got through a book every two or three days,' he said. 'I'm quite a fast reader!'

It was on one of those rest days that Chris reached his

lowest ebb, fairly early on. 'I was camped in a glen just below the Arrochar Alps,' he recalled. 'I remember waking up in the morning and it was drizzling, the midges were out and the glen in front of me was criss-crossed with power lines. There were road works going on close by and I just wondered what the hell I was doing there. I was almost overwhelmed by the enormity of what was ahead of me and it was the closest I came to chucking it.'

Chris also endured a wet and windy summer, with rain falling (enough rain to make him wear his waterproofs) on sixty-eight of the days. But it was the wind which took the greatest toll. During June and July, he was blown from the hills on several occasions.

So, what's next? A good rest, preferably on a beach with some hot sunshine? 'That's unlikely,' reckons Chris. 'Four months is a long time without getting any work done, so it looks like I'll be sitting down at the word processor in the next few days. There will be a book about the trip eventually, but meanwhile I've got a lot of work to catch up on.'

DONNIE MUNRO
JUNE 1998

There was a poignancy about the fact that the same week the rock band Run Rig were auditioning for a new lead singer, I was wandering the hills of Skye with their old vocalist, hearing of his hopes and ambitions for his new life without the band.

I was more than aware of a certain amount of emotion and sentimentality surrounding our chats, but they didn't come from Donnie Munro. I was the one who felt a little sad, for I've been a Runrig fan for a long time and, like many others, I will find it hard to contemplate the finest band to come out of Scotland for generations without him leading the line-up. But Donnie is more pragmatic in his outlook. At the age of forty-five he felt it was time for a change, for both him and the band, and by pursuing his other interests the others would be given an opportunity to take a different direction as well. One activity Donnie hopes to find more time for is wandering the hills and glens of his native Skye.

'I've grown up with this landscape,' he told me as we began our walk from Sligachan to Elgol. 'As a youngster going to school we would see the Cuillin in all her moods and sometimes we would be late because we just stood and stared at the wonder of it.'

At the age of fifteen Donnie became involved with the Skye Mountain Rescue Team. Some youngsters had gone missing and a policeman was rounding up every able-bodied person for the search. 'I was desperate to help,' he recalled, 'but my mother would have none of it. She said I was too young to be out on the mountains in bad weather, so I suggested to her that, if it was me who was missing, she would be gathering up every single person in the village for the search. She couldn't argue with that.'

His involvement with the mountain rescue team gave Donnie a keen awareness of the mountains and all their moods, an awareness that he believes is part and parcel of his native Gaelic culture. His love of the Gaelic language, the music and culture of the western highlands, and the landscape, are inextricably tied together and, if his ambitions as a politician come to fruition, he will be fighting tooth and nail for land reform in Scotland, come the Scottish Parliament.

In the last election he stood as a Labour candidate for his home constituency, and narrowly lost to the sitting member, the Liberal Democrats' Charles Kennedy. Come next May, he will be standing again, and hopefully for the Skye and West Inverness-shire seat.[3]

'I was born and brought up here,' he told me, 'and I desperately want to represent this constituency in the new Scottish Parliament. I left Skye at the age of seventeen to study at Grey's School of Art in Aberdeen and, after living there, Inverness and

3. After two narrow election losses Donnie relinquished his political ambitions to continue in his role at Sabhal Mor Ostaig. On a happier note, he has continued to perform as a solo artist.

Edinburgh, I came home to Skye again fairly recently. This is where I belong.'

At the moment, Donnie is Development Director at Sabhal Mor Ostaig, the Gaelic College on Skye which is now part of the new Highlands and Islands University. A new campus is in the process of being built, with buildings lining the coastline of Sleat and looking across the sea to the hills of Knoydart and Glenelg, an evocative and magnificent setting. Regular meetings with planners and builders, and endless fundraising, is a far cry from being a Highland Spice Boy, but Donnie Munro is more than content with his lot. On a recent visit to London, he was invited to a private meeting with Tony Blair. On entering the room, the Prime Minister shook his hand and commented how ironic life was. Here he was, someone who had wanted to be a rock singer all his life, meeting a rock singer who wanted to be a politician. I suspect Donnie will become a politician, and I suspect a damned good one at that.

BESS
JUNE 2000

My wife told me I probably love my dogs more than I love people, and I admit to a certain ring of truth in the accusation. In old Bess's case it was certainly correct.

For over a dozen years she was my constant companion. The only time she didn't trot along by my side was when I had to visit towns or cities. I never wanted to inflict that experience on her, but otherwise she was like a shadow. She was a quiet dog, a black Labrador but small for her breed.

I don't think I heard her bark more than a couple of dozen times in her life and the only time she was tempted into disobedience was when she found a pond of water. Bess should have been born with flippers; she loved to swim in any pond or pool, sea or ocean, and that was her only vice. When she swam, she liked to splash the water with her paws and then try and catch the drops in her mouth, an odd little routine that she loved enormously.

Unfortunately, from a distance, it looked as though she was in difficulty, and occasionally well-meaning people in boats would try to rescue her. On one occasion my late stepfather, taking Bess for a walk by Loch Insh, allowed her to go for a swim and was so convinced she was drowning he tried to wade out to rescue her, putting his own life at risk. He couldn't swim.

For twelve years she was a hill-dog, the perfect hill-dog. She walked by my side to a sharp command of 'here a'hint', and she would stay there all day if necessary, wearing a little dent behind my right knee with her polished nose. She was oblivious to sheep, chased nothing but splashes in a pond, and rarely ranged wide. She had a remarkable ability on steep rock and often found routes up the steepest of crags. All I had to do was follow her. Curiously, she appeared to be as fond of my company as I was of hers.

Her last mountain walk was on A'Chailleach in the Monadhliath and that night she stiffened up badly. For various reasons she hadn't been on the hill for a while, and she suffered for it. For a long time she made me suffer too. Every time I put my boots on she would place her head on my knee and plead with me to take her. I felt as though I was betraying her and for a long time my sorties to the hills felt incomplete.

But Bess had a forgiving nature. When I came home she was always there waiting, her tail wagging and love lighting her eyes. Her affection for me could not be concealed and I'll never know what I did to deserve it. Even in more recent years when her eyesight was failing, her instincts seemed to tell her when I was home and her welcome, although more subdued, was no less affectionate. Her basket sat below my desk and, even as I write this, I'm aware that she isn't curled around my feet as usual.

Over the past six years her walks became shorter and shorter and at the grand old age of eighteen we had to make the painful decision to end her life. She had become stone deaf and blinded by cataracts and her rear quarters had wasted away, with all the subsequent loss of dignity that entails. It wasn't an easy decision to make, in fact it was a bloody heart-rending experience that left me in tears, and I hope I never have to make that sort of decision about ending a human life.

Bess died peacefully, after a stroll and a sniff around her garden. She slept away quietly, albeit aided by an overdose of whatever it is the vet gave her, as gentle at the point of death as she was in life.

SYD SCROGGIE
FEBRUARY 2001

Congratulations to poet, author and mountain man Syd Scroggie who is to be awarded an honorary degree from Dundee University. The award, a Doctor of Laws degree, is in recognition of the example he has set to others by overcoming his disabilities. Despite a tin leg and being blind Syd has climbed the hills and mountains of Scotland almost all his life, and has written an excellent book and scores of poems about his love affair with the wild places.

I'll never forget our first meeting. I had been asked by BBC Radio Scotland to visit him at his home in Strathmartine, just outside Dundee, and interview him about a book he had written. Before I left home I phoned for directions. 'Nae bother man,' he told me. 'Jist get tae Strathmartine and ask anyone where the blind auld bugger lives.'

When I arrived in the village I saw a man working in his garden. 'Could you tell me where Syd Scroggie lives?' I shouted from my car. The man looked up. 'Ye've found him,' he said. 'Jist reverse your car back through the gate. I'll give you directions.'

So, there I was, reversing my car through a narrow gate when I suddenly remembered the stocky character I was watching in my wing mirror giving me explicit directions was completely blind!

During the Second World War, in Italy, just two weeks before the end of the war, Syd, at that time one of Scotland's most prolific climbers, was blown up by a landmine and lost a leg

1. Approaching Loch Errochty

2. Arkle, on the Sutherland Trail

3. Ben Tianavaig

4. By the Falls of Glomach

5. Cairn Toul and Sgurr an Lochain Uaine from Braeriach

6. Climbing Can a'Chlamain from Glen Tilt

7. Could Scotland's only reindeer herd be at risk because of climate change?

8. Eaval, North Uist

9. *En route* to Loch Dubh

10. Gylen Castle, Kerrera

11. Looking back towards the Cheviot

12. Looking south from the slopes of Ben Nevis

13. Looking towards Beinn Macdhui from Braeriach

14. Luxuriant Scots Pines in Glen Feshie

15. On the South West Coast Path in Cornwall

16. The bothy at Burnmouth, Rackwick Bay

17. The highly controversial mountain railway on Cairngorm

18. The Old Man of Hoy; some of the most amazing scenery on Orkney

19. The scrambling section below Carnedd Llewellyn

20. The Stack of Handa

21. The Table, in the heart of the Quiraing

22. Tryfan, from the slopes above Helyg

23. Upper Glen Feshie, rewilded and flourishing

and his sight. He was, as he recalls, fairly pragmatic about the accident. 'Stood on a landmine – bloody silly thing to do. There was light, then darkness. I can live without my sight, but never without my mountains.'

As we sat and chatted about his life one thing became apparent. Syd Scroggie is only blind in his eyes. His perceptions, his understandings, his awareness of movement and, above all, his imagination are as far-seeing as anyone's, more so than most, and when you talk to Syd his language is full of sight.

'Man, it was a great day! There were icicles hanging from every rock, the deer were richt doon by the roadside and white hares on the slopes. The ptarmigan were well camouflaged against the snow and the ice-crusted burn was aye chuckling.'

He relates his experiences with burning enthusiasm – those things he has seen through his other senses, and through the eyes of his walking companion, his wife Margaret whom he married following the death of his first wife in 1980.

For over forty years he has seen the sights of the Angus Glens and his beloved Cairngorms through the eyes of others. After a lengthy convalescence from his accident he was determined to return to the mountains. So, in 1958 he put the following advert in a Dundee newspaper:

> Blind hill man, due to senescence, indolence, hibernation, or house arrest of friends, requires patient, hardy companion for Clova weekend. Abominable snowman (tent trained) admirably suited, but no guide dogs need apply. Accommodation cramped; conditions appalling, hours endless, wages nil...

He returned to the hills with a succession of 'pairs of eyes', and tramped them for many years, becoming something of a celebrity. He has published several books and many poems about the Scottish hills, and appeared on the television programme *This Is Your Life*, but it seems he was surprised when told of the degree.

'I suppose I'm getting it because they think I'm some sort of example. It came as a bolt from the blue, but no-one could have been more delighted.'

Syd will receive his Doctor of Laws degree at a ceremony in July and no-one deserves it more.

FAY GODWIN
NOVEMBER 2003

A number of years ago I reviewed a book of stark, black and white photographs by a photographer who had just become President of the Ramblers' Association. Previous RA Presidents had been extremely vocal, campaigning, political-type figures but Fay Godwin's approach was different, as was this book she had just published.

Our Forbidden Britain, for that was the book's title, wasn't a documentation of lovely, pastoral scenes; of hedgerows and downland, moorland and mountain, but more accurately identified the realities of how we treat our countryside.

There were photographs of electricity pylons, goose-stepping their way across otherwise untainted landscapes. There were images of nuclear power stations, barbed-wire fences, overgrazed hill slopes, illegal fly tips, abandoned and rusting cars.

I remember that book made a powerful statement and, if a picture paints a thousand words, then Fay Godwin said infinitely more than her rather verbose presidential predecessors. I have to say that many of Fay's other books beautifully portray the more pleasant aspects of our landscape, and indeed encourage many people to go and see that beauty for themselves, but *Our Forbidden Britain* made an impact, not only with RA members, but with the public. People became aware that the 'green and pleasant land' was in dire need of first aid and, in some cases, emergency surgery.

Last week, I visited an exhibition of Fay's work in the National Portrait Gallery in Edinburgh and was once again reminded of how fine a photographer she is. What separates Fay Godwin's work from that of other landscape photographers is that each of her images makes a direct appeal to the viewers' senses, and shares something of the passion that informs her output. That passion, and a deep concern for the landscape, is blindingly obvious, or why else would such a talented photographer spend so much time recording stark images of land that has been closed to the public for selfish or commercial reasons? Why else collect such impressions of barbed wire strung across public footpaths, or keep-out signs, or once beautiful landscapes that have been mauled, scoured and pockmarked by military training?

It's because she cares. Because, like a visionary, she recognised that we have very few, if any, authentic wilderness areas, nothing of the bare and primeval landscapes that can be found in other countries, nothing that has remained untouched by agriculture, forestry, or urban growth, despite the fact that the British countryside, although largely artificial in landscape terms, was once regarded as a heavenly place, where farming and wildlife coexisted, a land that inspired artists and poets to tell the world that here, in this little island in northern Europe, was a fine example of a place where a dense population of humans could coexist harmoniously with nature.

Because of this vision, and the ability she had to touch people's hearts and minds through her photographs, Fay Godwin was an inspired choice to be President of the Ramblers' Association. This organisation, with its roots in the mass trespasses and socialist ideals of the thirties, along with a number of other non-government organisations, has steadfastly called for a more measured and sustainable management of the mountain and wild land environment in ways that recognise the needs and aspirations of the human communities who live there. This community involvement also features strongly in Fay's exhibition in Edinburgh. There are portraits of hill farmers, shepherds, keepers, shopkeepers – all those worthies of rural life, those who still hear the echoes of the land's call on their lives.

I suspect many people who go to the mountains and wild places still faintly hear those echoes in their own lives, and I have little doubt that photographs like Fay Godwin's might furnish a reminder of that elemental connection; that we are part of the web of life that we tritely call nature, connected to the rock and the air and the water of pre-life.

HEAVY WHALLEY
AUGUST 2007

Last week, the man known as Mr Mountain Rescue, David 'Heavy' Whalley MBE, BEM, retired from the RAF after thirty-five years of service, almost all of them with the Mountain Rescue Team.

I first met Heavy about twenty years ago, when I interviewed him for a radio programme. I bumped into him again when he climbed Ben Lomond with me in 1996 when I was celebrating the completion of my second round of the Munros and, at the same time, launching a book on the Munros, and spoke to him most recently when he was coordinating a search on the Rubha Mor peninsula in Wester Ross.

During an amazing career, Heavy has been involved in over a thousand mountain rescues and over eighty aircraft incidents in mountainous areas. He has also been a member of the Executive of the Scottish Mountain Rescue Committee for over twenty years, serving for three years as Chairman. In 2002 he was awarded the Distinguished Service Award for Service to Mountain Rescue.

A son of the (Church of Scotland) manse, he grew up in Ayrshire and learned to climb hills with his brothers and sisters under the care of their minister father. He joined the RAF in 1971 as a caterer and was posted to Kinloss to serve his first tour of duty. His first application to join the RAF MR team was rejected as, at seven stone, he was considered too light to join. He persevered and in February 1972, after passing the test, he finally joined the team, earning the nickname 'Heavy', which has stuck with him throughout his career.

In that same year he had his first experience of tragedy. On a search of Five Finger Gully on Ben Nevis for a missing French honeymoon couple, he was one of the first on scene and, as a very young lad, had to cope with not only the tragic death of the woman but also her distraught husband. Still in 1972 he attended a Viscount crash near Crianlarich with the loss of three airmen, and narrowly escaped death when he tumbled down a mountainside in an avalanche.

Over the years he has become a kenspeckle figure in Scottish mountaineering circles. He has climbed all of Scotland's Munros seven times and traversed the Scottish Highlands, from coast to coast, four times, two of them in winter. He has also participated in over thirty RAF expeditions to the Alps, Iran, Turkey, India, Nepal and Pakistan and was Base Camp Manager for the RAF Mountain Rescue Team's ascent on Everest in 2001. Seeing two fellow team members, Dan Carroll and Rusty Bale, make it to the top was a real highlight. He had trained Rusty in hillwalking skills in the early years of his mountaineering career.

'I have loved the mountains ever since my first hillwalk with my father and the more I have got into it the more I have loved it. The Mountain Rescue Team has a difficult job to do often in terrible conditions but the elation of finding people alive is fantastic and I'll miss it. I'll definitely miss the troops.'

There's little doubt that his colleagues at Kinloss will miss his indomitable spirit, his sense of humour and, probably most of all, his desire to help others. His very last job was coordinating the airlift of a heart transplant to London to save a baby's life. The last call he took before going off-shift was to hear that the plane had landed and the heart had arrived at the hospital. He was later delighted to hear that the baby had gone on to make a full recovery.

THE LADIES SCOTTISH CLIMBING CLUB
NOVEMBER 2007

I remember wandering the hills with the late Tom Weir when he asked me why I had never become a member of the Scottish Mountaineering Club. 'Never been invited', was my retort.

At that time Tommy was President of the SMC and he offered to propose me for membership. I didn't think much more of it until a few weeks later when it turned out there had been some embarrassment at the annual SMC dinner. It's traditional for the club to invite the president of 'kindred clubs' but that year one of the invited clubs had a female president. When this woman and her friend turned up there was widespread panic amongst some of the Club's older members. The Scottish Mountaineering Club, a men-only organisation, had never had a woman guest at their dinner before.

I found all this rather amusing and wrote about it, suggesting perhaps it was time the SMC dropped its Victorian attitude towards women and allowed females to become members of one of Scotland's most senior mountaineering clubs. A few days later Tom Weir telephoned me, said he had read my editorial and told me he wouldn't now propose me as an SMC member.

The SMC has since softened its stance and allowed women to join. I don't believe Tommy Weir was, in any way or form, a misogynist, or that he was coming from an anti-female stance. His lovely wife, Rhona, was a very active supporter of another of Scotland's senior clubs, the Ladies Scottish Climbing Club, and Tom simply felt that the women already had a club of their own and didn't want to see its membership affected in any way.

Next year is the centenary of that club, Scotland's oldest female-only mountaineering club. Women from all over Scotland will take part in a mass female assault on the Buachaille Etive Mor in Glencoe in May, after which many will disappear into the mountains for a hundred-and-fifty-mile wilderness walk. The Scottish celebrations will then be taken abroad as a female expedition sets out to tackle the peaks of Bolivia in July.

I remember speaking at an LSCC annual dinner a number of years ago, coming away with the thought that the ladies were a much more unruly bunch than their male counterparts in the SMC. It was a very lively affair, which I thoroughly enjoyed, and it was great to hear some of the climbing and mountaineering achievements of the members. These were certainly not women who merely followed their husbands or boyfriends up routes. They were pushing the boundaries in their own right.

The Ladies Scottish Climbing Club was originally set up in 1908 by three frustrated female mountaineers who were banned from joining the Scottish Mountaineering Club. Reflecting the gathering momentum of the suffragette movement at the time, they took matters into their own hands and set up their own club. Since then, members have blazed trails around the world, tackling some of its most daunting peaks. In 1955 three members formed the first all-female expedition to explore and climb in the Himalaya, achieving the first ascent of Gyalgen Peak (6151m/22,000ft) in the Jugal Himal. With subsequent expeditions including Greenland, Arctic Norway and Ladakh, the club has now set its sights on the six-thousand-metre peaks of Bolivia.

Today, even with females now allowed to join the Scottish Mountaineering Club, the Ladies Scottish Climbing Club is as active as ever and I'm delighted about that. They have truly earned their place in the pantheon of Scottish mountaineering history.

IRVINE BUTTERFIELD
MAY 2009

The last time I spoke to Irvine Butterfield was to congratulate him on being awarded the John Muir Trust's Lifetime Achievement Award. It was only the fourth Award made by the JMT, and the calibre of past recipients – Tom Weir, Adam Watson and Doug Scott – just shows how highly Irvine was regarded.

In typical Butterfield fashion, he muttered his appreciation before telling me off for not fighting hard enough about the wind-farms that are being proposed in Highland Perthshire. He later relented and admitted that he was worried about travelling to the John Muir Trust event at which he was being presented with his award. 'I'm not at all well,' he told me. He certainly wasn't, and he sadly passed away last week after a long fight against cancer.

Most hillwalkers will have known, or at least heard of, Irvine Butterfield. He was a weel kent figure in the outdoors scene in Scotland. A big, burly and often gruff Yorkshireman, he adopted Scotland as his home when his work as an exciseman brought him to Dundee. From there he moved to Perth where his colleagues at Dewars whisky introduced him to the Perth Mountaineering Club.

I guess Irvine fitted the description of a hill gangrel. He wasn't an athletic man; you wouldn't have seen him dangling on the end of a rope on a hard rock climb, or running around all the Munros in a single expedition. He was more pedestrian than that, but his character had all the steadfastness of the rocks he wandered over, climbing the Munros, following the footsteps of drovers and whisky smugglers, and searching out the tales of the hills in which he became something of an expert.

Irvine Butterfield was always good company, whether it was sharing a dram in a remote bothy (Irvine always had a flask of decent malt with him), walking the hills, or sharing a table in some committee room or other, and he spent a lot of his spare time doing exactly that. He was a past secretary of the Mountain Bothies Association, an early member of the John Muir Trust, an honorary lifetime President of the Crollachan Mountaineering Club, a founding member of the Scottish Wild Land Group and first President of the Munro Society. Possibly more important than all of these was the fact that, once he had retired from his Customs and Excise job, Irvine spent a number of years working voluntarily in the offices of the Mountaineering Council of Scotland. He did more for Scottish mountaineering than anyone I know.

In 1971 he completed his round of the Munros, the 105th person to climb all of Scotland's 3000ft mountains. He later wrote what is regarded as the finest of all the guides to the Munros and other big hills: *The High Hills of Britain and Ireland*. That was later followed by two fine photographic books: *The Magic of the Munros*, and *The Call of the Corbetts*.

Despite his dedication to the cause of several conservation

organisations, Irvine was never slow to criticise when he thought criticism was warranted. Indeed, on occasions he had the capacity to whinge for England, but such whingeing was usually based on frustration when things weren't happening quickly enough. On several occasions we had opposing views on various matters but that was never enough to make Irvine fall out with anyone. I always regarded him as a firm friend and always enjoyed his visits when he was in the Newtonmore area. His great hero, John Muir, once suggested that we 'do something for wildness and make the mountains glad'. Well, Irvine Butterfield took those words to heart more than any person I know. He'll be sadly missed.

CHAPTER NINE

Around the Edges

He calls himself the Island Man and he became the first person to sleep on every Scottish island of a hundred acres or more. Andy Strangeway, from Pocklington in North Yorkshire, had his Road-to-Damascus moment as he read yachtsman Hamish Haswell-Smith's wonderful book, *Scottish Islands*. I'm sure Hamish never imagined his island descriptions would set a fire burning in the heart of this self-confessed landlubber and land-locked Yorkshireman, but it did. 162 Scottish islands of a hundred acres or more are described in the book and Andy Strangeway spent a night on all of them. His final island was Soay on the St Kilda archipelago.

He suggested to me his island-hopping could be the 'next big thing'.

'The obvious thing to compare it to is bagging Munros,' he said, 'but this will be bigger than Munros because it will appeal to a cross section of people, not just athletic young lads. I love it when people say I must be crazy as I'm not particularly athletic.'

The first island Andy visited was Barra, but that was a comparatively simple expedition. He went there by public ferry from Oban. There are about forty-six islands that can be reached by public ferry and another fifteen or sixteen where people live permanently, leaving a large number of uninhabited islands with no obvious way of reaching them.

'I really had to think about this,' said Andy. 'There's no way a chap is simply going to come along and offer to take you and your little pack to any island of your choice. To be dropped on an uninhabited island and picked up the next day puts a lot of pressure on these local boat lads.

When I reached the forty- or fifty-island mark, people were still a little suspicious but when I went over a hundred it was a total green light. I got permission from all the island owners and I was totally transparent about what I was doing. With that transparency a trust was built up and that became very evident in the later stages.'

According to Andy there are about forty or fifty islands that are not served by public ferries or tourist boats and that are almost impossible to reach by chartering a boat. 'They really gave me a headache,' he told me. 'I eventually solved the problem, but I'm keeping that under my hat. It's called intellectual property I believe!'

A significant number of the islands Andy slept on are uninhabited. 'To some people that sounds like a nightmare, but I'm perfectly happy in my own company,' he says. There are ninety-five inhabited islands in Scotland with a total population of just under 100,000. While the total population of island-dwellers has fallen, the number of inhabited islands has increased from the eighty-seven recorded in a previous census.

The excitement was evident in Andy's voice as he described his most memorable island, Boreray in the St Kilda archipelago. He talked with a fiery passion about being attacked by bonxies, glimpsing the other islands of St Kilda through the mist and rain and spending the night alone with tens of thousands of sea birds. No-one had stepped foot on Boreray for years.

'You land and immediately have a steep incline to climb for about 120 feet. My first experience of rock-climbing was on Boreray and I had no idea what I was doing. I didn't think I was going to get off the island alive because I couldn't find my way down. If I didn't have a GPS I would have gone five hundred feet off a cliff. I've got no sense of direction.'

I know a number of Munro 'completers' who have taken up island-bagging once their hill days were over. I'm a bit of an island enthusiast myself but I've never quite promoted that enthusiasm into bagging mode.

My interest in islands is more or less confined to the hills I can climb on, or the coastal walks they offer, and that's what I've tried to reflect in the following essays. Just like our mountain ranges, Scotland's islands boast a wonderful diversity of landscape: Orkney and Shetland are completely different in character and in culture, and so different from the Western Isles. Even the Small Isles, albeit close together geographically, are incredibly different in nature. Eigg, Muck and Canna almost surround the larger isle of Rum, an island that boasts its own Cuillin ridge and what a mountain day it offers! The Isle of Skye boasts some of the best mountains in the country as well as the high and rolling escarpment of Trotternish but, much further south, in the waters of the Firth of Clyde, the Isle of Arran almost competes with the Cuillin in terms of a mountain range with tight, narrow ridges and vertiginous drops.

I've been lucky too, in that my television work has taken me to some of the more remote inhabited islands, like North Ronaldsay in Orkney, a remarkable place with its own bird-monitoring station or, closer to home, Handa Island off the north coast of Sutherland, a place of intense seabird breeding activity in the months of May and June, but probably the islands I know best are those of the Outer Hebrides. I've walked and cycled the length of the Outer Isles along the superb Hebridean Way, from Barra to the Butt of Lewis, and spent many happy hours exploring some of the byways of these wonderful islands. I think there will always be a small part of me that remains on the Isle of Harris. Here rise some of the most underestimated hills in Scotland. Rugged, rocky mountains that attract surprisingly few walkers. If you delve into the ancient byways that follow the glens, you'll come across ancient artefacts that underlie the spiritual history of these Outer Isles: the Holy Wells, the ancient ruins of chapels and 'teampaills', and the unusual sight of beehive shielings, curious small shelters that some scholars believe pre-date Christ.

Perhaps Andy Strangeway's notion of island-bagging will

encourage others to leave the hills behind for a while and take to their boats and kayaks. I really should get the maps out and check just how many I've visited.

ARRAN'S GOAT FELL
OCTOBER 1989

There's no better time to visit the Isle of Arran than early autumn. The woods around Brodick Castle glow gold in the evening light and the mountains echo to the roar of the red deer's annual rut.

I was due to give an audio/visual presentation in the evening, so I filled the afternoon with a wander up Goatfell, reluctantly turning my back on the delights, and fond memories, of the Cir Mhor – Beinn Tarsuinn traverse, the finest ridge in Scotland outside the Skye Cuillin and a place that was significant in my own mountaineering career.

During my talk I shared how the hills of Arran had played a vital role in my early mountaineering career for it was on that ridge, in the late nineteen sixties, that I first became intoxicated by the allure of the hills. It was a sun-soaked day and I had been thrilled by the tight and exposed crags and ridges – over Beinn Tarsuinn and Cir Mhor and the vertiginous delights of the A-Chir Ridge. My companions and I had spent too long on the sun-kissed granite, so we had to jog down the hill to catch our bus back to the Brodick ferry. As we loped down the hillside, exhilarated by our achievements on the narrow, exposed ridges, I made the decision that, somehow, I was going to spend the rest of my life amongst mountains. Ever since, the hills of Arran have been special to me.

The island has often been described as the 'highlands in miniature' but there's nothing miniature about its mountains. Beinn Tarsuinn, Cir Mhor, Caisteal Abhail and the island's highest hill, Goatfell, 874m, offer a challenge to any hill walker, no matter how experienced. These are serious mountains and Goatfell, although it's the highest, is also the easiest, and has a good path running all the way to its summit.

From the well-wooded castle policies, the path runs up through the heart of the hill's south-east corrie before emerging on the hill's Meall Breac ridge. From here the path quickly evaporates into a well-braided choice of routes, each little well-worn footpath easing its way upwards past slabs of granite and bristling spires of rock.

During my presentation I gently chastised my audience for allowing an English mountain name to dwell amongst the Gaelic. With names like Cir Mhor, A'Chir, Beinn Tarsuinn and Caisteal Abhail the name Goatfell jarred a little with someone like myself who believes it is important to cherish our Gaelic hill names. Later on, someone explained to me that the origins of Goat Fell were in fact Norse – geitar-fjall, and not Gaelic at all.

The view from the summit of Goatfell is varied and extensive. To the east and north-east the Firth of Clyde spreads out below. Beyond lies the Ayrshire coast, running all the way down to the Rhinns of Galloway and up towards the opening of Loch Long. Other islands include the Cumbraes and the Isle of Bute and the small island off the west coast of Bute is Inchmarnock, once known as the 'drunk man's island' because drunkards who persistently offended against Bute's laws of sobriety were banished there to serve a term of punishment.

To the west of Goatfell, across Glen Rosa, the rocky ridge of Beinn a' Chliabhain climaxes in the vertiginous slopes of Coire Daingean which, in turn, is joined to Cir Mhor by the great buttress of A'Chir. To the north lies Caisteal Abhail and the Ceum na Caillich, above Glen Sannox. Beyond Beinn a' Chliabhain lies Beinn Nuis and Beinn Tarsuinn. The view represents one of the finest concentrations of craggy mountains in all of Scotland.

THE PAPS OF JURA
NOVEMBER 1994

Jura is one of Scotland's more magical islands, highland in atmosphere but lying on the same longitudinal line as Glasgow.

It's about twenty-eight miles long by eight miles wide and the hills, the appropriately named Paps (breasts) of Jura, bunch together for protection in the southern half of the island. It's a curious geographical quirk that, from most directions, only two of three Paps are visible at a time, a fact that puzzles hillwalkers as they gaze across from Kintyre, or south from the Glen Coe hills. Those shapes drifting in the haze of the far horizon look like the Paps of Jura, but surely there are more than two of them? It's a common error.

Beinn a' Chaolais, 734m/2422ft, is the hill of the Sound of Kyle; Beinn an Oir, 785m/2590ft is the hill of gold and Beinn Siantaidh, 755m/2491ft, is the holy, or consecrated hill.

The quartzite domes of the three Paps are split by low cols and surrounded by low-lying moorland, much of which is extremely boggy. The name Jura is taken from the Norse words that mean deer island and the terrain is much more suited to those fleet-footed beasts than man. These are not easy hills by any means, and their traverse, including an add-on, Cora Bheinn, necessitates about 1645m/5400ft of climbing in about ten miles. A big day by any standard with many long slopes of greyish-white scree to negotiate.

The round begins at the bridge over the Corran River on the A846, the island's only road. Take a more or less direct line to the head of Loch an t-Siob, aiming right of a wood and across a shoulder, and down to the river just east of the outflow of the loch. From the head of the loch climb to the bealach left of the steep summit cone of Beinn a' Chaolais, then continue up steep quartzite rubble to the summit.

The route onwards starts easily enough on mossy ground, giving a false sense of security for the descent soon becomes tricky on shifting, unstable blocks. It feels like an unreasonably long descent to the bealach and, when you reach it, large quartzite blocks make the going difficult. It's almost a relief to get climbing again, up the scree-covered slopes to emerge onto the skyline to follow a pleasantly narrowing ridge to the summit. A causeway of stones continues north to the remains of some stone huts. There is difference in opinion as to the origins of the huts and causeway; some say they were built by observers who manned the summit during the Second World War, while others suggest they were created by Ordnance Survey workers during early triangulation work in the nineteenth century. From the huts, descend right towards the bealach below Beinn Shiantaidh: steeper slopes lower down can be outflanked by following a grassy terrace down to the right.

The ascent of Beinn Shiantaidh's west ridge is comparatively pleasant with another narrowing ridge leading to the summit. The views over the north of the island, towards the Corryvreckan and the island of Scarba, are magnificent. An early guidebook suggests you might be able to see both the Skye Cuillin and the Isle of Man, through 'dim to very dreaminess'.

At one time there was a box beside the cairn with a visitor's book in it, but I never found it. I did find the descent route though, even though its line is far from obvious. A lower cairn marks the route and then you must keep to the right, picking up a rather indistinct path that weaves its way through the quartz-ite rocks and screes. The bealach below Corra Bheinn will be welcome, keeping well to the right of its little lochan.

The ascent of Corra Bheinn, a lower 'fourth' Pap, is optional, but since it's less severe than the three Pap ascents it's worth going for. Descend eastwards to meet up with a path that offers an easy route back to the road.

ISLE OF KERRERA
SEPTEMBER 1995

We had been climbing a variety of Corbetts and Munros in the south-west highlands when rain and strong winds drove us off the high tops. As we drove up the coast towards Oban we post-poned plans of climbing Cruachan until the weather improved. Instead, we opted for a coastal walk, but one spiced with a touch of history, a pinch of tranquility and a definite feel of the Hebrides.

About five miles in length and forming a protective arm around the delightful Oban Bay, the island of Kerrera is separated from the mainland by a narrow channel, the Sound of Kerrera. Oban's bustling promenade and seafront was full of umbrellas and waterproofs as holidaymakers tried to make the most of the weather. In comparison, Kerrera could have been at the other end of the earth, such was its lush, green tranquillity. It's a hilly little island speckled with small crags, with a rocky coast where the seabirds wheel and skirl and seals pop their heads up to gaze at you, wide eyed and whiskered.

So, what of its history? Well, it was here, in 1249, that Alexander II of Scotland died of a fever when endeavouring to assert his authority on a race of people who regarded themselves as Norwegian, not Scots. The early inhabitants of Kerrera almost certainly saw King Haco's fleet of galleys join forces with the ships of the Lord of the Isles and those MacDougalls of Kerrera would have known that their direct ancestor was Loard, the brother of Fergus, who founded the ancient kingdom of Dalriada. Royal, certainly, was their race.

At the south end of the island lies the ruined castle of Gylen, a former stronghold of the MacDougalls. This Renaissance keep is perched on a rocky headland and is reached by a path from Lower Gylen. There are some interesting carvings on the north wall. An intriguing tunnel gives access through the castle to the cliff-girt headland beyond. Built in 1582 by the MacDougalls of Dunollie, Gylen Castle was destroyed in 1647 by General Leslie's Covenanting troops who carried off the famous Brooch of Lorne, an item of jewellery allegedly worn by Robert the Bruce in the fourteenth-century Battle of Dalrigh. Much later, the brooch was bought by General Duncan Campbell of Lochnell, who generously presented it back to the MacDougall family.

The island was also a staging post in the great cattle droves, when herds of black kye were landed on Kerrera en route from Mull to the mainland cattle trysts. They would have been landed at Port Dubh of Orasaig on the south-west of the island.

The interior of the island tends to be very hummocky, and

while the walk described is relatively low level it can be fairly strenuous. Once you land from the ferry turn left below the Ferry House and follow the road south towards Horseshoe Bay and then past the King's Field, or Dail Righ where Alexander II died. Continue past the Little Horseshoe Bay towards Upper Gylen, and then Lower Gylen. Just before you reach the farm-house leave the track through a gate on the left and follow another track that leads to the ruins of Gylen Castle above the twin bays of Port a'Chaisteil and Port a'Chroinn.

From the castle we followed the coast to Armore Bay where the main track can be rejoined. We passed the house at Ardmore and followed the old drove road above Port Phadruig to Barnabuck, the Ridge of the Roebucks. The route now weaved its way up over Am Maolan with superb views, despite the grey shrouds of rain that swept across the sea, up and down the length of the Firth of Lorne. On a clear day the hills of Glencoe, Ardgour and Morvern can be clearly seen in the north. From the high point the track drops gently downhill, past Balliemore, back to the ferry and the still bustling seafront of lovely Oban.

THE CARSAIG ARCHES
AUGUST 1998

A herd of feral goats grazed on the hillside only a few yards from where naturalist Dick Balharry and I lay against an old drystone wall. Some of the younger billies were locking horns in mock fights watched over by the full-bearded patriarch of the herd, a venerable old fellow like something out of the Book of Revelation.

Dick and I were enjoying a desultory wander along the coast of the Ross of Mull, between the tiny hamlet of Carsaig and one of the natural wonders of Mull, the Carsaig Arches. We had trawled the rock pools for crabs and starfish, identified a huge variety of seabirds and spent twenty minutes watching the astonishing aerobatics of a pair of golden eagles. This approach to the Carsaig Arches is only a four-mile walk and we were in danger of taking the entire day over it, below breathtaking cliffs with the rocky outline of the Garvellachs floating on the horizon of a crystal sea.

A couple of miles beyond Carsaig, a curious Sphinx-like rock stands guard over the hidden entrance to the Nun's Cave, or Uamh an Cailleachain, the cave of the old women. The entrance to the cave is partially hidden by a grass-covered bank. Tradition suggests that persecuted nuns, from Iona, were brought here for safety during the times of the Reformation. It's a large cave and according to an old account is capable of sheltering some three hundred people.

Carvings adorn the walls, mostly Celtic crosses, but it's difficult to make out those of antiquity from more modern graffiti. The oldest date that can be recognised is 1633 and, near the back of the cave, Dick found a clear carving of a sailing ship. Who knows how old it is? Dick also pointed out the mark of a mason. It's thought that stone used to build the Abbey Church on Iona was taken from this cave; indeed the quarrying here was worked from the Middle Ages right through until last century.

From the cave it's about an hour's walk to Malcolm's Point and the Carsaig Arches themselves. The coastline becomes increasingly wild the further you go west, and we gazed out to the dim outlines of Jura, Islay and Colonsay. Suddenly the path crosses a tableland of rock to a deep inlet where the sea surges into the first of the two Arches, a headland of columnar basalt with a sea cave that has eroded right through the rock like a tunnel. To the right a narrow track climbs up around a steep headland – the path is fairly exposed here – and drops steeply to a secluded bay where you can actually walk much of the way through the first arch. The other arch stands close by, a Cyclopean gateway through a tall and slim sea stack. Beyond lies an enormous table of rock known as Leac na Leum, the slab of the leap.

The return route above the cliffs involves a scramble on loose rock up Binnein Ghorrie, the next obvious break in the line of cliffs, to reach the moorland above the shore and cliffs. We didn't bother, there was still so much to see on the shoreline we were more than happy to return the way we came.

THE QUIRAING, ISLE OF SKYE
OCTOBER 2003

The first time I came across the Quiraing, one of the most amazing landscape features in the country, I was walking with my old pal Harry McShane of Crianlarich, down the length of the Trotternish Ridge on Skye, a two-day expedition that has been described as the finest ridge walk in Scotland.

We had been following the crumbling cliff edge southwards from Sron Vourlinn when, immediately below the great grassy mound of Meall na Suiramach, we came across a slanting rake that took us down through cliffs to the most amazing hidden valley that ran along the foot of the escarpment.

In complete surprise we wandered through this curious landscape of spires and bluffs, rocky formations so contorted and bent they looked like crooked fingers beckoning us toward some nether world. Above, immense crags, blocks and spires loomed high and scree slopes led us upwards into what appeared to be a giant amphitheatre. Great slices of rock, fissured, weathered and cracked, stood apart from the main cliffs. Behind and through them we could gaze out towards a scene of complete contrast – the pastoral green of the Staffin crofts, with the blue waters of Staffin Bay beyond.

Much of this Trotternish area of Skye is volcanic and you'll find huge landslips all down the length of the ridge between the Quiraing and the Storr. Apparently caused by the weight of basaltic lavas on top of older Jurassic sedimentary rocks causing the underlying rock to collapse, with the Quiraing the finest example of them all, a stronghold of Titan verticalities, surreal in its black and grey upthrusts.

I can't remember how long we wandered around this natural phenomenon, slack-jawed in amazement and, as though we hadn't been surprised enough, it seemed almost unreal to discover an elevated plateau of grass, as flat as a bowling green. This is The Table, the jewel of the Quiraing, and beyond it a wild flower garden hung from the cliffs. Yellow glove flowers, red and white campions, blue butterwort and sprays of golden roseroot contrasted with the glistening black of the dripping wet crags from which they grew.

We left The Table in silence and wandered down dark corridors of scree, past the highest of all the pinnacles, the towering spire of The Needle, 36m/120ft in height and tapering at both the top and the bottom. More slopes of scree slid us down to the track in front of another great feature, The Prison, a squat, square-shaped rock, the southerly outpost of the Quiraing.

I've lost count of how many times I've returned to the Quiraing (the name is taken from the Gaelic A'Cuith-Raing – the pillared cattle pen) but I've never failed to be delighted by my various companions' gasps of surprise. The normal route into the Quiraing follows a footpath from the Bealach Ollasgairte, the high point of the narrow Staffin–Uig road, the only east–west road to cross the Trotternish ridge. This route is not only safer than entering the Quiraing by its back door as we did on our first discovery, but is scenically far superior with views across the scattered croftships of Staffin and down the very impressive escarpment that rolls southwards towards Portree. Once beyond The Prison there are some steep slopes to negotiate before actually entering the Quiraing, but nothing that an able-bodied person shouldn't be able to cope with.

HILLS OF HOY
JULY 2005

Most outdoor enthusiasts of my vintage will recall the BBC's outdoor spectacular of 1967 when a team of rock climbers negotiated a number of routes up Orkney's formidable Old Man of Hoy. This 120m/394ft sandstone sea stack rises from the sea just off the west coast of the Orkney island of Hoy and was first climbed by Rusty Baillie, Tom Patey and Chris Bonington. The next year it became the subject of what was the BBC's most expensive outside broadcast to date starring those three famous climbers along with other household names such as Joe Brown, Dougal Haston and Hamish McInnes.

The sea stack itself is well worth seeing (The name Hoy comes from the Norse word for 'high') and Hoy itself is not only the second largest island in Orkney, but offers the best walking possibilities by far.

A magnificent coastal walk follows the western cliffs from St John's Head south to Rora Head, passing above the famous sea stack. The route offers a circular itinerary, and takes in the best of the coastal walking with a visit to the old (now virtually deserted) fishing community of Rackwick and a look at what is possibly the most northerly natural woodland in Britain.

A daily ferry runs between Stromness and Hoy and, from the pier at Linksness, a road, which gradually reduces to a track, straggles westwards towards Cuilags hill. You don't have to stay on the track for long and at this time of the year it's a delight to take to the moorland, still carpeted with wild flowers, principally sea pinks. These rough moors of western Hoy are dotted with small lochans, many of which provide sanctuary for a whole host of waders and ducks: red-throated and great northern divers, Slavonian grebes, mergansers and pintail. Hen harriers swoop low on ghostly flights over the moors, as do short-eared owls, and the mournful call of the golden plover provides a constant dirge.

From the outflow of the largest of these moorland lochs, Sandy Loch, it's an easy ascent to the summit of Cuilags, at just over 460m/1518ft the second highest hill on Hoy (Ward Hill is highest at 521m/1719ft). From the grassy summit the going is fairly easy and level for just over a mile to St John's Head, a spectacular viewpoint above steep cliffs which fall to the thunderous, crashing seas over a thousand feet below, a place alive with the cries of whirling fulmars.

The three-mile traverse of the cliff-tops south to Rora Head is the highlight, a highly dramatic and breathtaking route that passes high above the wide bay that's presided over by the Old Man of Hoy. From Rora Head the route continues along the cliff tops before descending to the stony beach at Rackwick, once a thriving fishing community but now no more than a couple of crofts and a fish farm. There is an air of desertion about the place. Empty, tumbled cottages scatter the hillsides, the doorways choked with nettles, but still Rackwick smiles on you, bright in its south-facing setting. One of the old buildings is now a bothy and the grassy field beside it is ideal for camping.

A road runs north from the old village and crosses the river. A path leaves the road here and heads north beside the river passing Berrie Dale on the left, with its rowans, aspens and birches of this natural woodland. Continue north, cross the river again and soon after you'll reach the western shore of Sandy Loch again. A short distance beyond and you'll meet the road you left earlier, taking you back to the pier and your return ferry to Stromness.

MACLEOD'S TABLES
AUGUST 2006

They're not only tabled but they're fabled, and many of the tales that are associated with these curious flat-topped hills of west Skye are to do with their names. It's easy enough to see why they're called MacLeod's Tables. Healabhal Mhor and Healabhal Bheag are isolated remnants of the vast basalt plateaux that once covered the island. Their flat tops and the series of successive steps in their flanks show how the molten basalt had flowed out in successive sheets from time to time.

That rather prosaic description has been given various shades of colour over the years ever since it was suggested that God himself sliced the tops off the hills to create a bed for his servant Columba. A more recent explanation involves a chief of the Clan MacLeod, Alasdair Crotach, who boasted to King James V that he had a finer table in Skye than the king had in Edinburgh. He claimed his hall was more spacious than the king's palace, his roof more lofty, his table more richly laden and his candles

more ornate. When the king later visited Dunvegan a feast was
laid out for him on the flat, moss-covered summit of Healabhal
Mhor, where, under the vast dome of a starry sky Alastair's
clansmen bore flaming torches to provide the lighting.

For a long time it was thought these two hills of Duirinish
had some ancient religious significance, as the name Healabhal
came from the Norse word Helgi – holy fell – but more recent
interpretations suggest the hills mean nothing more than the big
flagstone hill and the little flagstone hill.

In his new book, *Scottish Hill Names*, Peter Drummond tells
the story of a local man who, when asked by tourists what the
names meant, said 'one was a helluva big climb and the other
one even more so'. I'd happily concur with that view!

We'd gone to Skye to do something in the Cuillin, but gale-
force winds and rain put paid to that notion, so we ventured
north to a rain-soaked Old Man of Storr. By the next morning
we were keen to do something a little more energetic, so drove
round to Dunvegan, caught a glimpse of the flat-topped tables
through the cloud and went for them.

Let me say at the outset that these are not high hills. At
469m/1548ft and 488m/1610ft MacLeod's Tables don't make it
into any major lists of hills but, since you have to climb them
from sea level, and since both hills require a bit of a walk-in
over rain-soaked moorland, the ascents of Healabhal Mhor and
Healabhal Bheag, round the head of Glen Osdale, make for a
good, energetic five-or six-hour hill day. The bonus, should you
be blessed with fair weather, is wonderful views of sea, coast
and mountain, that wonderful blend that makes hill-bashing on
Skye such a memorable occasion.

Despite the gale-force winds and, frustratingly, low cloud on
both summits, we enjoyed the route in a kind of masochistic
way. Our best views were down onto Loch Bracadale and its
islands on the descent from Healabhal Bheag. Take care on this
descent though: the eastern ridge of Healabhal Bheag pulls up
abruptly at a blunt, rocky nose. You have to leave the ridge in
a northerly direction before the steep bit. After that it's an easy

descent all the way back to the start provided you stay as much as possible on the high ground. We made the mistake of wandering down into the depths of Glen Osdale where heather made walking difficult. Between that and the relentless wind we were more than ready for a beer in Dunvegan by the time we got back to the vehicle. Despite the difficulties we felt we had achieved something from a weekend that had initially threatened to blow us into the sea. Roll on the winter, it's got to be better than this past summer!

BLA BHEINN
SEPTEMBER 2007

As we topped the low rise above the lovely bay of Camasunary on the Isle of Skye, the south ridge of Bla Bheinn rose to the sky in a series of rocky steps. I was in the company of Alistair MacPherson, the local land manager for the John Muir Trust who own about 12,500 hectares of land in this part of Skye. He was telling me of the work he had been doing taking sheep from the slopes of Bla Bheinn to allow regeneration of plants and woodland. He remained true to the party line, but I suspected such an action must have caused a hint of remorse in someone whose grandfather was a shepherd on Skye in the early years of last century, a man who was born and brought up in a black house at the foot of Marsco in Glen Sligachan.

If he had any regrets about the removal of the sheep, Alistair didn't reveal it, but instead took delight in showing me some of the plants on the hill that, after years of browsing by sheep, are flourishing again. Better still, he took my arm, pointed upwards and said those magic words: golden eagle! This was the first of three golden eagles we were to see and this one was intent on showing off. It would spiral high before closing its wings and dropping like a stone, before spreading its wings again into another glide and upwards spiral.

The south ridge of Bla Bheinn not only offers a great route to the south summit of the mountain, but avoids the endless screes of the usual Munro-baggers' route from Coire Uaigneich. The views across to the Black Cuillin are astonishing. Alastair, a Skye man born and bred commented on its Tolkienesque quality and he was right; nowhere else in all the mountain regions of the UK can you witness such savage grandeur.

Bla Bheinn, 929m/3045ft, is the most southerly of the Red Cuillin and not only offers a splendid platform from which to gasp at the audacious outline of the Black Cuillin but also gives you the opportunity to appreciate the subtler curves of their pink-red neighbours. On a day of gusting winds and racing clouds a few years ago I struggled up the eastern ridge and broke the summit ridge skyline just as the wind tore a great gash in the low clouds. Through that hole the sharp, tortured peaks of the Cuillin appeared as crooked remnants of some hyperborean wilderness, but through the roar of the wind I heard something else. It was the cacophony of geese, no doubt disoriented by the racing cloud and the wind. Their music was clear, blending with the gusts into a natural melody that had me trembling in delight.

Alastair and I reached the south summit in a surprisingly quick time and saw the north summit, the true summit, only a few metres away. However, things are not as simple as they seem. In between the two summits there is a deep and steep chasm, and the descent and ascent to the main summit involved a rough scramble, a fairly delicate traverse on wet rock and another short, but steep, climb to the summit cairn and trig point. Indeed, you have to do it twice for the best descent route from the mountain – down the slopes of the south peak, down to where a very eroded footpath takes you down to Coire Uaigneich and the badly eroded path back to the John Muir Trust car park on the shore of Loch Slapin where we had left a car earlier.

BEN TIANAVAIG
NOVEMBER 2007

I've been working on a television project for BBC Scotland on the Isle of Skye, a long walk through the island from Rubha

Huinish in the north to Broadford and we spent so much time dodging weather systems that I reckon I've become an expert in the island's coffee shops. Look out for the guidebook . . .

I was trying to link two of the most amazing landscapes in Britain. Everyone knows of the spectacularly impressive outline of the Skye Cuillin, a mountain range that once prompted Sorley MacLean to describe them as 'the mother-breasts of the world, erect with universe's concupiscence', but fewer are aware of the geological extravaganza that is the Trotternish peninsula. A twenty-odd-mile basalt escarpment runs south from Rubha Huinish to Portree and volcanic landslips on its eastern side have created such landscape curiosities as the Quiraing and the Storr rocks, two of the most remarkable places in Scotland.

Linking the two landscapes of Trotternish and the Cuillin is an area of fertile loveliness known as The Braes, where the last battle on British soil took place in 1882. It involved local crofters armed with sticks and stones and fifty policemen who had been sent north from Glasgow to quell a longstanding dispute about grazing rights. The incident caused such strong feeling among the people of Skye that Prime Minister Gladstone eventually set up a Royal Commission to investigate the crofters' grievances. The result of that was a document known as the Napier Report, the blueprint for much of today's crofting legislation.

During my various sorties to Skye this past summer I've gazed longingly at a little hill that dominates this area of The Braes. It's a hill that rises immediately south of Portree Bay and forms a continuation of the basalt escarpment of Trotternish. Its cliffs are home to a pair of sea eagles and there are wild goats resident on the hill's slopes. It's called Ben Tianavaig, and it's a mere 413m/1355ft above sea level.

I had to return to Skye last weekend so took the opportunity, on a grey and misty early winter day, to climb the hill. Because of the weather I couldn't expect great views but was rewarded with a feeling of great exposure above the grey-green waters of the Sound of Raasay and a sense that on a good day the ascent of little Ben Tianavaig would be a real classic. Take this hill, transplant it in the Lake District and guidebook writers would be eulogising about it. Here on Skye it's dwarfed, both physically and aesthetically, by the rugged grandeur of the Cuillin.

Nevertheless, it's a grand outing for the short days of winter and there was an other-worldly feel to the tiny crofting hamlet of Camustianavaig as I left the stony beach, with inquisitive seals peering out of the bay at me and an equally inquisitive crofter wondering where I was going. 'Take care,' he said when I told him. 'A geologist fell from the cliffs and was killed just last summer.' With his words ringing in my ears I did take care.

There are certainly one or two spots where the basalt rock, made treacherously slippery by the rain, could be hazardous and the cliff line that you follow all the way to the summit is, in places, well exposed.

Despite that the route is straightforward, although the mists began to wrap themselves around me as I climbed higher, reducing visibility to a few feet. By the summit trig point I was rewarded with a brief opening of the clouds, revealing Portree in its harbour setting away below. Once known as Kiltaraglen, the town was renamed Port an Righ, the King's harbour, following a visit by James V in 1540. Indeed, the hill's name, Tianavaig, means the harbour at the foot of the hill.

EAVAL, NORTH HARRIS
SEPTEMBER 2008

After forty years of hillwalking in Scotland I had long since given up hope of being surprised by a mountain-top view again, but the panorama from the summit of diminutive Eaval on North Harris simply took my breath away.

It wasn't my idea to climb this little 347m/1145ft hill. I was in the Hebrides, cycling and hiking between Vatersay in the south and the Butt of Lewis in the north. Having badly wanted to climb the South Uist hills of Beinn Mor and Hecla, bad weather and the requirements of a television programme meant turning my back on them. Instead, I walked up the wonderful Machair Way on the west coast of South Uist. The ascent of Eaval was consolation for missing the southern hills and it was the idea of local artist and film-maker Andy Mackinnon.

Last year Andy and fellow artist Chris Drury made a two-day trans-Uist journey by Canadian canoe across the island, from the south-west coast to Lochmaddy in the north-east, a journey that made extensive use of the Uists' lochan-splattered landscape. The result of that very physical experience is an extensive show in Lochmaddy's Taigh Chearsabhagh Art Centre that includes the amazing installation of a suspended canoe that has been woven from heather, willow and salmon skins. Andy suggested to me it acts as a kind of open vessel for ideas, sensations and the material landscape. He wanted to show me the route of his canoe trip and where better to view it from than the summit of a hill?

As we walked by the mirror-like surface of Loch Euphort on a heaven-sent morning Andy reminded me that this is an inhabited and named landscape going back to Neolithic times. As such, naming it and the language used embeds it within the culture of an area that is often described as 'wilderness', but of course isn't, and another exhibit of the art show proves that. Using digital technology Andy and Chris have recreated an image of the landscape as a lacework of words in Gaelic, Norse and English, naming all the lochs, islands and hills seen from Eaval.

Stags were roaring their autumn challenges as we threaded our way from the road end at Clachan Bhiurabhal around the various promontories and inlets of ragged Loch Obasaraigh. It was surprisingly difficult walking, leaping over lively streams, negotiating slippery stepping stones and avoiding the worst of the bogs, but conditions rapidly improved as we left the shoreline to climb the north-east ridge of the hill. Almost immediately I became aware that I'd probably never before hiked through a landscape like this. It was as if there was more water on the land than land itself, and you can only see that from above. To the east a narrow strip of tumbled land separated the slopes of Eaval

from the sparkling waters of the Minch but that strip of land
was pockmarked by a myriad of lochans too, each deep-set and
reflecting the blue of the sky.

A pair of vocal ravens welcomed us while, below, on one of the
lochs, a pair of whooper swans, newly arrived from the Arctic,
sailed serenely. On one of the loch's beaches we had noticed the
prints of an otter but the most thrilling wildlife encounter was
yet to come.

Although it's only 347m/1138ft, Eaval has a character that's
out of all proportion to its height. Viewed from the east it
appears as a giant wave about to break over the watery landscape. Andy described it as the Mount Fuji of North Uist, and
I can understand why as it dominates the flat islands of North
Uist and Benbecula. To add a touch of rock climbing to the day
we elected to scramble up its ancient gneiss ridges as much as
we could. The scrambling took us directly to the summit trig
point and the surprising panorama that ranged from the hills of
Harris, over the loch-infested waters of North Uist and across
Grimsay and Benbecula to the big hills of South Uist and beyond
them to lovely Eriskay and Barra. Behind us the hills of Skye
and Wester Ross were perfectly clear, and Andy told me that if
it had not been for the haze we would have seen St Kilda on the
Atlantic horizon. However, the best was yet to come.

As we drank from our flasks in the lee of the trig point/cairn
a golden eagle flying overhead began a series of diving displays,
folding its wings back against its body and dropping like a dive-
bomber before soaring upwards again on great, finger-tipped
wings. Sensational barely describes it, but that eagle display put
the seal on what was one of the best hill days I've had for many
years.

CHAPTER TEN

More Than a Day

I will arise and go now, and go to Innisfree,
And a small cabin build there, of clay and wattles made:
Nine bean-rows will I have there, a hive for the honey-bee;
And live alone in the bee-loud glade.

And I shall have some peace there, for peace comes
    dropping slow,
Dropping from the veils of the morning to where the
    cricket sings;
There midnight's all a glimmer, and noon a purple glow,
And evening full of the linnet's wings.

I will arise and go now, for always night and day
I hear lake water lapping with low sounds by the shore;
While I stand on the roadway, or on the pavements grey,
I hear it in the deep heart's core.

The distant, shifting mists of memory obscure the circumstances of my introduction to W. B. Yeats's 'Lake Isle of Innisfree', but the spirit of the poem has been drifting in my consciousness for as long as I can remember. The words still resonate with the promise of better times, a simpler life and a return to the natural world. In Yeats's case it was a world he longed for when he was domiciled in the city: 'While I stand on the roadway, or on the pavements grey'.

The lake isle itself is a small, uninhabited island in Lough Gill, in County Sligo, Ireland, where Yeats lived as a child and it's very likely he visited it in his youth. I suspect it is a pretty ordinary place as islands go, but the poet's fertile imagination created something special, a blend of nostalgia and spirituality that can be traced in oblique biblical references (I will arise and go . . .) and a desire to be alone. In such solitude he could commune with the natural world, a more peaceful, slower, less complicated world, that perhaps lay within the deep core of his heart and being.

Jim Perrin once sent me a recording of Yeats reciting the poem. To the crackle of an early wireless recording the words are recited slowly and deliberately, like an incantation, the cadence of a woven spell. As I listened to it, in all its archaic simplicity, the hairs on the back of my neck bristled.

For a long-time gangrel like me there is a simple magic in the words, 'I will arise and go now . . .'. They suggest the first steps to an adventure, the beginnings of a journey, the start of something exciting, and there was something of the clay and wattle cabin that caught my childhood imagination. I didn't even know what wattle was, but in my mind's eye I could see that cabin in the woods, with wood smoke drifting from the chimney, the smell of it mixing with the scent of damp leaves and earth.

A home in the wilds with the beasts and birds as neighbours, a secret place I could call my own. There were definite echoes of Henry David Thoreau's wilderness cabin at Walden Pond where the American author lived simply in natural surroundings in his own 'bee-loud glade'.

In a personal sense I've enjoyed a similar connection to wild places by camping in a tent. On expeditions both long and short, at home and abroad, the simple tent became my 'clay and wattle cabin'. I guess a more likely comparison with Yeats' cabin would be a bothy, but such accommodation isn't as convenient as a tent. It doesn't offer the same privacy, doesn't offer the independence of a tent, and doesn't allow the same freedom of movement. Bothies have their value, there's no doubt about that, but I feel more at one with my surroundings when I'm only separated from them by a skin of thin fabric. There's something very rewarding about looking out from a tent to see the 'midnight's all a glimmer', or fall asleep to the sound of 'lake water lapping with low sounds by the shore'.

I've enjoyed living in a tent on a huge number of long walks: the John Muir Trail through the Sierra Nevada mountains of California, the Tour of Mont Blanc, The Walkers' Haute Route between Chamonix and Zermatt, the GR20 across Corsica. A tent has been my home during many treks in far-flung corners: Everest Base Camp, Around Manaslu, the Annapurna Trail, the Singalila Ridge of Kangchenjunga, across the Atlas Mountains of Morocco, in the Wadi Rum desert of Jordan, ascents of Kilimanjaro and Elbrus and Ararat and many others. During those expeditions, whether solo, with Gina or with a group of trekking clients, the tent has been my home, my shelter, my office, my place of security and privacy, my very own 'clay and wattles cabin'.

Here in Scotland, I've habitually preferred a tent over other forms of accommodation on the Sutherland Trail, the Skye Trail, on a number of coast-to-coast journeys and along the Scottish National Trail from the Scottish Border to Cape Wrath, but the real value of a lightweight tent is for shorter weekend or overnight trips when the weather looks favourable. On impulse, I just 'arise and go'. No need to book accommodation in advance, no need to worry if a bothy is likely to be overcrowded, no need to become concerned that I might not reach my chosen destination. A tent allows you to be extremely flexible in your planning, or in not planning at all.

I've always loved the notion that here in Scotland we can climb most of our hills and be down in the pub by opening time, but there is something distinctly magical about walking into the upper confines of a wild and beautiful mountain corrie in early evening and camping on a little patch of clumpy grass, sheltered perhaps by a low moraine. At times like this I go onto automatic pilot. The well-practiced procedures of setting up camp and arranging everything for the night have become so ingrained that I could probably do them with my eyes shut. Which is as well, for so often I find myself at this point of the day tired and thirsty, and there have been times when that well-oiled routine has meant the difference between a comfortable night and a grim one – especially in bad weather.

The pack comes off and I pull the tent from its stuff sack, leaving everything else I need inside the pack so I don't lose anything. When choosing a campsite I usually check the ground by lying down on it, to see if there is a slope. The tent poles and pegs live in the same stuff sack as the tent, so I pull them out and connect the pole ends together. I then stake out one end of the tent so it doesn't blow away if a gust of wind should catch it. The poles go through the sleeves, I pull the tent panels out firmly to avoid creases in the groundsheet, then stake out the corners and the guy lines.

Once the tent is erected it's time to pull out the sleep-mat, inflate it, and lay it inside the tent. Next comes the sleeping bag. I pull it out of its waterproof stuff sack, give it a shake or two to fluff the down and inflate it a bit, then I lay it on the sleep mat. Next job, before I finally crawl inside the tent, is to take my two water bladders and fill them in a nearby stream.

I then take out my stove, pots, knife and spoon and the rest of the things I might need for the night: a bag of food, a book, tomorrow's map and a headtorch. By this time I am ready to lie down. After a day's backpacking and all the bending down involved in pitching the tent I find my back tends to stiffen, so it's great to lie down inside the tent for a few moments and stretch it, a moment of bliss.

Next comes the best moment of any wild camping experience. Lighting the stove, putting on a pot of water and anticipating the first brew. After that, the evening passes as so many of them do, in a fuzz of eating and drinking, between long periods of simply gazing out of the open tent door. More often than not I have a wee dram, and I always carry a book, but I'm also amazed at how little reading I actually do. After the last brew I snuggle down in the sleeping bag, rearrange my pillow and drift off to the sound of the breeze and the musical tinkle of the stream, into the deep sleep that only a hard day's exercise in the fresh air can provide.

LOCH EINICH HORSESHOE
MAY 1986

Loch nan Stuirteag lay just below the glassy platform where I'd pitched my little tent, shining in the moonlight like pewter. Beyond it the fold of the hills dropped away into the long, narrow confines of Glen Geusachan, the haunt of golden eagle and red deer.

The moonglow had a magical effect on the night landscape, with cloud shadows floating gently across the still surface of the loch and stars pinpricking a velvet sky.

A few hours earlier I'd arrived by the lochside, footsore and weary after a long walk of seventeen miles over three Munros. For some time I'd looked at the big horseshoe route that runs over the hills that flank Loch Einich in the Cairngorms: Braeriach, 1296m/4252ft, the UK's third highest mountain on one side and Sgor Gaoith, 1118m/3668ft and the long Sgurans ridge on the other, and I reckoned I could extend it by adding Sgor an Lochain Uaine, 1258m/4150ft and Cairn Toul, 1291m/4236ft as well. Total distance was slightly short of thirty miles, so a high-level overnight camp would morph it from a long, hard hill tramp to a weekend wild land experience.

I don't think you can claim to know a mountain until you've slept on it and I've lost count of how many times I've camped in the high folds and sheltered crannies of the Moine Mhor, the great billowing plateau that spreads out from the cliffs at the head of Loch Einich. This 'great moss' is home to ptarmigan, dotterel and snow buntings, all birds of the high Arctic, and the wilder qualities of the place are intense, despite the presence of the bulldozed track that has ripped the plateau apart.

Most Munro-baggers, I suspect, tackle Braeriach, Sgor an Lochain Uaine and Cairn Toul from the east, from the deep cleft of the Lairig Ghru, but my own preference has always been to take the long walk-in through Rothiemurchus Forest to the dark and deep-set Loch Einich, from where an old stalkers' path climbs steadily up into Coire Dhondail. From there a long and steeper grassy ramp tops out on the Braeriach plateau where the infant River Dee bubbles up from the ground and begins its long journey to the sea at Aberdeen.

Up here on the roof of Scotland winter had not yet released its grip. Snow cornices rimmed the corrie edges and the head-walls of An Garbh Coire, one of the truly great corries of Scotland, were still swathed in white. The walk around these corrie rims, from Braeriach, over Sgor an Lochain Uaine to Cairn Toul is one of the finest high-level walks in the land and the extravagance of the mountain scenery was highlighted by moving cloud shadow and sunlight creating dramatic vistas of rainbow-enhanced views and Brocken spectres.

My original intention had been to descend Cairn Toul and make my way by Loch nan Stuirteag to the head of Gleann Einich, but by the time I reached the loch I was done in and famished. It was raw delight to peel off my socks and slide into a sleeping bag.

Next day was bright and sunny but great thunderhead clouds in the south suggested the good weather might not last. I was packed up and away by eight and on the summit of Sgor Gaoith before ten. Drifts of mist spiralled around me like great geysers of steam and as I followed the long ridge over Sguran Dubh Mor and Sguran Dubh Beag the clouds threatened to boil up and spill over the edge of the great chasm that cradles the dark waters of Loch Einich.

On past the Clach Choutsaich and the granite tor that commemorates the forces of the Duke of Argyll, the Clach Mhic Cailein, I decided my easiest option was to drop down into Coire Bhuidhe and follow the slopes down into Rothiemurchus, but that decision proved to be a wrong one. The combination of deep heather, tussocky grass and thick juniper slowed progress to a crawl, and I soon lost count of how many times I stepped through the heather into hidden streams. By the time I reached the track that runs to Loch an Eilean I was well soaked from the knees down but at least I managed to reach my car at Coylumbridge minutes before the first big thunderous deluge of the afternoon.

BEN ADEN
JUNE 1987

It was flaming June and for me that means my annual visit to the hills of Knoydart. Bounded in the north and south by the fjord-like Loch Hourn and Loch Nevis, the western peninsula of Knoydart is nevertheless firmly attached to the mainland, held forever in the grip of a rugged tract of mountains known as the Rough Bounds.

Kinloch Hourn, which is better served by boat than it is by the switchbacked, single-track road from Glengarry, lies at the head of Loch Hourn while the head of Loch Nevis has no need of a road at all. Only a mountain bothy (Sourlies) and a ruined farmhouse greet you after a four-hour trek along the rough footpaths of Glen Dessarry. Between Kinloch Nevis and Kinloch Hourn steep-sided mountains form a wall of impregnability, most notably the knobbly summit of Sgurr na Ciche, the popular jewel of Knoydart, and a squat, muscle-bound mountain called Ben Aden. If Sgurr na Ciche is the most public symbol of the Rough Bounds of Knoydart, then Ben Aden is its most sacred private icon.

Ben Aden, 887m/2910ft is, to use the parlance of the Scottish Mountaineering Club, one of the most retiring of all the Corbetts. That means it's remote and difficult to get to. The baggers' route treks round the western extremity of Loch Quoich from the Kinloch Hourn road, climbs the hill and gets you back out in a day, but any other route requires an overnight or two in a tent or bothy; no hardship in an area where lingering is well rewarded.

Treat yourself to a two/three-day backpacking trip and take a long, circuitous route around Ben Aden, exploiting the old deerstalkers' paths that lace this area, camping out in the company of drumming snipe and warbling curlews. Backpacking, with simple needs carried on your back, is the only practical way to explore the Rough Bounds. But solo backpacking can be a mixed blessing.

My route took me from Strathan, at the head of Loch Arkaig, over the Bealach Feith a'Chicheanais to Glen Kingie. From there a wonderful stalkers' path runs up towards the head of the glen before turning back on itself to zigzag over a high pass between An Eag and Sgurr Beag. In a little Corbett-bashing spree I left my pack on this pass and nipped, unladen, over the Munro of Sgurr Mor to Sgurr an Fhuarain and back again before dropping down into Coire Reidh and Loch Quoich.

Camping at the head of the loch I was in a perfect position to climb Ben Aden next morning by way of Coire na Cruaiche and its rocky east-north-east ridge. This approach from the north is a dramatic one, much preferable to the long slog up the south-west face of the hill which seems to be the popular route. Close to the head of Loch Quoich a slit-like trench holds the dark waters of Lochan nam Breac and, above it, Ben Aden hurls down knolls and corries, dark crags and tumbling ridges, a mirror image of those exaggerated Victorian paintings that epitomised the era of the Celtic Twilight.

It's up through those corries and tumbling crags that the route climbs, easily at first over yellowed deer grass and rocky slabs before the ridge rises in a series of bluffs and craggy steps. The route rises with it, maniacally zigzagging from one side of the ridge to another in an attempt to avoid the steeper crags, before the ground finally drops away on all sides and the small summit cairn heralds a magnificent viewpoint. Loch Hourn and Loch Nevis naturally draw the eye out to Skye, Rum and Eigg in the west, and almost every peak in the north and west highlands becomes visible: An Teallach and Ben Wyvis, the Kintail and Affric hills, down to the blue waters of Loch Quoich and the neighbouring hills of Sgurr Mor, Gairich and Sgurr Thuilm.

The rest of the day was more relaxed. A late lunch by Lochan nam Breac, old shielings in the narrow pass through to Glen Carnoch, fields of wood anemones, the tangy scent of the Carnoch salt flats and another camp, this time by Finiskaig at the head of Loch Nevis where I drifted off to sleep to the sounds of gulls and the sea.

Next day the weather broke, and the ten miles over the Mam na Cloiche Airde back to Glen Dessarry and Strathan were spent in the over-hot huddle of waterproofs. I considered myself fortunate to get at least two good days out of three; that's not bad in these Rough Bounds of Knoydart.

THE MINIGAIG
OCTOBER 1988

It had been a few years since I'd hiked the Minigaig, the ancient byway that climbs over the wild hills between Atholl and Badenoch.

Two ancient routes link the villages of Blair Atholl and Kingussie. The Minigaig replaced the older Comyn's Road some time before the seventeenth century. It seems probable that Comyn's Road fell into disuse because the Minigaig was more direct and slightly shorter. Seventeenth-century maps show it as the sole route across the Grampians.

Drovers, soldiers, poets and vagabonds have all tramped this high-level route but nowadays you're unlikely to see anyone other than the odd stravaiging gangrel, or a gamekeeper going about his business. You might not see many others, but in the course of a couple of days I saw hundreds of red deer, the stags still heavily in the annual rut, skein upon skein of migrating geese, dainty dippers on the high-level burns and, most surprising of all, a salmon grilse in the shallow headwaters of the River Bruar.

I had been enjoying a bite of lunch by a shallow tributary of the Bruar when my attention was taken by something splashing in the water. It was a salmon grilse, about a foot in length, flapping its way from pool to pool as it made its improbable way upstream. When it became aware of my presence it leapt into the mainstream and I was simply amazed at its efficiency and strength in negotiating the fast-flowing waters head-on.

Taking the Minigaig head-on at this time of year requires the use of a tent. Thirty-plus miles in the restricted daylight hours of late autumn could be difficult, and with strong winds and rain forecast I wasn't too keen on camping out on the elevated and extensive plateau that makes up the higher reaches of this route. The words of a modern guidebook resonate with warning. 'The Minigaig . . . is perhaps the bleakest and most featureless terrain crossed by any major hill track.'

This great plateau spreads itself aimlessly, a lofty tableland patched in the black and white of peat hags and remnants of early snow. Captivated by the place I stood and stared at the still and silent spread of it, inimical under the milky grey skies.

Since this high-level section of the route follows a long walk up the length of Glen Bruar you really have to make sure you leave Atholl at a fairly early hour. To shorten the route a little, and to treat myself to a slightly different start, I began the route at Bruar, rather than Blair Atholl, passing the scenically splendid Bruar Falls, at their most majestic following a bout of wet weather. The long walk up Glen Bruar got the best of the day's weather before a herringboned sky clouded over and threatened rain.

I scampered across the high-level section of the route under these threatening skies, aware that low-level cloud or mist could pose a real navigational problem, despite the line of white quartzite stones that pick out the route. Like all cairned routes, it's easy to be lulled into a false sense of security. As I reached the far edge of this great plateau a sudden impulse made me veer off to the right to climb the Corbett of Leathad an Taobhain, 912m/2991ft, and instead of returning to the Minigaig to descend into Glen Tromie I descended, by Meall an Uillt Chreagaich and Lochan an t-Sluic, into Glen Feshie, one of the most beautiful glens in Scotland.

The second day was shorter: thirteen miles, down Glen Feshie to Stronetoper, along the right of way to Druimguish, then by way of the Badenoch Way to Ruthven and Kingussie.

COMYN'S ROAD
APRIL 1996

It may have been the first weekend of British summer time but there was no disguising the fact that winter still lay heavily on the uplands of Atholl.

I was walking on a compass bearing, throwing snowballs into the mist in front of me, eager to find something to point my compass needle at. Occasionally a tuft of heather or a rock would break the snow's surface, but I may as well have been walking with a white shroud over my head. Visibility was reduced to a matter of a few feet and I simply couldn't discern between the snow-covered terrain and the mist. I was, to all intents and purposes, walking blind.

To add to my growing consternation, it was also eerily still and silent, and not for the first time I remembered that I was heading into the most supernatural place in Scotland.

I was walking the ancient Comyn's Road, a fourteenth-century hill track that runs over the marvellously remote Grampians between Blair Atholl and Kingussie. A sixteenth-century manuscript, *MacFarlane's Geographic Collections*, refers to ' . . .a way from the gate of Blair in Atholl to Ruthven in Badenoch made by David Comyn, for carts to pass with wine, and the way is called Rath na Pheny, or "way of wagon wheels"'.

That route eventually became known as the Rathad nan Cuimeinach, or Road of the Comyns, and it fell into disuse during the sixteenth or seventeenth century when the shorter Minigaig pass became the standard route between Atholl and Badenoch. At one point the twenty-seven-mile route runs through a district known as Gaick, an area that, according to that wonderful old Scots sennachie Seton Gordon, is the haunt of occult and dark forces.

In his book, *Highways and Byways in the Central Highlands*, Gordon tells the stories of Gaick. Of the Leannan Sith, the fairy sweetheart who tempts hunters to their doom, the tiny elfin-like Sprite o' Gaick and of the Comyn's Road's historical link with the evil forces. The highlands, of course, abound in such tales and even in these mercifully emancipated days it's all too easy to allow childhood bogies to rise up and affect our judgement. I wasn't so concerned with the supernatural, but I was growing increasingly paranoid about getting lost in this vast upheaval of snow and mist, a lofty tableland that spread itself aimlessly in all directions.

When I became aware that I was walking downhill the mist, and my paranoia, began to evaporate. Below me lay the slit trench that held the waters of the Allt Gharbh Ghaig and a footpath that ran north-west into the Gaick glen itself, where I planned to camp for the night, despite the ghosts.

Comyn's Road offers a fairly challenging two-day walk between Blair Atholl and Kingussie, much of it on good tracks and paths. The potentially difficult section is over the high and exposed 820m/2690ft Sron a'Chleirich above Glen Bruar and along the edge of the undulating tableland that stretches north towards Glen Feshie, an area of high ground that was described at a recent John Muir Trust conference on wild land as 'the wildest tract of land in Scotland'. This is not an area to become lost in!

The second day of Comyn's Road is much more straightforward. A good track runs north beside Loch an t-Seilich to Glen Tromie where you can either follow the tarmac road to Tromie Bridge, then by road to Ruthven, or cross the River Tromie and follow the old right of way over Sron na Gaoithe and its high moorlands to Ruthven. Whatever you do, try and avoid two-foot-high people wearing green siren suits. If you do spot such an individual then beware, you've seen the Sprite o' Gaick, and you might never be the same again!

THE GREAT GLEN WAY
JUNE 2002

During last year's foot-and-mouth crisis it became apparent just how important the West Highland Way is to the economy of the villages it passes through. The ninety-six-mile route between Milngavie and Fort William is believed to be worth in the region of ten million pounds per year and supports a healthy number of jobs. That there is a vast tourism potential in such long-distance walking routes is no longer questionable, and an enormous number of walkers, from home and abroad, happily embrace the concept of officially designated walking routes. It would appear that collecting, or 'ticking off' long distance trails has the same trainspotting appeal as bagging Munros!

Later this week, at a reception in Inverness, the Great Glen Way will be added to the West Highland Way, the Southern Upland Way and the Speyside Way to make up Scotland's quartet of officially sanctioned trails. There are about fifteen in England and Wales.[1]

The creation of this route, which runs from Fort William to Inverness along the line of the major geological fault that almost separates northern Scotland from the rest of the country, has taken an inordinate amount of time, primarily due to local access problems. All now appears to be resolved, the new signposts are in place, and the first guidebook was published last year.

Commenting on the early publication of his book, *The Great Glen Way*, last autumn, Tony Dyer, Senior Countryside Officer with Highland Council said, 'This is the first officially supported publication for the route and although in advance of the formal opening it will be very valuable. People have been walking up the Great Glen for years and this will direct walkers onto the route agreed with all the landowners.'

Tony Dyer's comments and the access problems hitherto

---

1. There are now twenty-nine Scottish Great Trails, long-distance walking routes that have been approved by NatureScot, formerly Scottish Natural Heritage.

are interesting. There are still many walkers in Scotland who fervently believe that such 'official' trails effectively corral walkers onto a linear route, a form of 'managed access' that could ultimately erode the de facto public right of access we currently enjoy in Scotland.

Indeed, such managed access is exactly what the Scottish Landowners' Federation and the National Farmers' Union of Scotland are calling for during the current debate on the Land Reform (Scotland) Bill. The only difference is the landowners and farmers want people to stick to such footpaths and not leave them. Thankfully, it appears highly unlikely that the access provisions in the Land Reform Bill will allow landowners to have their way and there is nothing in Scots law that would prevent anyone leaving a route like the Great Glen Way and wandering up an adjacent hillside.

Much of the route follows the towpath of the Caledonian Canal. Other sections utilise forestry tracks and paths and, while there are some slightly more challenging sections, this certainly isn't a route for the wilderness walker or lover of solitude. What the Great Glen Way does offer is an extremely pleasant multi-day coast-to-coast route that passes through some lovely areas of the highlands.

Early sections along the canal towpath towards Loch Lochy offer panoramic views of Ben Nevis, the Aonachs and the Grey Corries and, in high summer, the canal itself is always bustling with cruise boats and fishing boats taking the inland route between the North Sea and the waters of the west. Of course, the *pièce de résistance* for many will be the high routes that look down on the vast open waters of Loch Ness. You never know what you'll see!

The route itself is seventy-three miles long and would probably take the average walker five or six days. The route is well served by guest houses, hotels and youth hostels and there are camp sites in places like Gairlochy, Fort Augustus, Invermoriston, Drumnadrochit and near Inverness.

ARRAN COASTAL WAY
MARCH 2003

It's only a dozen miles across the Firth of Clyde but those twelve miles represent a crossover from one world to another.

As the Caledonian Islands ferry sliced through the calm waters of the Firth of Clyde I stood near the ship's bow and watched the dim outline of Arran's mountains appear through the haze. The evening sun, a golden orb, hung lazily over Goat Fell.

Arran has always held a special significance for me. It was while descending the granite slabs of the A' Chir ridge some thirty-odd years ago that I decided I wanted a job that would allow me to spend the rest of my life climbing mountains. The sun-kissed hills of Arran richly blessed me that day, but I wasn't visiting Arran to climb mountains this time. I had been invited to open a new long-distance trail, the Isle of Arran Coastal Way, and spend a few days walking sections of the route that was created by two local men, Hugh McKerrell and Dick Sim.

While the mountains of Arran have always attracted climbers and hillwalkers, many are a little overawed by the steep and narrow ridges of the island's main peaks. For every climber who has been thrilled by the sweeping granite slabs and steep, soaring pinnacles of the likes of Cir Mhor and Casteal Abhail there are dozens of walkers who would rather tackle something less dramatic, less technically taxing, but challenging enough to make their outing an adventure. So, the sixty-five-mile Isle of Arran Coastal Way was conceived.

The coastal route can be treated in several different ways. Diehard backpackers can wander round the island carrying a tent, sleeping bag and everything else needed for survival, dossing down in one of the island's many caves or bivouacking below the night skies. Others might prefer a little more comfort, spending the nights in a guest house or hotel. Others again might prefer to walk the route over a number of weekends, tackling one or two sections between villages each time.

Arran has, in a sense, been ideally created for coastal path walking. A raised beach, like a shallow coastal fringe, encircles the island, even below the steeper cliffs of the island, and the Coastal Way follows this raised beach virtually all the way. While much of the route follows well-used footpaths and stretches of beach, occasionally you have to follow the road, albeit a very quiet and pleasant road, mostly on the west of the island.

My own favourite section was probably the toughest part of the route, from Kildonan to Whiting Bay past Dippen Head. No footpath tames this part of the walk, although the difficulties can be avoided by following the road at the top of the cliffs. With steep 91m/300ft cliffs on one side and the open sea on the other, this part of the coastal fringe is an enormous boulder-field. Some of the boulders are the size of a double-decker bus.[2] The route passes the Black Cave, the largest cave on the island, and although great care is required as you leap from rock to rock there is something rather satisfying in the uncompromising nature of the terrain that made me, essentially a mountaineer, feel very much at home. Rocky reefs run out towards the little lighthouse island of Pladda and, beyond, floating on the horizon, is the great volcanic plug of Paddy's Milestone, the Ailsa Craig. It isn't hard to believe these parts have seen regular encounters between excisemen and smugglers over the years. The contraband trade once thrived on these south shores of Arran.

I suspect archeologists and geologists feel pretty much at home on Arran too for this island is a living archive. A nineteenth-century geologist once wrote: 'The number of rock formations, sedimentary and plutonic, which are found within this limited space is truly remarkable, perhaps unparalleled in any tract of like extent on the surface of the globe.' That's maybe why, on stepping ashore at Brodick pier, you feel as though you're entering an older, more peaceful world, another world indeed, although only a dozen miles from the Ayrshire coast.

2. The boulder-hopping section from from Kildonan to Whiting Bay past Dippen Head has now been re-routed to avoid the difficulties.

SGURR NAN EUGALLT AND SGURR A'CHOIRE-BHEITHE, KNOYDART, JUNE 2004

It was meant to be a birthday treat but a thought suddenly flashed through my mind that if I didn't take care there might not be any more birthdays.

I had just slid down an innocuous-looking slab of rock on a hill called Sgurr a'Choire-bheithe in the Rough Bounds of Knoydart. No harm done, other than a hole in my new Gore-tex jacket but here I was, on my own, in dreadful weather conditions in one of the roughest, toughest hill areas in the country. A measure of prudence was called for.

Earlier I had climbed Sgurr nan Eugallt, 894m/2950ft, (grimly translates as the peak of the death streams) which, thanks to the superb stalkers' path that climbs almost all the way to the summit, is probably one of the easiest of the Corbetts. Occasional clearances in the mist showed a wild, tumbled landscape, steep slopes pockmarked by rock outcrops and wild, foaming streams. The rain was relentless.

My birthday plan was to camp wild somewhere between Sgurr nan Eugallt and Sgurr a'Choire-bheithe, two Knoydart Corbetts whose summits are the high points of long, knobbly ridges that run roughly parallel from Loch Quoich to Glen Barrisdale. An overnight camp would break up a long eighteen-mile route in very rough terrain. This overnight bivouac was the essence of the birthday treat, the ascent of the hills only a little icing on the cake, for a wild camp in the heart of the Rough Bounds of Knoydart is always a memorable experience, the wildest, most heart-achingly beautiful region of Scotland.

The descent from Sgurr nan Eugallt, like most descents in this area, proved more awkward than difficult, down spongy slopes between crags and foaming burns to the rain-soaked bealach between Glen Barrisdale and Gleann Cosaidh. Red deer squelched off into the watery wilderness at my arrival.

The plan was to camp as close as possible to the Druim Chosaidh, the long ridge that bounds the south side of the glen, and climb Sgurr a'Choire-bheithe, 913m/2999ft, first thing in the morning, but a glance at the map suggested the morning walk out could be long and difficult enough on its own. Sgurr a'Choire-bheithe would have to be an evening ascent.

A quick brew and a bite to eat and I was off up the hill, eager to reach the narrow crest of the Druim Cosaidh with its knobbly tops and rocky knolls. By this time the mist had become less dense and every so often the grey vapours would rise to reveal breathtaking views of the surrounding peaks: Ben Aden, Sgurr na Ciche, Luinne Bheinn, Ladhar Bheinn, and deep, glaciated, summer-green glens.

It was scrambling down one of the rocky tors that I slipped on a slab of wet rock and performed a very inelegant bum-slide down the rest of the crag. It was enough to remind me of my potentially perilous situation. On my own on a remote mountain in wet and slippery conditions with most of my gear in a tiny tent fifteen hundred feet below me. After that, like the biblical character Agag, I trod delicately.

The rounded summit of Sgurr a'Choire-bheithe, (only a foot short of Munro height) gives a fabulous view down into Barrisdale Bay. Two hundred years ago it wasn't uncommon to see several trading ships at anchor there, but that was before the Clearances and thanks to one Josephine MacDonnell and her factor Alexander Grant, Knoydart folk suffered more than most.

After my little slip I was uneasy about retracing my scrambles over the Druim Chosaidh so instead I slowly descended a series of grassy gullies back to the depths of the glen and my tent. Never did a camp supper taste so good, or a sleeping bag feel so comfortable.

Torrential rain greeted me in the morning, the Abhainn Chosaidh had risen by a couple of feet and was now a white, swirling melee and a flowing moat of water had appeared around my tent. It was a long and wet walk out down to Loch Quoich and around its shoreline to the Kinloch Hourn road. Three miles on the road back to the car, in more hospitable weather, helped me dry out a bit and by the time I had finished every limb knew that I'd survived another tussle with the Rough Bounds of Knoydart.

CARN A'CHLAMAIN
OCTOBER 2006

I sat and watched a swollen River Tilt, the colour of blended whisky, forcing its way through a narrow, rocky channel. I could have spent all day here, leaning against a giant oak, watching the spumes of spray, the flowing eddies and the way the waters poured over the submerged rocks and into the deep stoppers before gathering themselves for the remainder of the descent, as though swollen and drunk with power.

I was making my way slowly up Glen Tilt towards the head-waters of the river where a thousand small feeder streams, grown boisterous after overnight rain, fed the river and set it on what was now a tumultuous course. My idea was to find a spot to tuck myself away for the night, somewhere I could hear the roaring of rutting stags, and out of the roar of the wind that had been shrieking over the hills for the past few days.

The great Scottish mountain writer W. H. Murray once suggested that the walker will never find his or her interest flagging in Glen Tilt. 'The river is continuously lively, the woods are mature and varied and there is a continuous, gradual change from the lower fertility to an upper desolation.'

South-east of Glen Tilt, the Beinn a'Ghlo massif rises to its four tops, described by ecologist and mountaineer Adam Watson as 'one of the most beautiful and mysterious hills of Scotland'. In contrast, the high, peaty area to the north of the Tilt is dominated the Ring of Tarf, a quartet of Munros, Beinn Dearg, Carn a'Chlamain, An Sgarsoch and Carn an Fhidleir, which offers the hillwalker a long and arduous expedition involving many miles of tough, remote walking. Most Munro-baggers are happy enough to break the round into at least three expeditions.

I had wandered up the glen in a desultory sort of way, with only a vague intention of climbing Carn a'Chlamain, 963m/3159ft, the Munro that lifts its head shyly from the Tarf plateau to gaze across Glen Tilt to the Beinn a'Ghlo massif.

My original plan was to camp somewhere near the Falls of Tarf in the upper reaches of the glen, and in the morning climb Carn a'Chlamain from the stalkers path that zigzags its way up the hillside from Forest Lodge in Glen Tilt. This is one of the popular routes to the Atholl Munros that the estate keeps open to walkers during the stag-shooting season.

The next day being Sunday I knew I was in no danger of inter-rupting stalking, so on the spur of the moment I followed a track that broke away from the main Glen Tilt route and climbed over high ground and down to the lonely Tarf Water. All of a sudden, a new plan of action became clear. Two miles upstream lay the splendid Tarf Bothy, an old and very remote shooting lodge. I intended camping close to it and, next morning, crossing Carn a'Chlamain from north to south, giving me a new perspective on a hill I had climbed several times before.

I didn't hear many stags during the night, although there were plenty of hinds about, roe deer too. Next day the wind was as strong as ever and I climbed up from the bothy, over the spur of Meall Tionail, and onto the scree-covered slopes of Carn a'Chlamain. Now and again the wind teased the mists away, revealing an immense landscape that stretched away to the north under a massive domed sky, yellow deer grasses bright and intense in colour, with every feature picked out and etched by the smile of a shy sun, ridge over ridge, horizon over horizon, rolling moor and shadow-stained glens, clear-cut land and glis-tening waters. This was the tumbled lands of Atholl and Bruar, one of Scotland's wildest and remotest quarters.

I dropped back into Glen Tilt by courtesy of Carn a'Chlamhain's south-west ridge, delighting in the contrast between the upper desolation and the relative fertility of the Glen. Almost immediately I met walkers on the track, and felt like a prophet who had just come down from the wilderness.

THE SUTHERLAND TRAIL
DECEMBER 2008

If you're anything like me you'll suffer from an occasional longing to cast off the shackles and escape to the hills for several days at a time, to jettison all the everyday routines and head off on a multi-day backpacking trip that takes you through some of finest landscapes imaginable.

At this time of the year, after reflecting on this year just gone, it can be exciting to look forward and plan trips for the coming year. With the help of a television show to be broadcast on Boxing Day, I can heartily commend a five-to-seven-day walking route through the northern county of Sutherland.

The Sutherland Trail is the subject of an hour-long documentary that I spent much of the summer working on, and what a way to spend the summer. My wife and I walked the route earlier this year, from Lochinver to Lairg, climbing Suilven, Foinaven and Ben Loyal en route, a distance of about seventy-seven miles, and I later returned with a crew to film the route for the BBC.

Pragmatically, it begins in the west-coast fishing port of Lochinver, but aesthetically it starts on the summit of Suilven, the uncontested showpiece of Sutherland, and finishes on the summit of Ben Loyal, which lies in isolated splendour at the head of the Kyle of Tongue. The route takes a meandering line: to the limestone region of Inchnadamph and its caves, fossil remains and chambered cairns, up to the Eas a Chual Aluinn waterfall, the highest falls in Britain, before descending to Kylesku and some of the best langoustine dinners you can imagine.

It then crosses the Kylesku Bridge to Kylestrome and a magnificent highway up and over the wild Reay Estate to Achfary, in the shadow of those wonderful mountains, Ben Stack, Arkle and Foinaven. You have the option of climbing any of these hills en route before another hill path wriggles its way through Strath Luib na Seillich, over the Bealach Feithe and down to Gobernuisgach Lodge and the road to the historic Strath More.

Passing the ancient Dun Dornaigil, one of the finest of our remaining brochs, you might like to climb Ben Hope, the most northerly of the Munros, before picking up the Moine Path[3] to Kinloch where you can either head for the route-end at Tongue or finish by climbing Ben Loyal, the Queen of the Highlands, according to a Statistical Account of 1842.

What I particularly enjoyed about this route, other than its breathtaking landscapes, was the discovery that Sutherland is almost reinventing itself. This old county, the South Land of the Vikings, has always had a reputation for being bleak and boggy, a midge-infested place that earned the reputation of 'the empty lands', but what we discovered wasn't so much a 'wilderness' in the normal sense but an area of vast potential, both for those who live there and those who come to these northern parts to take part in a multitude of outdoor activities and adventure sports.

People are returning to the glens, not in great numbers yet, but as the tensions and strife of urban Britain become increasingly intolerable more and more people are searching for an alternative lifestyle. Like the former hairdresser who has become a breeder of langoustine, or the Danish artist who finds inspiration in the colours and shades of her newly adopted home, or the shepherds and prawn fishermen who wouldn't want to live or work anywhere else.

Traditional crofters too have discovered a new purpose and meaning, freed from the feus and pressures of tenancy. The Assynt Crofters Trust made history with the first community buyout of land their families had crofted for generations. Their story is an inspiring one, and led the way to similar buyouts on Eigg, in Knoydart, in the Western Isles and in neighbouring South Assynt. There is a new momentum at work in the highlands and the finest way to experience it is to walk the land, to

---

3. Sadly, the wonderfully atmospheric A'Mhoine, which the Sutherland Trail crosses, looks likely to be the site of a satellite launching station. The UK Space Agency said it could pave the way for future space flights.

read its small print and connect with it. The Sutherland Trail allows you to do just that.

THE EASTERN CAIRNGORMS
AUGUST 2010

Such is the vastness of the Cairngorms that it's very easy to bite off more than you can chew, your ambitions thwarted by huge distances, difficult terrain and uncompromising weather.

My old pal Hamish Telfer had a couple of Munros to complete in the area, Bynack Mor, which I wrote about last week, and nearby Ben Avon. In a moment of unblemished overconfidence I suggested that we could climb both hills in a two-day sortie from the north, camping high somewhere on the Beinn a'Bhuird plateau.

As most hillwalkers are aware, the best-laid plans aft gang awry, and strong winds swept away any notions we entertained of a high camp. As we climbed towards Bynack Mor from the Pass of Ryvoan we soon became aware of the increasing intensity of the wind and by the time we stumbled across the summit ridge, we could barely stand up in the roar and bluster of the gales.

By the time we reached the Fords of Avon bothy, the old howff that stands close to the River Avon, we were still reeling from the battering we had taken and thought it might be sensible to put Plan B into practice. Rather than climbing up onto the Beinn a'Bhuird plateau via the high point of the Lairig an Laoigh we decided to stay comparatively low-level and follow the River Avon eastwards towards the bothy at Faindouran Lodge where we could set up camp. Depending on the weather we could either climb Ben Avon from the north, or wait until the morning before climbing it.

The weather gradually improved as we picked our way along the waterlogged path along Glen Avon and in no time at all we were both enthralled by the open skies, long hill slopes rolling out towards rounded summits and a real feeling of remoteness.

We pitched our tents outside the bothy, had a brew and a bite to eat and made the decision to go for Ben Avon. Now this wasn't as simple as it sounds for the slopes of the hill were on the opposite side of a raging, in-spate River Avon. A quick check on the map showed a footbridge downstream and from there a long climb would take us to the Stob an t-Sluichd summit of Beinn a'Bhuird. From there we reckoned on a high-level trek around the rim of the Garbh Choire, the big, rocky corrie above the Slochd Mor, before a final ascent to the granite tor called Leabaidh an Daimh Bhuidhe that marks the summit of the multi-topped Ben Avon.

Unfortunately, we were only a few metres short of Stob an t-Sluichd when we realised we were moving slower and slower. The sky was getting dark with heavy, ominous clouds and we knew we didn't have too long until darkness fell. Even if we made it to the summit we'd still have faced about seven miles of difficult mountain country to get back to the tent. Swallowing our pride we reluctantly called it a day, turned our back on the summit and high-tailed it back to Faindouran Lodge, the end of a long nineteen-mile day.

It was the right decision, although both of us are well past the point of believing that reaching Munro summits is essential. We'd had a long and superb day of wild walking in a marvellous part of the country, topped by a great walk-out: back to Fords of Avon, a climb up to The Saddle above Strath Nethy, another ascent of Cairn Gorm, and a long descent via the mountain's Sron an Aonaich ridge (what the funicular train company insists on calling the Windy Ridge) and the Allt Mor path back to Glenmore. By the time we reached the car we both knew we'd had a good bit of exercise!

CHAPTER ELEVEN

Protect and Preserve

The dog-eared flap of cardboard hung from a fence post, stained by lengthy exposure to the elements. The words scrawled on it were stark and unfriendly: 'Keep Out, By Order'. Similar notices once hung on gateposts and fences throughout Scotland, messages with feudal overtones that displayed an attitude far more pernicious than a desire for privacy. Such signs resonated with a subliminal message, a refusal to acknowledge that responsible access to Scottish land is hereditary and time-honoured, enshrined in tradition, a civil right that has long been valued by the Scottish public.

However, in the years prior to the publication of the Land Reform (Scotland) Act 2003 there was a growing tendency amongst many Scottish landowners to disregard such de facto access rights. With growing numbers going to the hills, many people felt intimidated by threatening trespass notices, especially those with little knowledge of Scotland's hill-going traditions. As a result, there was a growing call for access rights in Scotland to be changed from de facto to *de jure*.

There is still a general presumption that Scotland's right-to-roam legislation was 'gifted' to the people of Scotland by the brand new Scottish Parliament, but that's far from the truth. Initially the omens were good. During a debate in the Parliament in November 1999 the then Deputy Justice Minister Angus MacKay said the Executive (nowadays called the Government) wanted to 'codify' what was already happening in practice. This was exactly the aspiration of the Access Forum and Scottish Natural Heritage (now Nature Scot), who had made recommendations to the then Scottish Office in 1998 on new legislative arrangements for access. The Access Forum, set up in 1994 by SNH, had brought together land-managing and recreation interests, along with public bodies, and had an impressive track record in reaching agreement on access principles for the hills, including the provision of information to the public during deer stalking and other projects which helped to harmonise countryside interests.

All this was before the new Scottish Executive's civil servants got their teeth into the legislative process. Shock waves reverberated through the outdoor community when the Draft Bill was published in February 2001, just a day before the foot-and-mouth epidemic raised its ugly head. Proposals included powers that would criminalise access and allow landowners to suspend the public's new statutory right of access. It also placed a number of obligations on the public to act 'responsibly', with no reciprocal obligation placed on land managers and farmers.

It soon became clear that both Liberal Democrat Jim Wallace and Sam Galbraith of Labour, the coalition ministers responsible for the Draft Bill, had not at that stage fully understood the finer detail of the draft legislation and its wider implications. Not for the first time, civil servants had run rings around their political masters. Fortunately, Wallace, along with other Labour Ministers, (by this time Sam Galbraith had retired) began to get a grip of the process, influenced partly by a massive public consultation response. But it was something else entirely that convinced Jim Wallace that the Scottish public could be trusted to act responsibly in the countryside while the landowners and farmers couldn't. The dark cloud of the foot-and-mouth epidemic had a silver lining as far as Scottish access was concerned.

Wallace made it clear that he had become concerned at the way Scotland's landowners 'abused' the access closures, even months after the crisis had died down. Indeed, Robert Balfour, the erstwhile convenor of the Scottish Landowners' Federation, had spent hours of media time telling his members that if they were not seen to be co-operating with the spirit of the foot-and-mouth Comeback Code they would pay a heavy price. He later admitted to me that Scotland's landowners had shot themselves in the foot.

In the company of Dave Morris, Director of Ramblers Scotland, I was in attendance in Edinburgh when Jim Wallace, disgusted that 'Keep Out' signs still decorated the Scottish countryside months after the crisis ended, made his media announcement about his changes to the Draft Bill. The resulting legislation was everything we hoped for and created a wonderful climax to decades of political wrangling about the legal status of access in Scotland.

Although many individuals were involved in the campaign for access, notably the late Rennie MacOwan of Stirling, there is little doubt in my mind that it was Dave Morris[1] and the late Alan Blackshaw who spearheaded the campaign. It was Dave's campaigning skills and political nous, along with Alan's forensic research, that finally won the case and gave the people of Scotland what is arguably the finest access legislation in the world. As President of Ramblers Scotland in the three years running up to the publication of the legislation, it was quite an experience to be involved, and to witness the dedication, knowledge and sheer perseverance of these committed campaigners.

As a writer and mountaineer I had always found it difficult, nay impossible, to separate my love of the mountains and wild places from political activism, and as a newspaper columnist, and radio presenter on a weekly BBC Scotland environmental programme called *In the Country*, I had sufficient media presence to help further the cause of countryside conservation and public access. I also served for two three-year terms as President

---

1. I was delighted when Dave Morris, the former Director of Ramblers Scotland and one of the chief architects of Scotland's access legislation, finally had his achievement recognised when he was awarded an Honorary Fellowship of the Royal Scottish Geographical Society and was later given the Scottish Award for Excellence in Mountain Culture, both in 2021. Sadly, his colleague Alan Blackshaw OBE passed away in 2011.

of Ramblers Scotland and later spent six years as Chairman of the Nevis Partnership, a coalition of landowners, community groups and NGOs with an interest in the protection of our highest mountain, Ben Nevis, and Glen Nevis. Both of these roles propelled me to the forefront of wild land conservation at a time when we witnessed such issues as the campaign for public access, the foot-and-mouth crisis, the extension of skiing development and the proposals to build a funicular train on Cairn Gorm, the campaign to reduce deer numbers to help create more natural woodland and the proposed sale of the Cuillin of Skye.

There were ongoing issues too, like litter and an explosion of waymarking cairns, the misuse of bothies, the argument as to whether such shelters should be listed and publicised and, of course, the widespread creation of onshore windfarms and power lines. These were all issues that I regularly wrote about during my twenty-year editorship of *The Great Outdoors* magazine. I was determined to use that UK-wide platform to campaign on behalf of walkers, ramblers and mountaineers. We had a number of successes but always in spite of a large number of readers who thought politics, even green environmental politics, should be kept out of what they saw as a leisure magazine. Some of my publishers weren't too keen on this political content either, not because they opposed the views but because they couldn't turn it into advertising revenue.

My long run as a columnist in the Strathspey and Badenoch Herald gave me the opportunity of commenting on numerous issues in one of the conservation hotspots of Scotland and I'm saddened that even today, forty years on, some of the most serious issues have never been resolved. Highlands and Islands Enterprise still clutch on to their ownership of Cairn Gorm, ski developments on that mountain are still suffering because of a lack of snow, the funicular train is still draining the public purse of millions upon millions of pounds and some landowners are still building fences to protect areas of woodland. All within just one of our National Parks.

The managers of Scotland's other National Park, the Loch Lomond and Trossachs National Park, didn't do the reputation of Parks any favours by creating by-laws that criminalised 'wild camping' in an attempt to stop littering and vandalism on the east shore of Loch Lomond, a section of the lochside that contains the popular West Highland Way. Ignoring the fact there was already considerable legislation in place to deal with such issues the Park decided to disenfranchise most of Scotland's outdoor public and ensured the conservation spotlight would thereafter shine directly on them and their activities.

Concerned by the Park Board's apparent disregard for the access benefits of the Land Reform (Scotland) Act, which covered wild camping, a former Board member of Scottish Natural Heritage and a former President of the Mountaineering Council of Scotland, Nick Kempe, initiated a website called Parkswatch Scotland, a watchdog-type website that regularly reports on National Park issues and how they are dealt with. I think it's fair to say that while both Parks have done excellent work they are far removed from the original international concept of National Parks. For a start neither of our National Parks are in public ownership, a deep flaw that vastly reduces the power and ambition of the Park Boards, and National Park legislation requires them to view development with the same importance as conservation. I suspect John Muir, a son of Scotland as well as father of the worldwide National Parks movement, regularly birls in his grave.

BOTHY PROBLEMS
SEPTEMBER 1995

Have you ever heard of the Sgordrum Wrecking Crew or the Blackhill Antisocial Hillwalkers? Although I profess no intimate knowledge of these groups, and the stories of their activities could well be apocryphal, they nevertheless portray the darker side of outdoor activities in Scotland.

These groups are said to represent a direct backlash against years of 'urbanisation of the mountains', and have apparently torched or vandalised several bothies in the Lochaber and Sutherland area in protest against 'rowdy youngsters and bloody foreigners'. Sadly, the only people who really suffer are those lovers of the hills who know and love the bothies as simple shelters which allow them to explore some of the remoter areas of the Highlands. But do the Blackhill Antisocialites have a point?

I think they have, although I am repulsed by their method of objection. Destroying other folk's property to make your protest is a low place to sink and does nothing to promote your point of view. But it's important to know that other folk have been destroying such property for years. Many bothies have been vandalised and litter strewn by hillwalkers and climbers. Damage ranges from wooden partitions being torn down for firewood to bothy rooms being used as public lavatories.

The Mountain Bothies Association is not entirely innocent either. Formed as a maintenance organisation, enthusiasts would spend weekends and holidays rebuilding and repairing old barns, unused keeper's cottages and the likes for other hillwalkers to use. They have been a victim of their own success. Barely a week goes by that I don't get a letter or phone call from someone asking for the address of the MBA. Always, on questioning, the inquirer admits to wanting a list of bothies. They think the MBA is some form of youth hostel association, except that bothies are free.

What is more worrying is that there is a faction within the MBA which wants to publish lists of the bothies, to promote them as if they were theirs to promote.[2] They are not. The MBA does not own a single brick, all the bothies are owned by landowners, and some of them are becoming sick of having a midden of a bothy in their backyard. The owners of Corndavon Bothy, east of Ben Avon in the Cairngorms, recently closed it down,

2. Lists of Scotland's bothies are now publicly available on social media and a book, *The Bothy Bible*, was published in 2017.

not because of vandalism, but because of misuse, mainly a series of drugs and booze parties. The owner of Barisdale Bothy in Knoydart recently told me that he was concerned that a university group turned up for a weekend 'with more booze than I stock in my London wine bar'. His keeper later reported that the group tore up a new bridge over the Barrisdale River for firewood.

On a visit to a couple of bothies in Lochaber recently I was amazed to find them occupied by what I could only describe as New Age travellers. They were nice enough people, but their occupancy would have made it difficult for any innocent member of the public coming off the hill looking for shelter. Last year Ruigh Aitcheachan bothy in Glen Feshie was being used a week at a time by a school from England, like some sort of outdoor centre. Commercial walking groups use them, Scouts and Guides use them, and Duke of Edinburgh parties use them too. Of this I am not entirely innocent. I took a group of Scouts to a bothy a few years ago to find it inhabited by two hillwalkers, a young couple obviously newly in love. My dozen Scouts spoiled the peace and romance of their weekend, and I swore I would never again take a group of more than two people to a bothy.

As an enthusiastic lightweight tent user I've never really been much of an advocate for bothying, but I am aware that occasionally they do save lives. I am also aware of the social camaraderie of bothy life, but times are changing and it could soon be that bothies as we know them will be a thing of the past. If it rids the hills of some of the people they obviously attract, I for one won't lament their passing.

FENCING – THE BARBED TRUTH
OCTOBER 1997

There is a mania for fence building sweeping the Highlands. No matter where you go there are fences surrounding fields, fences stretched out in an endless march across mountainsides and fences around wee clumps of bushes and trees. I suspect they are costing you and me an awful lot of money.[3]

Fences for keeping animals in, fences for keeping animals out, fences which have a secondary effect of keeping walkers and ramblers in their place, and in many of the cases Scottish Natural Heritage is happy to grant-aid these structures. It seems to be the new tool of conservation. Build a fence around a clump of trees or a wad of vegetation, keep the nibbling deer and sheep at bay and perhaps, just perhaps, we can recreate our great forests of yesteryear.

Now, that's a noble cause, the Great Pinewoods of Caledon must have been wonderful places with luxurious undergrowth, rich in flora and fauna and a home to such exotic species as wolves, boars, bears and other creatures which have long since been extinct from these shores.

Unfortunately, our desire to build great ships and to exterminate these dark, damp places (which also offered a home to marauding thieves and vagabonds) meant that our ancestors, less appreciative than ourselves perhaps, saw little problem in burning and chopping down thousands of acres until very little was left. Browsing sheep and deer, which replaced people in the Highlands, left little hope of new seeds taking hold. Now, hundreds of years later, we are trying to recreate the great woods by keeping the deer and sheep away from the tender young shoots.

Nobody loves trees, especially the wonderful Scots pine, more than I do, but clumps of natural, indigenous forest are grossly spoiled when they're surrounded by miles of deer fencing.

I happened upon one particularly obnoxious example

---

3. Fences are going up again all over Scotland thanks to the Scottish Government's Forestry Grant Scheme. Despite the massive successes of woodland restoration at places like Creag Meagaidh and Glen Feshie, where no fences had to be built, most Scottish landowners refuse to cut down on the number of grazing animals, which would allow regeneration of our woodland without the need for fences. We appear to be going backwards in terms of the environment in Scotland.

recently. There is a lovely clump of birch woodland of which I am very fond, a therapeutic sort of place which lies below the great frowning crags of Creag Dubh. My first inclination that something was afoot was when a fine stretch of footpath through the wood was crudely torn up to allow vehicles to reach a small water dam. Some weeks later the same footpath was further despoiled by fence builders' vehicles. Now, running up through the woods and onto the open hillside is a long, long line of fencing. It's like an open sore on the face of the hill, deer fencing topped by that most evil invention of urban man: barbed wire.

What hideous mind ever thought up the idea of these crude barbs? Barbed wire is synonymous with concentration camps and prisons, not the Scottish countryside. The effect of stumbling against such an indictment of man's inconsideration to man is depressing. The first impression is that of feeling unwanted and pariahed, as barbed-wire fencing is more bitter in the statement it represents than any 'Keep Out' notice.

The second feeling is anger: anger at the people who have ordered such a thing, anger at the planning authorities for allowing it, and anger at SNH for putting up the money, taxpayers' money, to grant-aid it. Then there's anger at the insensitive nature of it and anger at generations of landowners who have allowed the deer and the sheep to become such a threat to our native woodlands in the first place.

THE CUILLIN FOR A TENNER?
JUNE 2000

I went to the Isle of Skye last week to make what some folk might describe as an audacious offer to John MacLeod of MacLeod[4] to buy the Cuillin from him, if indeed he does actually own it.

---

4. John MacLeod of MacLeod died in 2007 and his successor, Hugh Magnus MacLeod of MacLeod, managed to find new funding for the work at Dunvegan. The ownership of the Black Cuillin is still in dispute.

He has put the iconic mountain range on the market in a bid to raise money to pay for repairs to his ancestral home, Dunvegan Castle.

In my role as President of Ramblers Scotland I was launching a new Skye and Lochalsh group and took the opportunity to make my offer. If MacLeod doesn't own the land (there is some doubt), then I suggested the Crown Estate should offer it at a peppercorn annual rent of ten pounds, to the people of Skye.

By the end of August we should know the outcome of the ownership investigations. Doubt has been expressed as to the legality of MacLeod's ownership and after the Scottish Parliament effectively dismissed the claims it took a Westminster Labour MP, Brian Wilson, to encourage the Scotland Office in London to look into the case. The Crown Estate Commissioners have since taken it up but, whether or not MacLeod of MacLeod has legal title or not, I believe we must ensure that the future of the Cuillin lies safely in the hands of the local community, not exposed to the potential free-for-all of a grasping land market.

Provided MacLeod owns the land, I was prepared to offer him not ten million but ten pounds, on the basis that if BMW can sell Rover for a tenner[5] then surely I could buy the Cuillin for the same sum? If he accepts then I have no doubt the Scottish public will support him enthusiastically in raising the funds for the repairs to Dunvegan Castle and I'll be happy to pass on the Cuillin to the local community to be managed in cooperation with various Scottish conservation organisations.

Whatever ultimately happens to these mountains, it is only right and proper that the local community is given the opportunity to manage the estate, and to that end I deposited my ten-pound note in the Clydesdale Bank in Portree to open up a fund for the future community management of the Cuillin.

I hope this could be the start of something bigger. We badly need a new approach to land ownership and management in

5. In May 2000, BMW sold Rover to a business consortium called Phoenix in an attempt to save thousands of jobs and retain car production at Longbridge in the West Midlands

Scotland. We've seen the good, the bad and the ugly of both private ownership and ownership by national conservation bodies. Surely, we've had enough of Maruma and his ilk, the artist who briefly and drastically owned the Isle of Eigg. Do we really need the ongoing hassles of issues like Glen Feshie[6] where a bid from a coalition of conservation organisations was rejected in favour of an overseas businessman who is now trying to get massive sums of money from the public purse to erect yet more needless deer fencing? Surely, we should be seeking a new agenda where communities can take charge of areas like the Cuillin and, with the support of recreational and conservation bodies, ensure they are managed for the public good. The Ramblers' Skye and Lochalsh group will provide a new focus for land-use campaigning at a local level and we will be actively promoting this opportunity for a joint initiative between local interests and outdoor recreation bodies.

FOOT-AND-MOUTH : A BUREAUCRATIC DISASTER
APRIL 2001

I wonder how much longer the tourist industry in the Highlands and Islands of Scotland can be sacrificed by our elected representatives both local and national? The current foot-and-mouth crisis is a disaster and, while we all fully sympathise with those farmers whose livestock has been destroyed, one can't help but wonder if the so-called cure could eventually have more serious consequences than those of the disease itself?

As I write this, the countryside is in a state of acute confusion caused by conflicting advice from the Scottish Executive. Last week, Ross Finnie, the Minister for Rural Affairs told us all to 'keep out of the countryside'. This led to Scottish Natural Heritage, no doubt out of sympathy for the farming community, 'closing' all of its mountain properties. This led to a domino

---

6. Glen Feshie was eventually sold to the Danish businessman Anders Holch Povlson who has drastically reduced deer numbers and is effectively re-wilding the estate.

effect as the National Trust for Scotland and the John Muir Trust went into copycat mode. The Forestry Commission, probably pressured by the SNH decision, closed its forests to the public. Since then, private landowners have followed suit and more recently the Highland Council has posted signs all over the place telling the public there is 'No Access'.

Curiously, the no-access paranoia that is sweeping the nation has little basis in the scientific advice given the by veterinary service, or MAFF,[7] or the Scottish Executive's website or helpline. These sources have consistently advised people to steer clear of livestock everywhere and avoid areas where foot-and-mouth is present or suspected.

Let me reiterate again that the outdoor recreational organisations have been completely responsible through all of this, and remarkably patient. The Ramblers Association was the first recreational organisation to advise its members to cancel walks that went near farms with livestock. The Mountaineering Council for Scotland has been equally understanding, but the wholesale ban on the countryside that now exists is becoming intolerable, and not only because people can't go for a walk or enjoy a bit of climbing.

The fact of the matter is that walking and mountaineering are part of a burgeoning tourism industry that is, after only a couple of weeks of access restrictions, looking into an abyss. Tourism is much larger in terms of economic viability and future potential than either livestock or arable farming in the Highlands and Islands of Scotland. I'm not trying to set one industry against another here, nor am I being unduly critical of the agricultural industry or the NFU in their time of need, but I am saying that our elected representatives, both locally and nationally, must start looking at the bigger picture.

Outdoor centres, bunkhouses, hostels, guiding companies, walking tour operators and outdoor shops have lost millions of pounds already. The bed and breakfast establishments, the

---

7. Ministry of Agriculture, Forest and Fisheries

guest houses, the hotels, the pubs and the food shops that rely on this market outside the normal tourist season are suffering too.

With Easter coming up the future of our tourist industry is at stake. To save it the government must immediately listen to its own scientific advice and ease restrictions on access as soon as possible. It has to lay down its emotional and public relations-oriented attitude and become more pragmatic. It has to start listening to the desperate cries of a tourist industry that, like the farming community, has been kicked in the teeth time and time again by the strong pound, high fuel costs and the perennial problems of the Scottish weather.

What will happen if our politicians don't act? The answer to that is barely acceptable, and it is this: in time the government will have to listen to the tourist industry, simply because of that industry's size and the effect its demise would have on the country. By that time the government may well have to sacrifice the agricultural industry instead, but by acting quickly it has an opportunity to save both, and surely that's what everyone wants?

TIME TO GO
JUNE 2002

I felt as though I was gate-crashing a party I hadn't been invited to. The sun shone and the razzamatazz was in full flow as tourism minister Mike Watson MSP formally opened the Cairn Gorm funicular railway. It wasn't the time to raise old arguments.

I was on Cairn Gorm at the invitation of the BBC, and not the Chairlift Company or Highlands and Islands Enterprise. I attended the party to call on HIE to give up their landholding in the northern Cairngorms, a call that fell on surprisingly receptive ears.

HIE and its predecessors the Highlands and Islands Development Board, has been the driving force behind the funicular and other controversial projects on Cairn Gorm, including proposed, and ultimately unsuccessful, westward expansions of skiing facilities in the 1980s and 90s. Indeed, in recent years HIE's ownership of this estate has been the root cause of much of the disharmony that has made Cairn Gorm a byword for conservation controversy.

If we look at ski centres in other parts of the world, notably in the USA, we see that local communities have ownership and control of the ski grounds. In Switzerland, the local cantons run the ski business. Why not here in Scotland? It's absurd that a Government quango like HIE own such an estate. Now is the time for HIE to give up their landholding and arrange for it to be transferred to the local community or the incoming Cairngorms National Park Board. The Board will be in a far better position to build consensus over future development options and avoid the mistakes of the past.

I think there is little doubt that the funicular train is here to stay, probably for decades, and all interested parties have to work together to make the best of the present situation and the most of future possibilities. But I would add a corollary to that statement. We have to remember that HIE has succeeded in building a facility which is clearly not the best development option for the mountain and one which now creates an enormous financial burden for CairnGorm Mountain Ltd, the operating company. The train might be with us for decades to come but so will the financial burden.

Let's not forget that the construction of the funicular railway and associated buildings cost over twelve million pounds, most of this coming from public funds. CairnGorm Mountain Ltd has loan repayment charges substantially in excess of a hundred thousand pounds per annum to HIE and Highland Council and, at the time the project was approved, were approaching their two million overdraft limit with the Bank of Scotland.

Other, better, development schemes have been put to HIE in the past, but the Enterprise Board refused to sit down with voluntary organisations and discuss a better way forward. HIE has been at the forefront of community buyouts in Scotland, from Assynt to Eigg, so they are obviously not against the concept of community ownership. Alternatively, the new National Park Board, with both appointed and elected local members along with those appointed for their national and international expertise, will be in a far better position to decide on the future management of the northern Cairngorms. However, my guess is HIE are not willing to release their grip on Cairn Gorm any time soon.[8]

A RIGHT OF RESPONSIBLE ACCESS
JANUARY 2003

I have to admit that for much of my outdoor career the traditions of Scottish access have served me well. I've rarely suffered altercations with landowners, but I have been all too aware of a tendency amongst landowners to take advantage of the public's general ignorance about Scottish access law.

Over the past hundred years even so-called experts have disagreed on what we can or can't do. Walkers' guide books have offered conflicting advice about access, the majority of such advice reflecting the English version and, more recently, Environment Minister Ross Finnie suggested to me that if you asked a hundred lawyers if we had a law of trespass in Scotland they wouldn't be able to agree. Is it any wonder that when walkers are faced with a sign that says 'Keep Out' they would rather retreat than risk a fight with a truculent landowner?

In the past week access campaigners in Scotland have been celebrating the completion of the Land Reform (Scotland) Act. Since the publication of its first draft over two years ago the Bill has been on a tremulous course, but now, after over a hundred years of campaigning, the new Act secures the public a right of responsible access to all land and inland water and gives Scotland some of the best access arrangements in Europe, comparable with the much-admired 'allemanstratt' of Scandinavia.

8. Twenty years on since writing this column and after years of mismanagement HIE still maintain ownership of the Cairn Gorm Estate. Such is the glacial speed of land reform in Scotland.

Commenting on the legislation's final stage through the Scottish Parliament the chair of the Ramblers Association in Scotland, Alison Mitchell, said: 'This is an historic occasion, the final stage in a process which will secure, in statute, Scotland's traditional freedoms to take responsible access to land and water for outdoor recreation.

'The campaign to give legislative protection to our right to roam extends back to the 1890s when James Bryce MP placed the first of many Private Member's Bills before the House of Commons. It has taken the establishment of the Scottish Parliament, with its commitment to land reform, to turn that vision into reality.'

During the two years of the Bill's passage through the Scottish Parliament, MSPs, government ministers and civil servants have subjected the Bill to intense scrutiny and debate. The Parliament has also consulted widely with the Scottish public. The results of those consultations have delighted access campaigners and the subsequent Act will form the foundation for the new access arrangements, securing the public's traditional right to roam as well as providing a modern system for protecting footpaths and developing new path networks.

The Scottish public has always enjoyed a de facto right of access to the wild areas of the country. This right has been partly based on a mutual tolerance under which walkers are free to wander over wild land while not interfering with the landowners' use of his property (including stalking) or his reasonable privacy.

A crucial point in the legislative debate was the Parliament's acceptance that this historical right of access should become a defined, legal right. Detailed evidence at the committee stage of the Bill from mountaineer and former civil servant Alan Blackshaw, representing Scottish Environment LINK[9],

9. Scottish Environment LINK is the forum for Scotland's voluntary environment community, with over forty member bodies representing a broad spectrum of environmental interests with the common goal of contributing to a more environmentally sustainable society.

convinced the Parliament that such traditional liberties of recreation and passage already existed, and the Bill should simply codify what was already happening in practice.

Against stiff opposition from the Scottish Executive, Scottish Natural Heritage, the Scottish Law Society and the Scottish Rights of Way Society, the parliamentary committee, following an in-depth review of the law, chose to accept Alan's evidence. This decision was crucial to the final shape of the Act, ensuring a win-win situation for walkers in Scotland. It simply meant that no matter what restrictions to access, if any, ended up in the final legislation, there would still be a common law right for people to walk the land for recreational purposes.

The new legislation extends to all land, with a few common-sense qualifications. For example, the right will not extend to the curtilage of buildings, the curtilage depending on the size, setting and use of the building, although in most cases it should be fairly obvious on the ground. Neither does the right extend to land on which crops are growing; however, you are perfectly entitled to exercise the right around the margins of any field in which crops are growing and in woods and forests. Sports pitches and playing fields are out of bounds when they are in use and other no-go areas include places where access is restricted by the law on grounds of safety, health or the national or public interest, or places that are managed as a pay-to-enter attraction.

The new legislation also gives Scottish Natural Heritage the responsibility of drawing up a Scottish Outdoor Access Code, a Highway Code-type document that is designed to provide the reference point for responsible behaviour under the Bill. In essence, the legal dos and don'ts will be provided for in the Act, and the advice as to what constitutes responsible behaviour will be contained in the code.

As far as hillwalkers are concerned the contents of the Land Reform Act clear up much conflicting advice on the rights of individuals and issues like trespass. In areas like Glen Lyon where prominent signs tell walkers to 'Keep Out', the landowner will be asked by the local authority, under the provisions of the new legislation, to remove them. If he doesn't, the authority will have the power to remove them instead. It's hoped than in time the practice of placing such 'Keep Out' or 'Trespassers will be Prosecuted'-type signs will become a thing of the past and responsible walkers will be allowed to experience the full wealth of Scotland's scenery and natural heritage.

A RIGHT TO ROAM – A MIXED RESPONSE FROM THE PRESS
JANUARY 2003

In the aftermath of the Land Reform (Scotland) Act it's been interesting to see how some of the national newspapers have responded.

'Oiks, 1 Toffs, 0, as access becomes the trespasser's flexible friend', was the heading in the *Scotsman*, a newspaper that has become distinctly anti-Scottish Parliament, if not purely anti-Scottish, under the leadership of Andrew Neil.[10] It's little surprise the paper's circulation has, in recent times, gone into freefall. On the other hand the *Herald*, the Glasgow one that was[11], praised the Bill as flagship legislation and its approval by MSPs (except the Tory group) as representing a great day for the Scottish Parliament.

Sadly Magnus Linklater, whose work I have often admired, allowed his true-blue political colours to affect his normally accurate journalistic skills. Writing in *The Times*, he made the assertion that the legislation abolished 'Laws of Trespass' and repealed existing criminal laws. I'm not terribly sure what 'Laws of Trespass' Linklater was referring to, but it would seem to me that it is virtually impossible to be prosecuted for

10. It's been interesting to reread the crass comments by journalists like Neil, Linklater and Cochrane, the very same voices that today whinge and moan about the possibility of Scottish independence. True-blue journalists to the end.

11. The *Glasgow Herald* was changed to *The Herald* in 1992 following its purchase by Caledonia Newspaper Publishing.

trespass on land where the public has always enjoyed a de facto right of access, a common law right. This right has been partly based on a mutual tolerance under which walkers have traditionally been free to walk over land while not interfering with the landowner's use of his property, or his reasonable privacy. The new legislation simply takes that right out of the de facto bracket and places it firmly in the *de jure* one, or put another way, that right is now enshrined in legislation, as well as in tradition.[12]

Magnus Linklater's stated opinions were well wide of the mark, scaremongering in fact, as was his interpretation that the public now had a right to walk over any land at any time without any consideration for land management needs. Can I remind him that the new access provisions are for 'responsible' access for people taking recreation, and the legislation will be backed up by a Scottish Outdoor Access Code which will clearly lay out in simple terms how people should behave. Perhaps Linklater's biggest faux pas, inexcusable really for a journalist of his calibre, was his statement that 'privacy will henceforth be against the law'. This is flagrant tabloid nonsense unbefitting a newspaper with *The Times*'s reputation.

Astonishingly, he went on to say that the Justice Two Committee which dealt with the Bill paid 'little heed to the practical implications'. Once again, if he had taken the trouble to speak to some of the members of that committee he might have met someone like the Liberal Democrat MSP George Lyon, a former president of the National Farmers Union of Scotland, who played a very important role in the Committee's deliberations because of his own practical experience as a farmer.

Across the City, Linklater's fellow Tory, Alan Cochrane,

---

12. There are no laws of criminal trespass in Scotland. Trespass is a civil law. Where a member of the public accesses land which is not covered by the access provisions of the Land Reform (Scotland) Act 2003, they are trespassing. A court can therefore make an order to prevent trespassers from entering the land. Breach of such a court order could become a criminal offence.

writing in the *Daily Telegraph*, had obviously decided not to let the truth stand in the way of a good snipe against the Scottish Parliament. For example, he stated that the legislation was a result of 'furious prodding from the Ramblers Association'. As President of that organisation in Scotland I must write and thank him for the compliment – oh, that we had such power – but the truth of the matter is that Ramblers Scotland was only one part of a much larger group that conceived the blueprint for the new access arrangements, a wide array of land managing and outdoor recreation organisations as well as public bodies. That group had been established by Scottish Natural Heritage and was called the Access Forum.

Cochrane also insisted that landlords will now be 'made liable for the safety of walkers on their land'. He should have known that landowners already have a duty of care to anyone on their land, as a result of 1960s Westminster legislation. The Land Reform (Scotland) Bill has introduced nothing to change that.

Cochrane, who is the *Telegraph*'s Scottish Political Editor, claims the legislation 'will do nothing to improve the lot of ordinary Scots'. This is symptomatic of the view that the access provisions of the new Act will only be of benefit to climbers and walkers. The right of access that has been secured by the Land Reform Act is a public right of access for everyone, and that includes the family who would like to take a picnic by a riverside, or the retired couple who want to take a quiet ramble through the woods. More importantly, this legislation will provide much-needed protection for our remaining footpaths and provide opportunities for local communities to work together with farmers, crofters and landowners to develop new footpath networks appropriate to modern Scotland. Footpaths like the marvellous Badenoch Way, or Newtonmore's Wildcat Trail, or the excellent network of paths in Nethybridge, path networks that will bring enormous benefit in terms of healthy exercise and rural development.

PARK BOARD DISAPPOINTMENT
MARCH 2003

Along with a couple of dozen others I was interviewed for a place on the Cairngorms National Park Authority. The civil servants, perhaps not surprisingly, decided the new authority could cope quite happily without me.

The publication of the ministerial appointments to the authority has given a heavy hint as to why I wasn't appointed. Obviously, recreational interests are not seen as being of any importance to the National Park.

I must admit I read through the list with a sinking feeling: no mountaineers, no hillwalkers, no backpackers, no horse riders, no skiers, no paddlers to represent the biggest single group of individuals who have an interest in this mountain area. Instead, we get a mixed bag of individuals ranging from the usual clutch of consultants to farmers, a retired solicitor and surprise, surprise, an ex-convener of Highland Council. And an ex-chair of the Scottish Labour Party. Who would have imagined that?

Before I go on let me make two things clear. Firstly, I send the members of the new authority my very best wishes for the future, and extend those compliments to the council nominees and elected members. My overriding concerns are that the National Park is a complete success, that the continual degradation of the Cairngorms will be halted, and that the authority can avoid the kind of controversies that have haunted this area for decades.

Secondly, I accepted an invitation to apply for a place on the authority because I felt that recreational interests should be represented. When the letter arrived to tell me I had been unsuccessful I wasn't too concerned, feeling pretty sure there would be others invited who could serve recreational interests better than I. Sadly, that is not the case and those people who have campaigned for national parks in Scotland for decades have been snubbed in favour of career consultants, farmers and local politicians.

In a sense, I shouldn't be surprised. It was only a last-gasp amendment from Fergus Ewing MSP that ensured recreation appeared among the park's four main aims and objectives in the first place, even though mountaineering and walking tourism contributes some four hundred million pounds to the Scottish economy. I don't know how much walkers, climbers, skiers and paddlers contribute to the Cairngorms area, but I bet it's a damned sight more than any other single industry, traditional or not. The representatives of that market will not get an opportunity to influence the working of the new park.

It would appear that the Scottish Executive has learned little from the last three years. It was during the foot-and-mouth crisis that mountaineers and walkers convinced Ross Finnie that outdoor folks were not to blame for the outbreak and were capable of acting responsibly in the countryside. This pressure resulted in Finnie's famous U-turn and his subsequent plea for climbers and walkers to respond to his Comeback Code, to return to the villages of the Highlands and spend some money. Even today, there are Highland businesses suffering from the financial draught of that crisis. What's more, many of those land closures would still be in existence if it hadn't been for the lobbying and campaigning successes of Scotland's outdoor recreational groups.

More recently, Scotland's much-vaunted Land Reform Act wouldn't have contained the widely welcomed access provisions if it hadn't been for people like Dave Morris of the Ramblers and Alan Blackshaw, a mountaineer and campaigner of long standing. These men were representatives of LINK, a multi-interest consortium representing walkers, mountaineers, pony trekkers, ornithologists, paddlers and many others. The great bonus of those access provisions of the Land Reform Act will be that more and more people will come to the Highlands to enjoy areas like the Cairngorms. Such people will also spend money, lots of it, ensuring the future prosperity of our local communities.

Rather than recognise that fact, it would appear the Minister (or most likely Westminster-employed civil servants) decided the Park Authority would be better served by others, many of whom have historically fought against the needs and aspirations of walkers, climbers and those who cherish the Cairngorms not as an economic altar, but as a place of inspiration and quiet recreation.

WAYMARKING CAIRNS ON THE BEN
DECEMBER 2008

It's an age-old argument and it just won't go away. The question of lines of waymarking cairns on our mountains has split the climbing and hillwalking community, with people like me suggesting such cairns should be flattened and walkers encouraged to navigate by map and compass, while others insist such cairns are a lifesaving navigational aid and should be retained.

A few years ago, the Nevis Partnership,[13] a coalition of organisations with an interest in Ben Nevis, the UK's highest mountain, including local tourism organisations and landowners, produced a strategy document that included a recommendation that waymarking cairns should be provided, 'but these should be kept to a minimum'. Now, a Mountain Management Sub-Group of the Partnership is seeking consultation with climbers and hillwalkers on the subject as it strives to create an integrated policy for the summit plateau of the mountain.

The existence of waymarking cairns is not the only issue. There are many who believe there has been a proliferation of cairns on the summit of Ben Nevis, and not all of them are waymarking cairns. There are also abseil posts (signs that mark the top of particular gullies), and a summit emergency shelter that many believe should be removed. Indeed, there are those who would suggest the removal of the ruins of the old weather observatory, ruins that have been disintegrating since early last century.

---

13. The Nevis Partnership is nowadays known as the Nevis Landscape Partnership.

The Mountaineering Council for Scotland,[14] one of the organisations involved in the Nevis Partnership, is seeking the opinion of those who use the Ben. At the moment the Council has a 'holding position', which states: 'Support the retention of the main summit cairn, summit shelter and Peace cairn; to maintain a line of natural cairns (should be of natural construction with no cement or concrete) at 100 metre intervals along the mountain track from the summit to the 1200 metre contour; and to remove all other signs, cairns and posts including the No 4 Gully marker and the abseil posts and main marker at the top of Coire Leis.'

The Mountaineering Council of Scotland wants to gather views from all interested parties and points out two vital issues that have been highlighted during the debate so far.

First of all there are in excess of 100,000 people who climb Ben Nevis every year. Many of these people are tourists making a 'one-off' ascent because Ben Nevis is the highest mountain in the UK. Navigation on the Ben is often difficult because of poor visibility and many tourists simply don't have the necessary equipment or skills to cope in such conditions.

On the other hand, any cairns on the Ben Nevis plateau could cause accidents by encouraging people, who might otherwise have made the decision to turn back safely before reaching the summit, to continue, and who subsequently experience difficulty on more serious terrain or in deteriorating conditions.

These are issues that are vitally important and in many ways the situation on Ben Nevis is quite unique. There is a strong tourism interest. If tourists are encouraged to think that climbing the Ben is relatively safe and they won't get lost in the mist then more of them will attempt it. On the other hand, if they realise they have to navigate to the summit themselves many simply won't bother. There are also climbers who feel that navigating off the Ben, particularly in winter, can be particularly hazardous, and want to use waymarks. Having said that, others

14. In July 2016, in a rebranding exercise, the Mountaineering Council of Scotland became Mountaineering Scotland.

believe that mountaineering is about self-reliance and part of that self-reliance is being able to navigate in adverse conditions without having to rely on man-made contrivances. For those who climb mountains, such self-reliance should be fundamental.

Much of the current argument centres on the unique nature of Ben Nevis and its popularity with those who wouldn't call themselves mountaineers, but in actual fact the problem of waymarking cairns is much more widespread. You just have to walk up Beinn Macdui to realise there are similar problems in the Cairngorms.

FIXING PATHS ON BEN WYVIS
MARCH 2011

The letters page of a Cumbrian newspaper was recently the battleground between those who claim that the cost of footpath repairs on the Lake District fells was a waste of money and those who believe that such work is necessary to preserve the essential quality of the hills, and to protect the area from being literally loved to death.

We're fortunate in Scotland that comparatively few of our mountains suffer the same amount of people-pressure as the popular Lakeland fells, and footpath repair programmes are generally regarded as a way of regenerating vegetation and reducing the visual impact of overerosion, rather than simply improving access for walkers.

One mountain that does get a lot of foot traffic is Ben Wyvis in Ross-shire. Over the years footpath schemes on the mountain have attempted to find a solution that will balance access and nature conservation. About two years ago it was recognised that the problems caused by increased visitor numbers on the mountain have exacerbated the need to protect the fragile moss heath of the summit ridge, a habitat that attracts birds like the ptarmigan and the relatively rare dotterel.

Most of Ben Wyvis is owned and managed by Scottish Natural Heritage as a National Nature Reserve and the mountain is a

Site of Special Scientific Interest. But it's also the closest Munro to Inverness and attracts some 8,000 hillwalkers a year whose trampling boots have left their mark on the moss heath of the summit ridge. Two years on and the work on the summit ridge has proved successful. A £42,000 programme to repair and upgrade a section of the approach path to the mountain has also been completed.

A number of years ago I had the pleasure of officially opening a stretch of footpath on the lower slopes of Ben Wyvis that had been 'improved' by the Dingwall-based Footpath Trust. That section of path runs up from the roadside to a forestry fence on the moorland below Wyvis's An Cabar ridge and is a delight to walk on, but once over the fence you found yourself in a quag-mire of mud and peat.

Now that section has also been repaired, all the way from the entrance to the Ben Wyvis National Nature Reserve to the steep section below An Cabar on the south-west flank of the mountain.

'The popularity of this route had taken its toll in recent years and the path had been badly eroded by many pairs of boots and the effects of surface water run-off,' Peter Beattie, SNH's area officer told me. 'Much work has gone into repairing the route to ensure that the scar of the old path will heal over in time and reverse the process of erosion. But erosion is not only a land-scape issue but a safety one as well. The upgraded path should now be durable for many years to come and allow for a more enjoyable and safe climb and descent.'

Construction work on the path was carried out by Axiss Conservation of Carrbridge and they've made a wonderful job of it, using local stone for cross drains and steps.

Ben Wyvis's main physical feature is the two great corries which are gouged out of the eastern flanks of the hill, the dark side of the mountain which is relatively unseen, and unfrequented. Here the snow lies late into the summer and John Mackenzie, Earl of Cromartie, and a keen climber to boot, told me that his ancestors used to rent their land from the Crown on condition that they could produce a snowball at any time of the year.

CHAPTER TWELVE

Furth of Scotland

I've borrowed this term from the Scottish Mountaineering Club, one of the rather quaint terms they use in their Munro-bagging definitions. It refers to those 3000-foot mountains that lie in England, Wales and Ireland. Munros, the 282 hills in Scotland over 3000 feet or 914 metres are, of course, uniquely Scottish.

I've lived all of my life in Scotland and I think it's fair to say there are enough walks and mountain climbs north of the Border to last several lifetimes, but occasionally I like to spread my wings and leave my Highland eyrie for a while. I've been fortunate enough to travel widely, from the Himalaya in the east to California in the west, but closer to home lie some hill areas I've become rather passionate about, particularly the English Lake District.

During my years as editor of various outdoor magazines I gradually discovered the outdoor delights of places like the Lake District and North Wales, and it didn't take me long to realise that the UK climbing world generally considered either Manchester, historically in Lancashire (with its close links to the Lakes and North Wales) or Sheffield in Yorkshire (where the gritstone edges of the Peak District beckon), to be the epicentre of the climbing world. Competition between the two cities is akin to the War of the Climbing Roses.

Northumberland and the Yorkshire Dales were other areas I grew fond of during my magazine years, and I always had a steady flow of readers of my *Sunday Herald* columns to remind me that it was easier to reach the Lakes and Northumberland from the Central Belt of Scotland than Glen Coe, Ben Nevis or the Cairngorms. So, it seemed reasonable to include a fellwalk from the North of England from time to time in the paper.

The other area of England I fell in love with, even though there are no mountains there, is its south-west toe that includes Devon, Cornwall, Somerset and Dorset. Over a period of a few years, Gina and I escaped Scotland's lingering winters by travelling to the glorious South West Coast Path that begins at Minehead in Somerset and follows the coast to Poole Harbour in Dorset. This Path is 630 miles long and we hiked most of it in several visits over a five-or-six-year period. There may be a dearth of mountains in this south-west peninsula of England, but don't mistakenly think there are no hills. The walking around this coastline is extremely up-and-down and we would often fall into our tent at night utterly exhausted, as though we had just climbed a Munro or two.

There are no mountains in the deep south of England but there are some grand mountains in the Lake District, some of which wouldn't be out of place in the Scottish Highlands. Helvellyn, the Scafells, Pillar, Great Gable, Blencathra and the Old Man of Coniston are all fabulous hills on whose flanks, ridges and summits I've enjoyed many a day, but I don't think it's solely the mountains that are responsible for the huge passion that many people have for this corner of England. Some have accused the Lake District National Park of trying to preserve the area 'in aspic', but I suspect it's exactly that old fashioned, Beatrix Potter feel that makes the area so popular. The slate-tiled stone farmhouses and drystone walls, the narrow lanes and cobbled byways, Wordsworth's daffodils and a sheep-shorn landscape that would be decried as 'overworked and overgrazed' anywhere else in the country.

Almost every hill in the National Park has lower slopes that are given over to sheep, predominantly Herdwicks, that graze every plant that dares raise its head above ground. The ecologist Frank Fraser Darling once described the Scottish Highlands as a 'wet desert' – I wonder what he would have thought of twenty-first-century Lakeland? Split between tourism and sheep farming the effect of the 'hooved locusts' doesn't appear to have affected the area's popularity and I wonder if it is the smaller scale of the farming units that has allowed this form of agriculture to dominate the culture of the region, a slightly 'olde England' way of life that, despite the obvious difficulties in these economically harsh times, attracts many modern-day romantics from the cities and towns.

Such tourism is not new. The Lake District was the home of the traditional romantic poets and just as Sir Walter Scott popularised Loch Lomond and the Trossachs through his writings his contemporaries in the North of England were doing a similar job in the Lakes. The Wordworths, John Keats, Samuel Taylor Coleridge and others extolled the beauties of Cumberland and Westmorland as they were then, and helped drive an expectant eighteenth-century tourist boom northwards into an area that was essentially poverty-stricken and backward. The same 'romantics' saw the hills and lakes through new eyes, a place of sublimity and wonder rather than a place where dragons dwelled, a natural world that reflected their own human emotions and feelings. Indeed, the poet and art critic John Ruskin was critical of this anthropomorphism, investing nature with human qualities, a style of art he dubbed the 'Pathetic Fallacy'. I think Ruskin's criticism was fair and that this condition is apparent in many of us who enjoy the outdoors even today.

Alfred Wainwright, the doyen of the Lakeland Fell-wanderer, appeared oblivious to such anthropomorphism. He was a man obsessed, driven by unknown forces to document every part of this scenic region, in words, maps and line drawings, guidebooks that have become recognised as works of art. I only met him once or twice but my good friend and long-time television producer Richard Else knew him well. It was Richard who encouraged A. W. to overcome his naturally reticent (some might say curmudgeonly) nature to appear in a number of television series. In a later biography, Richard makes the assertion that Wainwright likely suffered from Asperger's Syndrome, a form of autism that is characterised by significant difficulties in social interaction, along with obsessive and repetitive patterns of behaviour. Such an assertion would go a long way in explaining his often rude and unsocial behaviour.[1]

I've written about Wainwright in a couple of the essays that follow, but a contemporary of his that I did know well was Harry Griffin, a climber, local journalist and author of dozens of books about the Lake District. His 'Country Diary' column in the *Manchester Guardian* (and the *Guardian from 1959*) ran for an astonishing fifty-three years until his death in 2004, beating Tom Weir's forty-six-year-old monthly column in the *Scots Magazine* and putting my own meagre thirty-two years of weekly columns in my own local newspaper to shame.[2] Born in Liverpool Harry moved to Barrow-in-Furness as an infant and during the war rose to the rank of lieutenant colonel, serving in Burma. He later became the Northern editor of the *Lancashire Post* until his retirement in 1976.

Harry had an unrivalled knowledge of Cumbria and in particular the crags, cliffs, hills and mountains of the Lake District. His formidable literary output was essentially over-shadowed by Wainwright and whilst the two knew each other I was aware that Harry didn't have a lot of time for Wainwright. He found him rude and offensive, something that appalled Harry's rather conservative (with a small 'c') outlook on life.

While Wainwright's books are very much guidebooks, Harry Griffin's are more wide ranging, describing climbs and hill walks, the varied topography of Cumbria from the coast to the mountaintop, the daily routines and interests of those who lived and worked there, the heritage and folklore of the fells and dales and, above all, his deep passion for simply living amongst the fells he held dear.

---

1. Richard Else's thoughts on Wainwright's mental health can be found in his book, *Wainwright Revealed*, published by Mountain Media in 2017.
2. At time of writing, I have contributed a monthly column to the Scots Magazine for the grand total of eleven years. It's highly unlikely I'll match Tom Weir's forty-six never mind Harry Griffin's fifty-three.

As an outdoor magazine editor it was once my ambition to bring three old storytellers together, Tom Weir, Showell Styles from Wales and Harry. All agreed to the project and the plan was a simple one: put the three of them round a table with a tape recorder and let them blether. Oh, the stories and yarns that could have come out of that gathering! Sadly, it never happened. Ill health and difficulties of travel got in the way and Harry died in 2004, followed by Showell Styles the following year and Tommy a year after that, the three Grand Old Men of British outdoors writing. We'll never see the likes of them again.

CARTER BAR, BORDERS
FEBRUARY 1998

I'm sure you'll forgive me for this brief foray into England-shire although you can; if you feel strongly about such things, walk at least half the route on the Scottish side of the Border. It's a route that throws up an interesting comparison in legal access, but we'll come to that later.

We had driven through Northumberland to Carter Bar, the 415m/1371ft-high border point between Scotland and England, the historic barrier between Celt and Saxon. The writer H. V. Morton, in his fine book *In Search of Scotland* suggested that for a Scot, the view north from Carter Bar is 'as definite and unmistakable as the white cliffs of Dover to an Englishman'.

We didn't get much of a chance to appreciate the view. Leaving the warm comfort of the car we were blasted by the arctic chill of a northern wind as we squeezed into our boots and windproofs and searched for gloves and warm hats. It was a bitter, bone-chilling wind but we knew that within a few moments we would get a measure of protection as we climbed the short but steep slopes of Catcleuch Shin on the south side of the Wauchope Forest.

Warmed up and legs stretched, we were better prepared for the wind when we broke free of the trees and tramped over the frozen turf of Carter Fell where the full splendour of the view burst upon us. To the south the sinuous twists of Redeswire Dale dropped down to the Catscleugh Reservoir, deep in its conifer-covered cradle. Eastwards, straddling the border, lay the broad slopes of Redeswire, famous for its sixteenth-century skirmish between border families and, way beyond it, across the crumpled borderlands, lay the massive bulk of the Cheviot.

Grand as these views are, it was the view north that was most heartwarming, even though the view itself looked as cold as ice. Yellowed moors led the eye to the Eildon hills, early promises of what is to come as you travel deeper into Scotland. Beyond, from the Lammermuirs to the Moorfoots to the Tweedale, Teviotdale and Ettrick hills, everything was shrouded in white, gleaming brightly in the winter sun.

H. V. Morton's words came to mind as we rested briefly by the small cairn that marks the summit of Carter Fell. 'I feel that invisible things are watching me. Out of the fern silently might ride the Queen of Elfland, just as she came to Thomas of Ercildoune in this very country with 'fifty silver bells and nine' hanging from her horse's mane.'

It was far too cold today for any elfin queens so, anxious to keep warm, we continued over the broad whaleback of Carter Fell, following the border fence and aware that on one side of the fence hillwalkers can wander freely, and legally, while on the other, English, side I suspect we may have been trespassing. On a walk like this the legal aspects of access are almost meaningless.

Trespassing or not we were aware that the rough and frozen topography below our boots was once scraped and dug and quarried for coal, surely some of the most exposed and wild opencast mines in the land. Little is left to remember of the hardships and labours of those miners of old: the opencast areas have been scoured and raked by decades of wind and frosts and below, in the headwaters of the Bateinghope Burn, old ruins whispered their industrial heritage from a wild and bleak hillside.

We stopped awhile amongst the old stones, luxuriating in the windless shelter and gentle sun and remembered the border families whose sons may well have worked in these remote mines: the Scotts, Armstrongs, Elliotts, Douglas, descendants perhaps of those who reived and plundered and skirmished on either side of this ancient border.

From the old mine working an old track led us back along a natural shelf on the hillside high above Redesdale. Away below, the waters of Catscleugh Reservoir glinted in the sun but clouds were now pouring down from the north and the threat of snow was all around us. The exposed car park at Carter Bar wasn't the place to linger so we turned our backs on England and headed back to the icy north.

CARNEDD LLEWELYN AND CARNEDD DAFYDD, NORTH WALES, AUGUST 1999

What's in a name? Carnedd Llewelyn and Carnedd Dafydd are the highest and second highest peaks in the Carneddau of North Wales. It's generally thought the two names commemorate Llywelyn ap Gruffudd and his brother Dafydd ap Gruffudd, the last independent Prince of Wales. Or could the twin peaks be named after Llywelyn the Great, or Llywelyn ap Iorwerth and his son and successor, Dafydd ap Llywelyn? I guess the truth lies somewhere in the mists of time, and mist was certainly prevalent when we arrived in the Ogwen Valley to explore the rugged side of the Carneddau. From the Ogwen Valley road we couldn't see any of the tops for low cloud and rain.

We camped in the Gwern Gof Uchaf farm campsite so that seemed as good a place as any to start. Just along the road lay the Climbers Club hut at Helyg. A friend of mine, Geoff Milburn, wrote a fascinating book about the hut's history and its connections with the Climbers Club, so I was keen to have a look at it as we passed. Almost in the shadow of Tryfan, Helyg is steeped in the history of British climbing. It was the first climbing hut in the UK and was used as a base by the pioneers of British climbing for early ascents on Y Lliwedd and Tryfan and as a training base for the 1953 Everest expedition. Today, little has changed, and the Climbers Club has done a remarkable job in providing a modern, comfortable hut for its members, while keeping the exterior pretty much as it would have been in the days of Colin Kirkus and Jack Longland.

According to the Ordnance Survey there is a footpath between Helyg and the lower slopes of Pen yr Helgi Du's south ridge, but we must have missed it. It was a boggy start to the walk but once we got a bit higher, with marvellous views of Tryfan, things improved enormously, and so did the weather. By the time we reached the summit of Pen yr Helgi Du much of the cloud had blown away, the rain had stopped and the sun spasmodically appeared to light up the surroundings. Only the high tops of Carnedd Llewelyn and Dafydd remained hidden.

It's a steep drop from Pen yr Helgi Du to the bwlch (I'm slowly becoming familiar with the Welsh language) and my wife was already making sounds of complaint about the terrain. She was already missing the easy, smooth slopes of the northern Carneddau but it was almost outright rebellion when we started up the slopes immediately to the left of Craig yr Ysfa. A steep and rocky scramble, not for the faint-hearted, took us to a marvellously rock-girt viewpoint, looking down into the craggy depths of Cwm Eigiau. I convinced Gina that was the reward for the rough scramble but much to my chagrin the terrain then eased off considerably and it was a simple stroll to the summit of Carnedd Llewelyn.

It was still cloudy on the summit so we couldn't see round to Carnedd Dafydd. I had thought about visiting Yr Elen too, but decided to concentrate on Carnedd Dafydd, just in case there were any more scrambling surprises.

From the summit shelter on Carnedd Llewelyn we headed south to where the ridge began to narrow above Craig Llugwy. We caught the odd glimpse through the cloud down to the steel grey waters of Ffynnon Llugwy reservoir, deep-set in its little cwm below us.

The ridge walk to Dafydd was surprisingly easy, even in the cloud, but Gina had experienced enough scrambling for one day. Rather than take the steep route off Pen yr Ole Wen we backtracked a little from the summit shelters and descended south-east, then south into the depths of Ffynnon Lloer's cwm. From there a path dropped and took us back to the road just east of Llyn Ogwen.

THE HOWGILLS, CUMBRIA
MAY 2002

My good friend, the broadcaster Eric Robson, described it as one of the gentlest and most appealing mountain landscapes in Britain. Wainwright describes it as a herd of sleeping elephants. I guess most folk regard the Howgills as large, billowing swells of hills, and they are that, but they are also full of interesting little nooks and crannies, with some tight and narrow little valleys burrowing into the fells. There's history here too, and one or two impressive waterfalls. Plus, and most important, they tend to be off the beaten track of the most popular Lakeland fells. That, in itself, is a good enough reason to visit the Howgills. The classic route from Sedbergh is to wander along the River Rawthey to the Cross Keys Inn, a seventeenth-century temperance inn, and then climb up beside the tumultuous Cautley Spout to the high plateau. We were keen to get the climbing in first, before descending by a path that would give us good views of Cautley Spout. A brew at the Cross Keys was planned before gently completing the eleven-mile circuit along the bridleway back to Sedbergh.

The smooth flanks of Winder roll down virtually into Sedbergh's back door and the hill dominates the town. A good path climbs onto the hill behind the back alleys and gardens of Sedbergh's town houses and climbs to a cluster of flat-topped peaks, all linked together by rounded ridges that offer easy high-level walking mixed with ever-changing views. The highest point is The Calf, at 676m/2200ft or so, and what a wonderful viewpoint it is. The view to the west is expansive with Morecambe Bay standing out clearly, Black Combe and the whole Coniston range looking fantastic, Crinkle Crags, what looks like the Scafells, and all the hills in between.

We reached the flat-topped summit of The Calf fairly comfortably. A footpath passes close by the summit cairn and heads in a north-east direction, so we followed it for a while before dropping down the steep slopes of Hare Shaw to Bowderdale Head where another footpath plunges into the depths of the valley. It's certainly a steep path but it's well made and offers marvellous views of the thundering Cautley Spout, the most dramatic feature in the Howgill Fells. What might it have been like here several million years ago when the great glaciers were scouring out these U-shaped valleys! In my mind's eye I imagined a glacier biting into the mountainside where there was a small meandering stream going across the mountain tops. I then imagined the glacier diverting that northbound stream, turning it over the top of what we now know as Cautley Crag. Two thousand years ago, there was an Iron Age settlement down here, deep in the valley, and the people built a track, a good stone-edged road, all the way from their settlement to the foot of Cautley Spout where it stopped quite abruptly. What was its purpose? We don't know if some form of ritual cleansing took place here, we don't know if there might have been a big pool here where the people washed their clothes together or it might have had more of a spiritual significance. Perhaps they were just inspired, as we were, by the tumbling waters. All that remains of the settlement are some stones and an earthwork.

After our promised tea-break in the Cross Keys we followed a sequence of bridleways, tracks and quiet roads all the way back to Sedbergh where we headed for the Dalesman Inn for something just a little stronger.

PILLAR AND GREAT GABLE, LAKE DISTRICT
AUGUST 2005

I have sneaked across the Border this weekend to the Lake District, where the hills may be less rugged but are nevertheless worth the occasional foray. I'm very fond of the Lake District and when I was asked to make a DVD of a long walk around Wast Water in the Western Fells I had no hesitation in agreeing.

The walk begins and ends at the delightful Bridge Inn at Santon Bridge and follows riverbank paths to Crag House Bridge, Hollins and Stang End. We then crossed Birks Bridge to Nether Wasdale and Church Stile before tramping through fields to Buckbarrow Farm where we began the climbing, and there's a lot of it on this route.

It was a steep haul to the summit of Buckbarrow, high above Wast Water, the lake reflecting its famous Wasdale Screes, which fall down in a curtain of stone from Illgill Head and Whin Rigg, two hills we would traverse at the end of the walk before returning to Santon Bridge.

Further along the lake rose the crouched form of England's highest hills, Scafell and Scafell Pike, and to the north, across the gap of Sty Head, lay the conical shape of Great Gable, one of my favourite Lakeland fells. Our route was designed as a challenge-walk of some twenty-six miles, but my excuse for taking two or three days over it was simple. Filming is a long-winded and laborious affair, with a lot of stops and starts and too much sitting around chatting.

Once past the lovely Greendale Tarn we took a fell-runners' path to the col between Red Pike and Scoat Fell, then on past Black Crag to Pillar, the first time I'd been there. Pillar has a big plateau-like summit, that falls away sharply to the north into Ennerdale, and just over the edge, like a great knuckle of stone, lies Pillar Rock.

I was to meet an old friend of mine here. Ken Ledward is an ex-outdoor instructor and fell-runner who makes a living from testing equipment for outdoor companies. Ken was to show me an interesting scrambling route onto the summit of Pillar Rock. The Slab and Notch route is, according to the guidebook, 'a fascinatingly varied ascent ... a rope for protection is advised for all but competent rock climbers.'

We were both reasonably competent rock climbers, which

was just as well as we didn't have a rope with us. As it was the rock was warm and dry and we had little difficulty in negotiating the steep arêtes to the summit.

From Pillar Rock Ken led the way past the Robinson Cairn to Black Sail Pass from where we skirted the northern slopes of Kirk Fell to Beck Head where we climbed to Great Gable. He left me here, but I was to be joined by another old friend, the legendary fell-runner Joss Naylor, who led me over Scafell Pike and Scafell and down to Burnmoor Tarn, high above Wasdale, the valley where he's shepherded and farmed most of his life. I think it's fair to describe Joss as the greatest fell-runner of all time, having won about every fell race there is to win. When he was sixty he celebrated by running over sixty Lakeland summits in one long run. For his seventieth birthday he intends, if his wife gives her permission, to run seventy tops.[3]

The final section of our mammoth fell walk was over Illgill Head and Whin Rigg, down to Irton Pike, then back through fields to the Bridge Inn at Santon Bridge. Never did a pint of beer slide down so easily.

The video by the way, should be out before Christmas.

KINDER SCOUT, PEAK DISTRICT
MARCH 2006

About twenty years ago I took part in a Karrimor Mountain Marathon with my old buddy Chris Townsend: a fell-running-cum-orienteering event, in the Dark Peak area of Derbyshire. The route took us up onto Bleaklow and Kinder Scout and after two days of plodding through glutinous peat and trying to navigate along deeply eroded peat groughs, some of them six feet deep, I swore I would never soil my boots in the Dark Peak again and I haven't, until last weekend.

---

3. Joss Naylor's wife did consent and the following year, for his seventieth birthday, he ran seventy Lakeland fell tops, covering more than fifty miles and ascending more than 25,000 feet, in under twenty-one hours. Truly astonishing.

To many hillwalkers the Peak District National Park is iconic. Lying between the huge conurbations of Manchester and Sheffield, this vast area of high rolling moorland provides an escape for thousands of city dwellers and, if it lacks the mountain diversity and grandeur of the Scottish highlands, it is, at least, easily accessible to those who live in Lancashire and Yorkshire.

Access to these grouse moors has not always been so readily available. In the early years of last century gamekeepers and landowner's agents physically stopped walkers and ramblers accessing the moors and it wasn't until a group of walkers took on the keepers, and the police, in the infamous Kinder Trespass of 1932, that attitudes began to soften with regard to access to these peaty uplands.

Access to the hills of England and Wales has always been a contentious issue, especially compared with the de facto freedom to roam we've traditionally enjoyed in Scotland. Scotland's Land Reform Act of 2003 legalised that arrangement and we Scots can now boast some of the best access arrangements in the world. Go south of the Border though, and the access situation is still in the feudal Dark Ages, despite some improvements brought about by the recent Countryside and Rights of Way Act. I'm afraid the concept of 'trespass' is still greatly cherished by too many English and Welsh landowners, including a fair number of 'recently rich' pop singers, actors and businessmen.

It was to remember those brave souls of the Kinder Trespass that I returned to the Dark Peak last weekend. Next year is the seventy-fifth anniversary of that event and I was advising on a television documentary, part of a major series on Britain's mountains, to be broadcast by the BBC next year.[4] We weren't quite recreating the event of 1932, but simply recalling how those distant events had an impact that eventually helped give us the freedoms we enjoy today. With a huge group of ramblers and walkers we retraced the footsteps of the early trespassers, up

---

4. The television show was called Mountain and was broadcast on BBC1 in 2007

from the Bowden Bridge car park in Hayfield, along the edge of the Kinder Reservoir, up William Grough to Ashop Head from where the Pennine Way makes its tortuous route down to the Snake Pass and then on up to the godforsaken peat groughs of Bleaklow (never was a hill so well named). From Ashop Head it was an easy climb onto the Kinder plateau and across to the summit, an island in a soggy wilderness of brown/black peat.

We were led on our merry way by that well known jester Griff Rhys Jones, who had obviously done his homework and regaled us with tales of Benny Rothman, one of the Kinder trespassers who went to gaol for his troubles. What Griff didn't mention was that Benny wasn't even a particularly enthusiastic walker at the time. He was employed by the Young Communist League as a political agitator, and an illegal trespass was the ideal opportunity to stir up socialist values.

I suspect that didn't really matter too much to the other Kinder trespassers who were predominantly left wing anyway, in direct contrast to many of the walkers on last weekend's outing, the modern middle class, many of whom could be described as Thatcher's children. Certainly, the car park at Bowden Bridge wouldn't have been jam-packed with nearly-new cars in Benny Rothman's day.

Politics aside, it was good to join in the fun and remember that if it hadn't been for Benny Rothman and his mates seventy-five years ago, the access situation in England and Wales could be even worse than it is. I'll be back in the Scottish hills next week.

HAYSTACKS AND INNOMINATE TARN, LAKE DISTRICT
SEPTEMBER 2007

I was in the Lake District to give the Wainwright Centenary Lecture, a celebration of the legacy of Alfred Wainwright, England's most iconic fell wanderer. I thought it slightly curious that the Wainwright Society should invite a born, bred and patriotic Scot to give this lecture. We all know that Scots hill-goers are a wee bit contemptuous of good old A. W. and, occasionally, even slightly contemptuous of the busy Lake District itself.

Wainwright used his unique talents to portray an appreciation of a beautiful landscape that inspired him. His work, as Martin Wainwright (no relation) suggested in his recent BBC book, was a 'love letter to the fells, a love letter which others might share'.

Wainwright's favourite fell was Haystacks, above the head of Buttermere. 'For a man trying to get a persistent worry out of his mind, the top of Haystacks is a wonderful cure,' he once wrote. On another occasion he suggested, 'One can forget even a raging toothache on Haystacks.' So, what was so special about it?

'For beauty, variety and interesting detail, for sheer fascination and unique individuality, the summit area of Haystacks is supreme. This is, in fact, the best fell top of all – a place of great charm and fairyland attractiveness,' he wrote. 'The combination of features, of tarn and tor, of cliff and cove, the labyrinth of corners and recesses, the maze of old sheepwalks and paths form a design, or a lack of design, of singular appeal and absorbing interest.'

A stone's throw away from the summit of Haystacks, amid a tumble of rocky tors, lies the little expanse of Innominate Tarn, where Wainwright asked for his ashes to be scattered. It's a delightful spot, a little cusp on the broad, knobbly ridge that flows south-east from Haystacks itself, a reed-fringed tarn that acts as a reflecting foreground to the bigger hills that radiate out from Haystacks's central hub: Great Gable, Kirk Fell and Pillar, High Crag and Fleetwith Pike.

With a few hours available to reflect on what I was going to say to the Wainwright Society I couldn't think of a better walk than a traverse of the curmudgeon's favourite fell top, and a stroll by his final resting place.

From the head of Buttermere, just over the Wharnscale Beck bridge, I took the gradually rising packhorse route towards Scarth Gap. The trail makes its way through the gap before descending into Ennerdale but I left it at its highest point to climb up through the crags of Haystacks to its shaggy, multi-topped summit ridge, crowded with people. It was even busier down on the shores of Innominate Tarn, with little opportunity for peaceful reflections, but I knew how to escape the crowds. I simply left the footpaths behind, and took to the bracken-covered fellside instead.

From the quarry workings above Dubs Bottom I took a direct line to the summit of Fleetwith Pike and for a precious hour or so didn't meet another person, an hour that gave me the opportunity to understand why this was Wainwright's favourite corner of the world.

Away below, Buttermere stretched out towards the strip of land that separates it from Crummock Water, the steep slopes of Red Pike, High Stile and High Crag falling precipitously into its dale. Opposite rose the bracken-covered slopes of Littledale Edge, Robinson and Hindscarth, glowing bronze in the after-noon sun. In the opposite direction lay the big hills of Lakeland, Great Gable, with Scafell rising beyond, Kirk Fell and the rocky-faced grandeur of Pillar, perhaps the most dramatic mountain in the area. It was a peaceful and beautiful panorama and by the time I had descended Fleetwith Edge back to bustling Gatesgarth I felt a little more fondly towards the Lake District's pipe-smoking patron saint.

FAIRFIELD, LAKE DISTRICT
MARCH 2008

It was the English schools' half-term holiday and the M74 was nose to tail with cars slung all round with mountain bikes, canoes and caravans. It seemed as if the whole of England was migrating north so, in a mood of perversity, I thought I'd go in the opposite direction. I went to the Lake District.

Not surprisingly, it felt as though every English person who had decided against travelling to the Highlands had opted for a weekend in the Lakes instead. Every narrow street was jam-packed with cars, every tea shop had snaking queues and the hills had a human chain strung out over them. And it's not even Easter yet!

I suspect the weather had something to do with it. All week a system of high pressure had dominated, the skies were blue and the nights were cold and frosty. When we set out from Ambleside to wander round the ten-mile-long Fairfield Horseshoe the sun shone from a cloudless blue sky and the temperature was still below freezing. It didn't take us long to warm up.

A couple of years ago I guided a bunch of folks round the same route on a day of rain, low cloud and wind. Amongst the group were some lads I had met on a trek to Everest Base Camp and on that miserable day they had inadvertently become separated from the group, took a wrong bearing and ended up at the Traveller's Rest pub on the Keswick road. I strongly suspected they hadn't taken a wrong bearing at all.

Anyway, they were keen to complete the route this time and as we wandered along back lanes to High Sweden Bridge, an ancient packhorse bridge in Scandale, before the climb onto the ridge, they mentioned that they had all been training for various fell races. Off they loped up the fellside and sweat was soon pouring from me as I tried to keep up.

The Fairfield Horseshoe is a marvellous walk and is undoubtedly one of the classic walks of the Lake District. Two long ridges enclose the narrow valley of the Rydal Beck and steep, craggy slopes close off the head of the valley below Fairfield and Hart Crag. The eastern ridge rises from the foot of Scandale and is formed by the crags of High Pike, Dove Crag and Hart Crag while the western ridge rises high above Dunmail Raise near Grasmere and Rydal, culminating in the peaks of Great Rigg and Heron Pike.

It was a steady climb to High Pike and my mate Rowly, a native West Cumbrian and resident of Ambleside, guided us past all the most eroded sections. Severe erosion is a common enough feature of these popular hills and, here and there, even the stalwart work of the footpath maintenance crews can't keep pace with pounding walking boots.

It's easy to become negative about the erosion but all of us who go to the hills contribute to it. I was, however, delighted to see a long line of waymarking cairns that used to line the route between High Pike and Fairfield had vanished. These cairns contributed to the erosion problem in another way. Thousands of people would traditionally lift a stone from the turf and add it to the cairn, leaving holes in the ground that slowly became bigger because of the effect of freeze/thaw cycles and running water. The route is all the better for the removal of these obtrusive waymarking cairns.

According to local guidebooks the Fairfield Horseshoe offers wonderful views over scenes of great beauty and the walking quality is first class throughout. While I would wholeheartedly agree with the quality of the walking route, we couldn't see very far because of a silky haze that rose from the valleys and dales. Only the very tips of the neighbouring hills peeked above the haze although we did get some good views of St Sunday Crag and Helvellyn from the summit of Fairfield.

Our return route to Ambleside followed the long undulating ridge over Great Rigg, descending to a broad col before climbing gently to Heron Pike. Here the haze was less dense and we could make out Coleridge's 'shining levels'. He was referring to the lakes and tarns that are visible from this ridge: the tiny Thirlmere Tarn, with its waterfalls, the distant meres of Windermere and Coniston, Rydal Water and Grasmere at the foot of the fell, all flashing like gems in the folds of the hills.

My racing companions enjoyed the view while waiting for me before plummeting downhill to the steep terminal of Nab Scar where a good path zigzags its way down to Rydal Hall and its marvellous tea shop. A field carpeted with golden daffodils made nonsense of the season.

THE CHEVIOT, NORTHUMBERLAND
AUGUST 2010

It's been called England's best kept secret and that might be the case for most general tourists, but many hillwalkers are familiar with the delights of Northumberland, particularly the wild and secluded upland areas that surrounds the ancient volcano known as The Cheviot.

I've climbed The Cheviot by its regular routes from the English side of the Border and have gruesome memories of wading through oozing, glutinous peat, but tackle it from the Scottish side and not only do you get a largely peat-free ascent, but a much prettier one. Indeed, the walk-in from Sourhope Farm in the Bowmont Valley near Yetholm is a sheer delight, wandering through narrow valleys that are rich in ancient remains and traversing sheep-grazed slopes by good paths.

About seven miles beyond the border twin villages of Kirk and Town Yetholm the single-track road comes to a dead end at Cocklawfoot, just below the high ridgeline that forms the Scotland/England border, the edge of a high and lonely plateau from which long ridges ease their way down into secretive sheep-cropped valleys.

We left the vehicle at a road junction above the Bowmont Water near Sourhope Farm from where we could follow farm tracks all the way up to the Border Ridge just south of Black Hag. From there, the ridge would carry us over The Schil, past the Mountain Refuge at Auchope and on to Auchope Cairn from where it's just over a mile of peat plodding to the summit of The Cheviot. From there we could return to Auchope Cairn and resume our ridge wandering south, over Score Head and King's Seat and onto Windy Gyle, almost ten miles from The Schil. From Windy Gyle a track runs north down Windy Rig to Kelsocleuch Farm and the farm road past Cocklawfoot and back to the start.

The tidy Sourhope Farm was all quiet as we walked through and found the track that would take us around Fasset Hill to the lonely farm of Auchope. Man has farmed these slopes since the fourteenth century and long before that Iron Age settlements were set up on the slopes of Fasset Hill itself. Today the farm is used as a centre for land use research, mainly the breeding of Cheviot sheep.

Beyond lonely Auchope Farm, tucked away in delightful isolation in its narrow valley, we struck uphill towards the main ridge that separates Scotland and England. Just before we reached Black Hag we left the path and climbed eastwards, keen to reach the main ridge and the easy climb to the tor-studded hill known as The Schil. At 601m The Schil just falls short of the 2000-foot mark but stands on the route of the Pennine Way. Indeed, it's the last real summit of the Pennine Way and may well have a poignant significance for those wayfarers who have hiked the two hundred and sixty-odd miles here from Edale in the Peak District. For us it was the first top of the day and a superb viewpoint with the North Sea on one side and the hills of Dumfries and Galloway on the other.

Descending south from The Schil we found ourselves walking along the line of paving stones that forms much of the Pennine Way route from Byrness in Northumberland. When they were first laid down these paving slabs caused some controversy, but I suspect most walkers prefer them to the boggy footpath that turns to mud after any period of intense rain.

I've never visited the temptingly beautiful College Valley whose upper reaches lie to the east of The Schil but it looked magnificent today, as did the dark and gloomy amphitheatre of the historic Hen Hole. This rocky recess boasts some climb-able crags and local tradition suggests that men and women are occasionally lured into its dark confines by sweet and beautiful music, never to be seen again.

A wooden mountain rescue hut lies at the foot of Auchope Cairn and we took advantage of it to shelter from the brisk breeze before tackling the stiff-looking climb to Auchope Cairn. Beyond the summit wooden duckboards float across the bogs to Cairn Hill and The Cheviot itself and I don't intend saying too much about The Cheviot's summit, 815m/2674ft, a wet, boggy and glutinous kind of place and we wondered why we bothered. We returned to our ridgeline as soon as we could, following the Pennine Way paving slabs through the heather to Score Head, King's Seat and then across the old drovers' road of Clennell Street to Windy Gyle, at 619m/2032ft, the third highest top to straddle the Border.

An easy descent took us down to Kelsocleuch Farm and from there the Cocklawfoot road took us back to the start, the end of a magnificent high-level stravaig across a quiet, unspoiled and beautiful section of the Borderlands.

MALHAM COVE, YORKSHIRE DALES
APRIL 2011

It was a still and misty morning and not even a full English breakfast was capable of lifting the dampers. We tugged on boots and tried to console ourselves with the fact it wasn't raining. Other than our campervan the car park was empty when we left and crossed the old clapper bridge onto the route of the Pennine Way. A middle-aged dog walker greeted us enthusiastically. 'You're the first walkers I've seen this morning,' she proclaimed. 'Pity about the weather, it was lovely yesterday.'

Our spirits rose significantly as we watched a white-bibbed dipper dart up the bubbling course of the youthful and boisterous River Aire. The pale walls of a stone barn appeared through the mist, with some rusting farm implements lending something to the faint air of desolation, then we were through a gate and into the damp atmosphere of Wedber Wood. Ahead of us the waters of the rain-swollen river were cascading over the tufa-rock into a wooded limestone gorge. This was Janet's Foss. Tufa is a smooth limestone deposit usually formed when water containing calcium carbonate passes over exposed rock and, while the tufa is easily explained, I'm not so sure of the significance of Janet, or Jennett, although tradition suggests she may have been a faery queen. The word 'foss' is old Norse for waterfall.

We climbed to the road beyond the cascades, trying to reconcile fairy stories with the popular conception of hard-nosed, straight-talking Yorkshiremen. It didn't quite fit, although not so very far away from here, near Burnsall in the Yorkshire Dales, a distinctly conical-shaped hill called Elbolton is said to be one of the Cracoe Reef Knolls (geological remnants of an ancient coral reef which formed in a shallow prehistoric sea many millions

of years ago) and possess weird magical powers. Known as the
'Hill of the Fairies', Elbolton is one of several supposedly supernatural places lying within the so-called Barden Triangle.

We crossed the road, went through a gate and I immediately
guessed we might face some difficulties getting up Gordale
Scar. I've never seen this normally placid burn so full of water.
It had risen over the banks onto the flats and, here and there,
helpless-looking sheep were trapped in little islands of green
grass. My fears were justified when we entered the steep-walled
canyon flanked by the sheer cliffs of New Close Knotts to the
left and Cross Field Knotts to the right, and followed it in an
anti-clockwise course into the cold heart of the chasm. It's said
the poet Thomas Grey 'shuddered with awe' when he reached
this spot, and I guess thousands of others have shuddered too.
Today we just shivered.

In normal circumstances the stream flows down the right side
(as you look up the Scar) of the centrally located staircase of
tufa, or crystallised limestone, that acts as a compressed plug
in the floor of the canyon. The usual scrambling route is up the
left side of the rock, but not today. The whole plug was running
with water and the polished holds were as slippery as seaweed.
Discretion, we decided, was the better part of valour. We made a
hasty retreat down the length of the valley, crossed over Gordale
Bridge and made our way up a green track, going through three
gates before meeting a road. We followed the road as it rose into
the mists then crossed a stile to the north where another green
track took us past the rucked wrinkles of some ancient settlement and past Prior Rakes to meet another road at the car park
at Low Trenhouse.

We were disappointed at not being able to climb through
Gordale Scar and the limestone pavements that dominate the
valley above it, but the setback was alleviated somewhat by the
prospect of better weather. The mist was lifting and there was
even a hint of sunshine for our descent to Malham and the other
geological delights of this walk.

It didn't take long for the swollen river we were following

to vanish from sight. This was the aptly named Water Sinks, and the river doesn't escape from its subterranean course until it reappears below Malham village. You can follow its ancient watercourse, a rugged, craggy and now very dry valley called Watlowes. It's an extraordinary feeling to trundle down this dry glen, knowing that somewhere below your feet, the river would be plunging through limestone caverns and hollows, eagerly seeking the light of day again.

Beyond the Dry Valley the next geological highlight of the walk was the incredible limestone pavement above Malham Cove. It's such an unusual phenomenon, the natural fissures of the rock enlarged and widened by millennia of rain and frost forming the characteristic clints, the blocks, and the deep clefts in between them, known as the grikes. It was too early in the season to search for the spleenworts and ferns and primulas that are often to be found deep in the fissures, well protected from browsing beasts, and it was obviously too early in the season to see the indigenous breed of rock-men and women who traditionally swarm to Malham Cove on warm summer evenings to tackle the steep limestone overhangs.

A long flight of rock steps descend the steep-sided cove into a different world. From the grey and craggy landscape you enter a placid world of green, followed by the well-manicured path along tree-lined riverbanks with the colossal limestone amphitheatre behind you. As we headed down to the village and the Buck Inn it was good to just remind ourselves of the antiquity of this place. The impressive Cove had been formed by ice and water erosion throughout the last million years. An excruciatingly slow process which makes humanity's little flirt with 'time' seem almost superfluous.

HIGH STREET, LAKE DISTRICT
MAY 2012

I was in Cumbria to give a talk at the Keswick Mountain Festival and couldn't think of a better warm-up to the event than a wander over the fells that lie to the south-east of Ullswater.

Much of my Lake District exploration is enjoyed in winter, when short daylight hours and the harshness of the Scottish hills makes a foray to the gentler south a welcome change of intensity. In summer, the Lake District tends to be too busy for my liking, but not today!

Gale-force winds and torrential rain showers kept most walkers to the lakeshore paths or the outdoor shops in Keswick, and the puddled car park at Hartsop was empty when I arrived. This little hamlet of traditional slate cottages lies at the foot of the Kirkstone Pass and makes an ideal start and finish point for a hike over High Street, a long grassy ridge that's been described by old Wainwright as a hill 'that has been known and trodden, down through the ages, by a miscellany of travellers on an odd variety of missions; by marching soldiers, marauding brigands, carousing shepherds, officials of the governments, and now by modern hikers'.

Certainly, the ancient Romans laid a road across the summit ridge: this was apparently their High Street between garrisons at Ambleside and Broughton. Later, horses were raced over these high tops and on older maps the summit is called Racecourse Hill.

The route from Hartsop follows a good trail beside the lively Hayeswater Gill all the way to Hayeswater. The path continues towards a hill called The Knott, from where High Street is only a few easy strides away across the Straights of Riggindale, but I wanted to make more of a circular walk, traversing the long High Street ridge, returning to Hartsop via the lovely Angle Tarn and Boredale Hause. This choice of route also runs contrary to Wainwright's guidebook advice: 'Enterprising pedestrians approaching from Hartsop may tackle High Street direct from the head of Hayeswater – but they will not enjoy the climb, which is steep, dull and overburdened with scree.'

Since the waters of Hayeswater were chopped into white horses by the blustery wind, and the cloud level wasn't much higher than the surface of the lake, I reckoned it wouldn't matter too much if this was a dull ascent. I wasn't going to see much anyway.

As it happened it didn't take me long to reach the high, slender cairn on Thornthwaite Crag, high above the Hayeswater glen. From there I had the wind at my back so I could stride out towards High Street, high above the depths of Bleathwaite Crag and Blea Water. Completely swathed in Gore-tex, the heavy showers didn't worry me too much, but those who had taken the Knott route from Hayeswater were having to battle and fight headlong into the blustery gales.

Once across the Straights of Riggindale and around the side of The Knott I came out below the clouds and could see my path ahead as it snaked its way between Saturday Crag and Brock Crags and down to Angle Tarn, one of my favourite spots in the Lake District. I found a sheltered niche beside some rocks and ate lunch there, watching the wildfowl on the loch, the calls of greylag geese competing with the sound of the wind screaming between the rocks.

It's an easy and gentle descent from Angle Tarn down to Boredale Hause below Place Fell and down the track to the valley floor at Beckstones, lush in its greenness, pastoral and remarkably pretty. It's this sudden contrast between the wildness of the fells and the gentle landscapes below that make the Lake District so remarkable, and unique. An hour earlier I had been battling with the foul conditions. Down here it was another world and I strolled back down the leafy lanes to Hartsop in a Beatrix Potter landscape of tilled fields, rich hedgerows and cuckoo calls.

Changing Times

History rarely takes a straight line. Events and issues create bends and loops along the way, and occasionally the route doubles back to create a sense of déjà vu that leaves us disoriented, confused and disappointed. Recent world events demonstrate that we are less than competent when it comes to learning lessons from the past and, even in the more confined world of Scottish hills and mountains, landscape and wild land conservation, history has a dreadful habit of repeating itself.

Reading through my old newspaper columns, it's clear that trends come and go, conservation battles are won and lost, and that the popularity of outdoor activities over the past forty to fifty years has seen peaks and troughs. One thing that is clear today is that outdoor enthusiasts are less likely to specialise in one activity than they did in the past, and instead enjoy a host of disciplines from Munro-bagging to paddling a sea kayak, wild swimming to paddle-boarding, bike-packing to packrafting, and winter mountaineering to bouldering. All that is good, but if there is one aspect of the outdoors that is shared by all of these activities it is access. If we cannot access the mountain, river or lochside, we can't participate in our chosen activity and, despite years of Scottish Government promises about land reform, most of our countryside is as privately owned as it ever was. In a few cases, it is just as jealously guarded.

Twenty years ago, it wasn't unusual for maverick landowners to try and curb access to their estates, even though the people of Scotland had a traditional de facto right to roam. Many walkers, especially those unfamiliar with these traditional rights, were perturbed and discouraged when they came across padlocked gates and signs telling them trespassers would be prosecuted. Thankfully, the access provisions of the Land Reform (Scotland) Act 2003 codified that de facto right, enshrined it in legislation, and gave the public a legal right to roam if they acted responsibly. The new laws were seen as progressive and amongst the best in the world.

The published legislation was accompanied by a Scottish Outdoor Access Code, a type of countryside Highway Code, which laid out the responsibilities of both the public and, most importantly, land managers. However, in the years since there has been a steady flow of attempts by landowners to erode the access provisions by building fences, padlocking gates and posting 'No Entry' signs. Most have been dealt with effectively by local council access officers and the courts, but the words of warning given by former Ramblers Scotland Director Dave Morris on the eve of publication of the legislation continue to ring true.

'The access provisions of the Land Reform (Scotland) Act have given us, arguably, the best access legislation in the world, but we will have to fight to maintain it as there will be those who, using every means possible, will try and oppose it.' When Dave Morris made that statement I don't think anyone in their wildest dreams imagined the most serious challenge to the access legislation would come from the leadership of Scotland's first National Park.

Holiday weekends have always created issues on the east shore of Loch Lomond where huge numbers of Central Belt citizens converge to picnic, barbeque and camp overnight There was already legislation in place to deal with the litterers, the vandals and the rowdies, so the local police inspector was able to devise schemes to deal with those who refused to act responsibly. However, the National Park management, with absolutely no policing experience and even less in dealing with a rowdy public, asked the Scottish Government to create local by-laws to stop people camping. This they are legally entitled to do under the provisions of the Land Reform (Scotland) Act, as they are to follow the West Highland Way, which runs along this same shore.

This decision was an attack on the public's hard-won access rights and, by taking it, the board not only eroded them but seriously damaged the reputation of Scottish National Parks. John Muir, the Scots-born father of the international National Parks movement, must have birled in his grave.

Despite opposition by Ramblers Scotland and Scottish Mountaineering, the by-laws were later extended to other areas in the National Park, running roughshod over Scotland's world-leading access arrangements. I pleaded with Scotland's Environment Minister, Aileen McLeod, to reject this plan but she seemed not to fully understand the traditions and import-ance of access in Scotland, nor the implications of the new by-laws. I even had a lengthy meeting with Scotland's First Minister, Nicola Sturgeon, on the same subject but to no avail. The by-laws went ahead and outdoor enthusiasts in Scotland felt angry and inexplicably betrayed by their own government.

It struck me at the time that outdoor recreation needed stronger political representation in Scotland. Traditionally, our case would have been taken up by Ramblers Scotland or Mountaineering Scotland, but campaigning does not appear to be as important to these organisations as it was in the past. There was a time when the very name of the Ramblers was a watchword for political campaigning, striking fear into the hearts of wayward landowners, but that no longer appears to be the case. Time after time, opposition comes from old firebrands like Dave Morris.

Outdoor recreation in the UK badly needs high-profile opinion formers and campaigners. Previously, outdoor maga-zines provided a platform for such individuals but, again, that is no longer the case. The dire need for advertising revenue and higher sales figures has seen our outdoor titles fill their pages with bland gear reviews and endless articles about the Lake District. Of all the outdoor magazines in the UK, at my time of writing, only one carries a conservation column. The opinion formers who still exist, and there are very few of them nowadays, are not getting any younger, so new campaigners are required to fight tooth and nail to protect the cherished access rights that many fought for so long to achieve. We desperately need a new John Muir.

I'm glad to say that some issues have improved over the years, remembering when the only females you saw on Scotland's mountains were trudging several paces behind their gung-ho male partners. Women now realise they don't need male companionship to explore our mountains and wild places, and it's commonplace to see groups of women hillwalkers enjoying each other's company. One woman told me she felt safer walking alone in the hills than she did in the cities. It's also encouraging to read more and more books and articles written by women. The female perspective offered is different from that of their bearded counterparts and, in my opinion, tends to offer a wider appreciation of the environment and a better understanding of the benefits of wild land.

Appreciation of those benefits on mental health and well-being has been one of the hallmarks of the Coronavirus (Covid-19) crisis that began in 2020. Locking people down in towns and cities for lengthy periods resulted in record-breaking levels of depression and stress and, although I wrote on this subject forty years ago, it's good that such recognition has at last become mainstream. This awareness has led to a huge increase in visitors to Scotland's hills and mountains, an annual invasion that brings its own problems. Many people newly visiting the countryside are unaware of their responsibilities, and some seem to believe that 'right to roam' means they can go anywhere and do as they like. The Covid years have witnessed clashes between visitors and locals in many of the popular areas and vociferous calls, no doubt encouraged by the actions of the Loch Lomond and Trossachs National Park, have been made for bans and by-laws.

Education is surely the answer. A media campaign every

spring should remind people of the old Countryside Code and how they should behave in the outdoors and, of course, I would welcome Government intervention to reduce the number of outdoor education centre closures. Many of my generation had a grounding in outdoor life and countryside behaviour at centres like Outward Bound and local authority outdoor centres, many of which are long gone. The Scouts and Guides, no longer fashionable, offered a similar education.

The problems resulting from release after Covid lockdowns have, however, resulted in a greater awareness of the need for improved infrastructure to cope with growing numbers of people, cars and campervans. We need better car parking at the foot of our popular mountains, and more camp sites and overnight stopping points to cope with the burgeoning numbers of campervanners who don't want to be stuck on the same campsite for a week or more.

I was delighted when the Scottish Government began to take a more positive and pragmatic approach in 2021 by helping local councils to finance car parks and overnight stopover places through their Rural Tourism Infrastructure Fund. However, some may ask, should we be encouraging people to use polluting cars to visit the countryside in the first place? Should we really be promoting 'road trips' like the North Coast 500? Shouldn't we be campaigning for an improved local public transport network? Of course, but that's only one issue we should be considering. The question mark that Covid-19 has posed is overshadowed by an even bigger and darker question mark. Because of climate change, ambient temperature, atmospheric carbon dioxide, and cloud cover are increasing and Covid-19 is not the only infectious disease linked to climate change.

The World Health Organisation has highlighted the link between changing environmental conditions and epidemic diseases. However, we don't have direct evidence that climate change is influencing the *spread* of Covid-19. What we do know is that climate change alters how we relate to other species, which matters to the risk of infections and therefore our health.

We also know that deforestation simultaneously adds to atmospheric carbon dioxide and forces bats, and other animals that may be carrying disease, into contact with humans, which is possibly how Covid-19 originated. In the longer term, global warming is likely to bring mosquito-borne tropical diseases such as malaria to more northern countries.

Climate change will also result in rising sea levels with potentially catastrophic consequences for coastal areas and cities like London, Aberdeen, Dundee, Glasgow and Edinburgh, which are built on tidal rivers. Increased heat and subsequent drought conditions have increased the possibility of wildfires which, in turn, will release more carbon gases into the stratosphere. Warmer air holds a higher water content so we can look forward to more extreme rainfall patterns, and, in turn, violent rainstorms create landslips, flooding and erosion.

It is tempting to think of our hills and mountains as inscrutable and implacable or, as the Navvy Poet Patrick MacGill suggested, 'Naked to the four winds of heaven and all the rains of the world, they (the mountains) had stood there for countless ages in all their sinister strength . . .' Unchanging they may be, but their spirit of ancient mightiness is not immune to the effects of climate change.

In my own lifetime I've witnessed the severe shrinking of glaciers in the Alps and the Himalaya, which leads to less water for consumption by the population, a lower hydroelectric energy generation capacity, and less water available for irrigation. More than 9.6 billion tons of glacial ice have melted in the world since 1961, according to a 2019 satellite study by the University of Zurich (Switzerland), and climate change threatens to evaporate over a third of all glaciers by 2100, according to the Worldwide Fund for Nature.

In the Scottish Government's climate change framework, a key consequence of climate change in our hills and mountains is identified as change to our ecosystems as some habitats and species are affected by changing snowfall and rain patterns. 'In addition, the climate space where certain habitats and species can exist is likely to shift,' it suggests. 'Some of these habitats and species are already at the edge of their ranges, with mainly northern or montane distributions, or they occur in habitats such as snowbeds. These species may have nowhere they can move to as their climate space in Scotland disappears. The challenge is to develop appropriate management for the uplands to increase the resilience of habitats, species and soil to climate change.'

This has not turned out to be the final chapter I originally envisaged. I wanted to complete this book on a note of optimism, triumphant in the knowledge that more people enjoying our hills and wild places would mean more protection for them. I wished to be positive in the belief that things had improved since I wrote my first newspaper column in the seventies. That the wild places would be loved by a new generation of hikers and climbers who would care for them. Most of all I wanted to declare we had learned lessons from the past. We haven't, but all is not yet lost.

Climate change may be the biggest threat to mankind since the last Ice Age, but we have the science, the skills and the knowledge to deal with it. What is urgently needed is political will and our personal acceptance of the challenges we face. So, what are those challenges? First, to be aware of how much we are reliant on the planet. That the fight against climate change is not only a fight to save the planet, it's also a fight to save mankind. The planet will roll on and heal itself. It's not reliant on us as we are reliant on it. It provides everything we need to survive and, if you don't believe me, try holding your breath for two minutes. It's the planet that sustains us and it's the planet that provides for us. We have to stop abusing it, for in abusing it we abuse ourselves and our grandchildren's future.

We can overcome the worst excesses of climate change, but we have to sing from the same hymn sheet. We need to stop worshipping at the altar of increased GDP and continual growth, issues that are simply unsustainable. We need to decarbonise our economy, consider changing to plant-based diets and travel less. Crucially, we need to consider our mountains, hills and wild land as cathedrals in which we worship, places where we are sustained and uplifted, rather than places to be conquered and controlled for monetary or personal gain. With ambition, a willingness to change and a desire to work together we can win the fight against climate change. What's more, we can be richly blessed in doing so.

Index